TUTOR GUILD

TUTOR DELIVERY PACK

ENGLISH

— YEAR 6 —

Pearson

Tutora

ENGLISH
YEAR 6

Contents

Page		Learning Objectives
3	How to use this pack	
5	Information for parents	
7	Curriculum guidance	
11	Revise mapping guide	
13	Needs analysis	
15	Progress report	
16	End-of-lesson report	
17	**1 Diagnostic lesson** *A mix of reading, writing and GPS objectives*	To find out how well the student reads and writes, and to understand their grammar, spelling and punctuation proficiency; to find out the student's preferences and attitudes
23	Source texts	
29	**2 Question types** *2a; 2b*	To become familiar with different types of question used in KS2 English assessments; to deal with different response types appropriately; use textual evidence
35	**3 Non-fiction features** *2b; 2f; 2h*	To become familiar with the features of non-fiction texts; to identify features of reports, news articles and explanations; to write a short report
41	**4 Finding answers** *2b*	To scan text to find answers; to retrieve and record information; to use PEE to answer open questions
47	**5 Character, theme and language** *2b; 2d; 2f; 2g*	To understand how writers portray character in a story; to look for sequences of events and patterns of ideas; to explain the main theme or message of a text; to explain the effect and meaning of the author's choice of language
53	**6 Meaning** *2a; 2d; 2e*	To make predictions using the text; to determine the meaning of single words in context and explain them using synonyms; to make inferences using evidence from the text
59	**7 Making comparisons** *2c; 2f; 2h*	To make comparisons within the text; to explain how narrative content is related and how it contributes to meaning; to summarise main ideas from more than one paragraph
65	**8 Poetry (similes and metaphors)** *2a; 2f; 2g*	To become familiar with poetic forms; to become familiar with a range of figurative language; to recognise and write similes and metaphors
71	**9 Poetry (other figurative language)** *2a; 2f; 2g*	To become familiar with poetic forms; to become familiar with a range of figurative language; to recognise and use personification, alliteration and onomatopoeia
77	**10 Audience and purpose** *Plan writing*	To understand the terms *audience* and *purpose* in relation to composition; to recognise the intended audience and purpose of texts; to write for a particular audience and purpose
83	**11 The writing process** *Plan writing; draft and write*	To plan a piece of non-fiction writing; to organise ideas into paragraphs; to draft non-fiction writing from an organised plan
89	**12 The editing process** *Evaluate and edit; propose changes; proof-read*	To edit a draft piece of writing; to check writing against a plan; to proof-read to check spelling and punctuation
95	**13 Writing: articles** *Plan writing; note and develop ideas; draft and write*	To revise the features of articles; to plan a news article from source material; to write a news article
101	**14 Writing: explanations** *Plan writing; evaluate and edit*	To revise the features of explanations; to plan an explanation; to write and evaluate explanations
107	**15 Writing: persuasive letters** *Plan writing; recognise formal language*	To recognise formal language; to use persuasive language; to plan and write a formal letter
113	**16 Writing: balanced arguments** *Draft, write, evaluate and edit*	To examine different sides of an argument; to plan and write a balanced argument text; to use cohesive devices to structure and develop arguments
119	**17 Writing fiction** *Plan writing; note and develop ideas; draft and write*	To use a stimulus to plan a piece of fiction; to organise ideas into paragraphs; to use dialogue; to write a short story
125	**18 Nouns** *G1.1; G1.3; G3.2; G5.1*	To differentiate between common and proper nouns and know when to use a capital letter; to recognise what makes a noun phrase or expanded noun phrase; to write a variety of expanded noun phrases in context, using capital letters where appropriate

ENGLISH
— YEAR 6 —

CONTENTS

Page		Learning Objectives
131	**19 Pronouns and determiners** *G1.5; G1.5a; G1.8*	To identify and use a range of determiners; to select pronouns to replace nouns appropriately for clarity and cohesion; to use pronouns to indicate possession
137	**20 Adjectives and adverbs** *G1.3; G1.6; G1.6a*	To use adjectives to add detail to nouns; to use comparative adjectives to compare nouns; to use adverbs and adverbial phrases to add detail to verbs; to use fronted adverbials
143	**21 Verbs – present** *G4.1a; G4.1b; G4.1d*	To use regular and irregular verb forms to express present time, including progressive and perfect forms
149	**22 Verbs – past** *G4.1a; G4.1b; G4.1d; G4.2*	To use regular and irregular verb forms to express past tense, including progressive and perfect forms; to select and use tenses consistently throughout writing
155	**23 Verbs – future and modal** *G4.1c*	To use modal verb forms to express degrees of possibility; to use modal verb forms to express future time
161	**24 Conjunctions and prepositions** *G1.4; G3.3; G3.4; G1.7*	To use a range of conjunctions to link words, phrases and clauses; to use a range of prepositions to express when, where or how; to distinguish between co-ordinating and subordinating conjunctions
167	**25 Sentence types** *G2.1; G2.2; G2.3; G2.4*	To recognise the four sentence types by their grammatical patterns; to punctuate the four sentence types accurately; to write questions and commands in a number of forms
173	**26 Subject and object** *G1.9; G4.4*	To recognise the difference between the subject and object; to recognise the difference between the active and passive verb forms; to change a sentence from active to passive and vice versa
179	**27 Clauses** *G3.1; G3.1a; G3.4*	To identify main clauses, relative clauses and other subordinate clauses; to link clauses using co-ordinating and subordinating conjunctions; to use commas to mark clauses
185	**28 Standard English** *G7.1; G7.2; G7.3*	To recognise Standard and Non-Standard forms of English, including dialect and slang; to recognise formal and informal language and structures; to use the correct subject-verb agreement
191	**29 Basic sentence punctuation** *G5.1; G5.2; G5.3; G5.4; G5.7*	To use capital letters to mark the start of a sentence; to use a full stop, question mark or exclamation mark to mark the end of a sentence
197	**30 Commas** *G5.5; G5.6a*	To use commas to separate items in lists; to use commas for clear meaning; to avoid splicing main clauses together with commas
203	**31 Parenthesis** *G5.9*	To identify and use pairs of brackets, dashes or commas to indicate parenthesis
209	**32 Colons and semi-colons** *G5.10; G5.11*	To use colons to introduce lists; to use semi-colons within lists; to use colons or semi-colons between clauses
215	**33 Apostrophes** *G5.8*	To use apostrophes to show possession; to understand the difference between plural and possessive –s; to use apostrophes to indicate a contraction
221	**34 Punctuating speech** *G5.7*	To use inverted commas to indicate direct speech; to understand how to order punctuation in direct speech; to change reported speech to direct speech and vice versa
227	**35 Hyphens and single dashes** *G5.12; G5.13*	To use hyphens to make meaning clear; to use hyphens to make compound words and add prefixes; to use a single dash between clauses to show an interruption in speech or thought, or a shift of direction
233	**36 Word families** *G6.2; G6.3; S38; S42; S43; S46; G6.4*	To classify words according to common root words; to add a variety of common suffixes and prefixes to root words; to recognise and write different plural noun forms accurately
239	**37 Synonyms, antonyms and homophones** *G6.1; S61*	To understand how words are related by meaning as synonyms and antonyms; to recognise homophones; to use the correct homophones depending on context
245	**38 Tricky spellings** *S58; S59; S60*	To spell frequently occurring words with unstressed vowels or silent letters; to understand and apply the *i* before *e* except after *c* spelling rule; to spell frequently occurring words that include the letter string *–ough*

ENGLISH
YEAR 6

HOW TO USE THIS PACK

The *Tutors' Guild* Tutor Delivery Pack gives you all of the tools you need to deliver effective lessons to Year 6 students, who are working towards the 'expected standard' in the Key Stage 2 national curriculum tests. Everything in this pack is available for you to download as an editable file. This means that every lesson can be edited to suit the needs of an individual student, but also that you can print off each resource as many times as you need.

LESSONS

There are 38 one-hour, six-page lessons in this Tutor Delivery Pack. Most tutors working for a full year will have around 38 lessons with a student. If you have less contact time, you can choose which lessons are most important to the student and build your own course, using the customisable digital version of this pack. Each lesson is standalone and can be taught independently from those preceding it.

If you have more than 38 lessons together, or your lessons are longer than one hour, you can incorporate assessment from the accompanying Tutor Assessment Pack (ISBN: 978 1 292 17250 7 for English). There is an *end-of-topic test* for every lesson in this pack, as well as *checkpoint challenges* and a *practice paper*. All of the papers can also be given as homework, used as diagnostic tests or incorporated into revision.

LESSON PLANS

The first page of each lesson is your *lesson plan*. It is designed specifically for tutors and is intended to guide you through a one-hour session in either a one-to-one or small group setting. It is not designed to be student-facing.

LEARNING OBJECTIVES AND CONTENT DOMAINS

At the top of each lesson plan, you will find two lists. The first – *learning objectives* – is a list of your aims for the lesson. You can discuss these with the student or use them for your own reference when tracking progress. They are informed by the national curriculum but may have been rephrased to make sure they are accessible to everyone. The second list – *content domains* – informs you which of the content domains from the test framework are covered in the lesson. You can find out more about content domains and the test framework on pages 7–10.

ACTIVITIES

The first five minutes of your lesson should be spent reviewing the previous week's homework. You should not mark the homework during contact time: instead, use the time to talk through what the student learned and enjoyed, and any difficulties they encountered.

The final five minutes should be used to set homework for the forthcoming week. There are three ways to do this: using the *end-of-lesson report* on page 16; orally with a parent or guardian; or simply using the *homework activity sheet* on the fifth page of each lesson.

In each lesson plan, you will find four types of activities:

- *Starter activities* are 5–10 minutes each and provide an introduction to the topic
- *Main activities* are up to 40 minutes long and are more involved, focussing on the main objectives of the lesson
- *Plenary activities* are 5–10 minutes each, require little to no writing and recap the main learning points or prepare for the homework
- *Homework activities* can be up to 45 minutes and put learning into practice.

In the lesson plan, you will find a page reference (where the activity is paper-based), a suggested timeframe and teaching notes for each activity. The teaching notes will help to guide you in delivering the activity and will also advise you on some common misconceptions associated with the topic.

ENGLISH
— YEAR 6 —

HOW TO USE THIS PACK

DIFFERENTIATION AND EXTENSION IDEAS
This pack is aimed at students who are working towards achieving the 'expected standard', but every child is different: some may need to be stretched in spelling but require a little extra guidance in punctuation and others vice versa. In this section, you will find ideas for providing some differentiation throughout the activities.

PROGRESS AND OBSERVATIONS
This section is left blank for you to use as appropriate. You can then use this to inform assessment and future lessons, as well as to inform *progress reports* to parents.

ACTIVITIES
There are four student-facing *activity sheets* for each lesson. On each sheet, you'll find activity-specific lesson objectives, an equipment list and a suggested timeframe. All activities are phrased for one-to-one tutoring but are equally as appropriate for small group settings. If you have a small group and the task asks you to work in pairs or challenge each other, ask the students to pair up while you observe and offer advice as necessary. Where appropriate, answers can be found on the sixth page of the lesson.

DIAGNOSTICS
The first lesson in this pack is a diagnostic lesson, designed to help you find out more about your student: their likes and dislikes; strengths and weaknesses; personality traits. As well as the diagnostic lesson, the *needs analysis* section (pages 13–14) allows you, the student and the student's parents to investigate together which areas of the subject will need greater focus. Together, these sections will help you deliver the most effective, best value tuition.

PROGRESS REPORTS
This can be used to inform parents or for your own planning as frequently or as infrequently as is useful for you. Spend some time discussing the statements on the report with the student.
Be prepared – some students will tell you there isn't anything that they enjoy about the subject!

END-OF-LESSON REPORTS
Parent participation will vary greatly. The *end-of-lesson* report is useful for efficiently feeding back to parents who prefer an update after each lesson. There is space to review completed homework and achievements in the lesson, as well as space for students to explain how confident they feel after the lesson. Finally, there is a section on what steps, including homework, the parent and student can take to consolidate learning or prepare for the following week. The *end-of-lesson* report may also be useful for communicating with some parents who speak English as a second language, as written instructions may be easier to follow.

CERTIFICATES
In the digital version of this pack, you will find two customisable certificates. These can be edited to celebrate achievements of any size.

ENGLISH
YEAR 6

INFORMATION FOR PARENTS

INTRODUCTION
Your child's tutor will often make use of resources from the *Tutors' Guild* Year 6 English series. These resources fit perfectly with the current national curriculum tests. The tutor will use their expert knowledge and judgement to assess your child's current needs. This will allow them to target areas for improvement, build confidence levels and develop skills as quickly as possible, giving your child the chance to succeed in the end of Key Stage 2 tests or in their Year 7 resits.

Just as a classroom teacher might do, your tutor will use lesson plans and activities designed to prepare your child for the new national curriculum tests, formerly known as SATs. Each set of resources has been designed by experts in primary English and reviewed by experienced classroom teachers and tutors to ensure it offers great quality, effective and fun teaching. All *Tutors' Guild* resources are fully flexible and adaptable so that your tutor can tailor the course to meet your child's needs.

GETTING STARTED
Before tutoring can begin, your child's tutor will need to know more about your motives for employing them in order to set clear, achievable goals. They will also try to learn more about your child to ensure lessons are as useful and engaging as possible.
To gather this information, your tutor will work through the *needs analysis* pages of the *Tutors' Guild* Year 6 Tutor Delivery Pack with you. It shouldn't take too long, but it will really maximise the value of the tuition time you pay for. You could also take this opportunity to discuss with your tutor any questions or concerns you may have.

LESSONS AND HOMEWORK
Each lesson will have the same structure: there will be a starter, which is a quick introduction to the topic; some main activities, which will look at the topic in greater detail; and a plenary activity, which will be used to round off the topic. Throughout the year, your child will become increasingly more confident with the content of the Year 6 English curriculum, but will also improve their speaking, writing, reading, listening and co-ordination skills through a carefully balanced range of activities.

At the end of each lesson, your tutor will set your child a piece of homework, which should take no more than 45 minutes to complete. If you don't want your tutor to set homework, please let them know. If you are happy for your child to be given homework, your tutor will either discuss the homework task with you at the end of the lesson or give you an end-of-lesson report. All of the homework activities are designed to be completed independently but if you would like to help your child to complete them, your tutor will be able to tell you how you can help.

FURTHER SUPPORT FOR YOUR CHILD
Parents often ask a tutor what else they can do to support their child's learning or what resources they can buy to provide extra revision and practice. As a Pearson resource, *Tutors' Guild* has been designed to complement the popular *Revise* series. Useful titles you may wish to purchase include:

- *Revise* KS2 SATs English Revision Guide – Expected Standard (ISBN 978 1 292 14601 0)
- *Revise* KS2 SATs English Revision Workbook – Expected Standard (ISBN 978 1 292 14600 3)
- *Revise* KS2 SATs English Revision Practice Papers (ISBN 978 1 292 14597 6)
- *Revise* KS2 SATs English – Grammar – Targeted Practice (ISBN 978 1 292 14594 5)
- *Revise* KS2 SATs English – Reading Comprehension – Targeted Practice (ISBN 978 1 292 14595 2)
- *Revise* KS2 SATs English – Spelling – Targeted Practice (ISBN 978 1 292 14596 9)

'Above expected standard' editions of the Revision Guide and Revision Workbook are available.

Using pages 11–12 of this pack, your child's tutor will be able to tell you which pages of the above Revision Guides are appropriate for each lesson.

ENGLISH
— YEAR 6 —

INFORMATION FOR PARENTS

WHAT'S IN THE TEST?
You may have heard a lot about the new national curriculum tests from your child's school, from other parents or in the media. Here is a breakdown of the tests that your child will sit at the end of Year 6.

GRAMMAR, PUNCTUATION AND SPELLING (GPS)
Your child will sit two tests that assess their grammar, punctuation and spelling ability:

Paper 1: questions
This is a 45-minute test in which your child will be given 49 questions to answer on grammar, punctuation and vocabulary. Some answers will be non-verbal (tick boxes) and some will be verbal (written words and sentences).

Paper 2: spelling
The spelling test is administered by a teacher and as such is not strictly timed. It consists of 20 words that your child will have to spell correctly. Each spelling is read aloud by the teacher several times and your child will be given a sentence in which to put the word. This will give your child the chance to think about the word in context.

READING
Your child will sit only one test to assess their reading ability. They will, however, also be assessed by their classroom teacher through the year.

Paper 1: English reading test
This test is one hour long, including reading time. Your child will be given a reading booklet with a selection of texts: non-fiction, stories and poetry. They will also be given an answer booklet which will have a number of comprehension questions worth 50 marks in total. Your child will have to answer all of the questions about each of the texts. As with GPS paper 1, some answers will be non-verbal (tick boxes) and some will be verbal (written words and sentences).

WRITING
Year 6 students no longer sit a writing test at the end of the year. Instead, your child's writing abilities will be assessed throughout the year by their classroom teacher. Their teacher will collect a variety of fiction and non-fiction pieces of writing to show a good range of your child's abilities.

RESULTS
On results day, your child will not receive a grade or level as students do for their GCSEs or A levels. Instead, they will be given a scaled score for each subject. It is scaled so that there is no difference from year to year. If your child's score is 100 or higher, they are thought to be working at the expected standard for their age. If their score is 99 or lower, they are thought to be working below the expected standard.

ENGLISH
YEAR 6

CURRICULUM GUIDANCE

The new 2014 national curriculum was assessed for the first time in 2016. The tests are no longer formally called SATs, instead they are known as national curriculum tests. Most students will only sit maths and English tests but, every two years, a sample of schools will be chosen to take a science test. Areas of the curriculum on which students may be tested are set out in the 'test framework'. This pack provides full coverage of the test framework for English, so you can be confident that you are giving the student the best chance of success in the tests.

THE NATIONAL CURRICULUM

The national curriculum was introduced in 1988 and must be offered by all state-funded schools. It aims to ensure each child is given the same standard of education; it combines a range of statutory and non-statutory areas of study and is intended to be broad-ranging, inclusive and balanced. At Key Stage 2, it comprises: English; maths; science; art and design; computing; design and technology; geography; history; languages; music and physical education. It is available to view in full on the government's website at www.gov.uk/national-curriculum/overview.

'WORKING AT THE EXPECTED STANDARD'

Students sitting the new national curriculum tests will no longer be given their results as a level. Instead, they are given a scaled score. If the scaled score is 100 or higher, the student is deemed to be 'working at the expected standard'. This roughly equates to a level 4 on the SATs tests taken by Year 6s until 2015. A scaled score is used so that results stay consistent across the years, regardless of any differentiation in the distribution of marks across content areas or perceived difficulty of any one test. Students will be given a separate score for all three areas of English: grammar; punctuation and spelling; writing and reading.

Page 17 of the reading test framework and pages 28–30 of the grammar, punctuation and spelling test framework provide lists of suggested skills for a student working at the expected standard, though it is acknowledged that different pupils have different strengths. Whilst you can use this as a guide, it should not be used prescriptively.

It has been suggested by the government that students who are not deemed to be 'working at the expected standard' may have to re-sit the tests in year 7.

THE ENGLISH TEST FRAMEWORKS

The national curriculum's statutory requirements for English have been used to create two English 'test frameworks': one for reading and the other for grammar, punctuation and spelling (GPS). The primary purpose of these documents is to inform test developers, but they are also really useful for ensuring your teaching programme covers all of the most important aspects of the English curriculum.

There are several sections of the test framework (detailed below) that may prove useful to you as a tutor.

CONTENT DOMAIN

The content domain explains which English topics may be assessed in the national curriculum tests. It has been used to construct the 38 lesson plans provided in this pack, which list the appropriate content domain areas. Areas of the content domain are not assessed in equal measures.

For more on assessment, see pages 11–12 of the accompanying assessment pack (ISBN 978 1 292 17250 7).

GRAMMAR, PUNCTUATION AND SPELLING

Pages 7–12 of the GPS framework detail the content domains for the GPS test, including key terms that students will need to know. More detail of these content areas and key terms can be found in the government's English Appendix 2. The testing of grammatical understanding is more prescriptive in the tests than previously, so it is important that students learn the key terms and know how to identify the grammatical features listed.

ENGLISH
YEAR 6

CURRICULUM GUIDANCE

Pages 12–13 detail the content domain for the spelling test. This is essentially a list of spelling patterns, phonological patterns, prefixes and suffixes. A full explanation of spelling patterns and word lists for Key Stage 2 can be found in the government's English Appendix 1. The majority of spellings tested in this pack's activities come from the statutory word lists in Appendix 1. However, other appropriate spellings will also be taught and tested, both in this pack and in school.

READING

For reading, the content domain tests comprehension:
- give / explain the meaning of words in context
- retrieve and record information / identify key details from fiction and non-fiction
- summarise main ideas from more than one paragraph
- make inferences from the text / explain and justify inferences with evidence from the text
- predict what might happen from details stated and implied
- identify / explain how information and narrative content are related and contribute to meaning as a whole
- identify / explain how meaning is enhanced through choice of words and phrases
- make comparisons within the text

The activities in the reading section of this pack will test the skills listed in the reading content domain.

Teacher assessment is also used to report reading skills to the DfE (Department for Education). Teachers will use the 'teacher assessment framework' to inform their judgments. This is so that skills such as reading aloud, which cannot be tested via written assessment, can be measured. A student must be consistently able to display all of the skills listed (on page 2 in the 'interim teacher assessment framework' for 2017 teaching, though this may change in later versions) to be deemed as working at the expected standard.

WRITING

Your student's writing skills are teacher-assessed in the new national curriculum tests. This means that the student's classroom teacher will collect pieces of writing from across the curriculum and decide whether the student is working at the expected standard. To do so, they will use the 'teacher assessment framework', which can also be found on the government's website. This document is updated for each new teaching year and so should be reviewed each summer.

As with reading, to be deemed as working at the expected standard, a student must be able to demonstrate their ability in all of the skills listed in the 'teacher assessment framework' (on page 4, though as with reading, this may change in future versions of the document). The writing assessment framework also contains a list of skills required of a student working 'towards the expected standard' and 'at greater depth within the expected standard'. The new national curriculum emphasises that those aiming higher than the expected standard should develop a greater understanding and ability within the national curriculum for Key Stage 2, rather than move on to Key Stage 3 areas of study.

Students with a physical disability or sensory impairment must be able to display all of the skills they are able to access. For example, a student with a physical disability that prevents them from holding a pen will not be tested on handwriting.

COGNITIVE DOMAIN

The cognitive domain explains the skills needed and processes undertaken to find the answer to a question. Further guidance on the cognitive domains and the tests themselves can be found in the *Tutors' Guild* Year 6 English Tutor Assessment Pack (ISBN: 978 1 292 17250 7).

ENGLISH
YEAR 6

CURRICULUM GUIDANCE

GRAMMAR FOR THE NATIONAL CURRICULUM TESTS

Much of the discussion around the new national curriculum tests has concerned the new, more prescriptive grammar requirements. We know that many tutors are not as confident teaching grammar as they are teaching reading or spelling. This might be because they haven't taught it in a long time or because they didn't learn it explicitly at school or university themselves.

If you need to refresh your knowledge of Key Stage 2 grammar ahead of teaching, you will find cross-references to the popular *Revise* series on pages 13–14 of this pack. Each page has a clear explanation and straightforward examples. Once you look at a page, you'll probably realise you knew what that particular feature was anyway, you just didn't know the name for it! You'll also find glossary entries for important words on the final page of each lesson, just below the answers.

Below is a list of the most important grammar features, with explanations and examples, from the content domain that your students will need to be familiar with for the GPS test. Students will be expected to know any terminology shown in bold.

- **Nouns** are names of people (*Melissa*), places (*Beijing*), things (*waistcoat*) or ideas (*happiness*). Nouns can be singular (*hat*) or plural (*hats*). **Proper nouns** – names for people, places, days and months – need a capital letter.

- **Verbs** are 'doing words' (*jump*, *walk*) or 'being words' (*have*, *think*). A verb should 'agree' with its subject (*I think*; *she thinks*).

- **Adjectives** are words that describe nouns. Adjectives can add detail (*the marvellous magician*) or compare two nouns (*Your cat is fatter than my cat*).

- **Personal pronouns** can replace nouns to aid **cohesion**: to avoid repetition and make sentences flow more naturally (*I ate the pie and it was yummy* versus *I ate the pie and the pie was yummy*).

- **Possessive pronouns** show ownership of something. They can work with nouns (*It is my car*) or they can replace nouns (*The car is mine*).

- **Relative pronouns** (*who*, *whose*, *that* and *which*) introduce **relative clauses**. Use *who* and *whose* to talk about people and *that* and *which* to talk about things. You never use a comma before *that*, but you always need one before *who*, *whose* and *which*.

- **Adverbs** are describing words. They tell you more about verbs (*He moved stealthily*) but can also describe adjectives (*His face was really pale*), other adverbs (*His heart was beating unusually quickly*) and whole clauses (*Finally, he saw it*). Students need to know that you add -ly to an adjective to create a regular adverb. They also need to know how to express time (*then*), place (*everywhere*) and cause (*therefore*), and indicate degrees of possibility (*possibly*) using adverbs.

- **Adverbials** are groups of words that act as an adverb. An adverbial phrase can tell you how (*She arrived by unicycle*), where (*She appeared from behind the wall*) and when (*After the show,*) something is happening.

- Students need to know how to use **prepositions** to express time (*before*), place (*under*) and cause (*because of*).

- **Determiners** come before nouns to make them more specific (*the*, *this*, *six*, *your*) or more general (*a*, *an*). Students should know to use *a* if the next word begins with a consonant and *an* if the next word begins with a vowel.

- **Modal verbs** come before other verbs to indicate degrees of possibility (*may*), certainty (*will*) and necessity (*must*).

- **Noun phrases** add extra information to a noun (*the picturesque Norfolk countryside*). Students should be able to expand noun phrases using adjectives (*the vicious cat*), nouns (*the litter of cats*) and preposition phrases (*the cat under the bed*).

- **Sentences** must have a subject and a verb. They do not have to have an object (*She smiled*).

- The **subject** of a sentence is who or what the sentence is about (*The boy ate all of his vegetables*).

- The **object** is the person or thing that the verb is being done to or done with (*The boy ate all of his vegetables*).

ENGLISH
YEAR 6

Curriculum Guidance

- There are four main **sentence types**:
  - **Statements** state a fact or opinion and usually end in a full stop (*My favourite frog is the red one*).
  - **Questions** ask something and always end with a question mark. Students will gain marks if they form a question using a question word (*What time is it?*), inversion (*Is it time?*) or by adding a question tag (*It's time, isn't it?*) but not by adding a question mark to a statement (*It's time?*).
  - **Commands** order or instruct someone to do something. A command contains an imperative verb (*Come away from the edge*). You can describe this to students as a 'bossy verb'.
  - **Exclamations** show strong feelings such as shock, joy and excitement. To be classed as a sentence, an exclamation must start with *what* or *how*, include a verb and end in an exclamation mark (*What a surprise that was!*) A minor sentence with an exclamation mark (*Happy birthday!*) will not be marked correct in the test.

- There are three main types of **clause**:
  - **Main clauses** have a subject and an object and must make sense on their own (*Jimmy laughed*).
  - **Subordinate clauses** are introduced by a co-ordinating conjunction (*Although*) and do not make sense on their own (*Although he knew he shouldn't, Jimmy laughed loudly*).
  - **Relative clauses** are a type of **subordinate clause**. They give more detail about the noun and always come after it. Use commas to separate a relative clause from the main clause. (*Jimmy, who had just seen Sanjay fall in the mud, laughed loudly*).

- There are two main types of **conjunction:**
  - **Co-ordinating conjunctions** join main clauses (*He huffed and he puffed*).
  - **Sub-ordinating conjunctions** join subordinate clauses to main clauses (*It rained so we went inside*).

- Students need to be able to use conjunctions to express time (*I had to finish my homework before I could go out to play*), place (*I went to Rome where there are lots of old buildings*) and cause (*I left early because I had to visit the dentist*).

- The **simple past tense** is used to talk about something that happened in the past. It usually ends in *-ed* (*I walked*) and always has one verb component (*I ran* versus *I have run*). The **simple present tense** is used to talk about something that is happening now (*I walk*) and also has one verb component (*I run* versus *I am running*).

- Verbs in the **perfect form** are used to say that something happened at an unspecified point in the past. The present perfect is formed with *have* or *has* before a past participle (*have visited, has seen*). The past perfect is formed with *had* before a past participle (*had visited, had seen*).

- The **present and past progressive tenses** express a continuous event in the present or past and have two verb components: a present or past tense form of *to be* and a present participle (*is working* – present, and *were playing* – past).

- Students will be expected to use **tenses** consistently throughout writing.

- Students should be able to recognise **subjunctive verb forms** and know they are appropriate for formal writing.

- Students should be able to use the **passive voice** in place of the **active voice** to affect the presentation of information in a text (*She stole the pie* – active, versus *The pie was stolen* – passive).

- Students should know that **Standard English** requires the use of standard verb forms (*I did* versus *I done*), standard pronouns (*those books* versus *them books*) and standard adverbs (*run quickly* versus *run quick*).

- Students should be able to recognise **formal** and **informal vocabulary** (*enquire* versus *ask about*) and **formal** and **informal structures** such as the passive voice and the subjunctive form.

ENGLISH — YEAR 6

REVISE MAPPING GUIDE

Pearson's *Revise* series provides simple, clear support to Year 6 students preparing for the National Curriculum tests. Parents may ask if you know of any independent study resources that they can work through with their child, or you may wish to provide such resources yourself. We have provided a mapping guide from each lesson in this pack to a corresponding page in the *Revise* series, to make such recommendations easier for you.

For students working towards the 'expected standard', we recommend the following titles:
- *Revise* Key Stage 2 SATs English Revision Guide – Expected Standard (ISBN: 978 1 292 14601 0)
- *Revise* Key Stage 2 SATs English Revision Workbook – Expected Standard (ISBN: 978 1 292 14600 3)

If you are looking to help pupils work at a greater depth, we recommend the following titles:
- *Revise* Key Stage 2 SATs English Revision Guide – Above Expected Standard (ISBN: 978 1 292 14599 0)
- *Revise* Key Stage 2 SATs English Revision Workbook – Above Expected Standard (ISBN: 978 1 292 14598 3)

The Revision Guides and Revision Workbooks for each level correspond page-for-page, so the page references are the same for both.

Lesson		*Revise* - Expected Standard		*Revise* - Above Expected Standard	
		What's in the book?	Page	What's in the book?	Page
1	Diagnostic	This lesson touches on many topics from the Revision guide		This lesson touches on many topics from the Revision guide	
2	Question types	Selected answers; Free answers	56, 57	Retrieving information; Selecting an answer; Free answers	57, 58, 59
3	Non-fiction features	Non-fiction features	60		
4	Finding answers	Retrieving and recording; Point, evidence, explain; Summarising	61, 62, 63	Retrieving information; Using evidence; Inference; Prediction; Summarising themes; Making comparisons	57, 60, 61, 62, 68, 69
5	Character, theme and language	Character; Theme; Author's language	66, 67, 72	Author's language; Inference about characters; Summarising themes	63, 67, 68
6	Meaning	Finding meaning; Inference; Predicting	68, 69, 70	Inference; Prediction; Word meanings	61, 62, 66
7	Making comparisons	Making comparisons	71	Making comparisons	69
8	Poetry (similes and metaphors)	Similes and metaphors	75	Similes; Metaphor	76, 77
9	Poetry (other figurative language)	Personification; Alliteration and onomatopoeia	76, 77	Alliteration; Personification; Onomatopoeia	73, 74, 75
10	Audience and purpose	Audience and purpose;	45	Audience and purpose	44
11	The writing process	Planning and organising; Writing and editing	46, 47	Planning and organising; Drafting and improving	45, 46
12	The editing process	Writing and editing; Checking	47, 48	Drafting and improving; Proof-reading	46, 47
13	Articles	Writing articles	49	Instructions and reports	50
14	Explanations	Writing explanations	50	None	
15	Persuasive letters	Writing persuasive letters	51	Persuasive writing	49
16	Balanced arguments	Writing balanced arguments	52	Persuasive writing	49

ENGLISH
YEAR 6

TUTORS GUILD

REVISE MAPPING GUIDE

Lesson		*Revise* - Expected Standard		*Revise* - Above Expected Standard	
		What's in the book? / Page		What's in the book? / Page	
17	Writing fiction	Writing stories	53	Writing stories	48
18	Nouns	Nouns; Noun phrases	1, 2	Noun phrases	2
19	Pronouns and determiners	Pronouns; Possessive pronouns; Determiners	3, 4, 5	Pronouns; Possessive pronouns; Determiners	1, 3, 4
20	Adjectives and adverbs	Adjectives; Adverbs; Adverbial phrases	6, 12, 13	Adjectives and adjectival phrases; Adverbs; Adverbial phrases	5, 12, 13
21	Verbs – present	Present tense; Perfect and future tenses; Tense consistency	7, 9, 10	Verbs; Present and past tense; Present and past perfect tense	6, 7, 10
22	Verbs – past	Past tense; Perfect and future tenses; Tense consistency	8, 9, 10	Verbs; Present and past tense; Present and past perfect tense	6, 7, 10
23	Verbs – future and modal	Perfect and future tenses; Tense consistency; Modal verbs	9, 10, 11	Future tense; Modal verbs; Future perfect tense; Subjunctive	8, 9, 11, 17
24	Conjunctions and prepositions	Conjunctions; Prepositions	14, 15	Conjunctions; Prepositions; Prepositional phrases	14, 15, 16
25	Sentence types	Statements and questions; Commands and exclamations	16, 17	Questions; Commands and exclamations	18, 19
26	Subject and object	Subject and object; Active and passive	18, 19	Subject and object; Active and passive voice	20, 25
27	Clauses	Phrases, Main clauses; Subordinate clauses; Relative clauses; Subject-verb agreement;	20, 21, 22, 23, 24	Phrases and clauses; Main and subordinate clauses; Compound and complex sentences; Relative clauses	21, 22, 23, 24
28	Standard English	Standard English	25	Standard English verbs; Standard English tense and voice; Standard English Grammar	26, 27, 28
29	Basic sentence punctuation	Capital letters; Ending a sentence	26, 27	None	
30	Commas	Commas in lists; Commas for clarity	28, 29	Commas for clarity	29
31	Parenthesis	Parenthesis	30	Parenthesis	30
32	Colons and semi-colons	Colons; Semi-colons	31, 32	Colons; Semi-colons	31, 32
33	Apostrophes	Apostrophes: possession; Apostrophes: contraction	33, 34	Possessive apostrophes; Apostrophes for contractions	33, 34
34	Punctuating speech	Punctuating speech	35	Direct speech	35
35	Hyphens and single dashes	Hyphens and single dashes	36	Hyphens and ellipses	37
36	Word families	Word families; Prefixes; Suffixes; Plurals	37, 38, 39, 41	Prefixes; Suffixes	38, 39
37	Synonyms, antonyms and homophones	Synonyms and antonyms; Homophones	40, 44	Synonyms and antonyms; Homophones and homonyms	40, 43
38	Tricky spellings	Tricky spellings; More tricky spellings	42, 43	Tricky spellings: silent letters; Tricky spellings: pronunciation	41, 42

ENGLISH
— YEAR 6 —

NEEDS ANALYSIS

For parents

We have a tutor because …
(Briefly explain why you have employed a tutor.)

Where we are currently …
(Briefly explain how your child is currently progressing. Has the school given you any feedback?)

For students

(Use this space to tell your tutor about yourself.)

I am …

Quiet ☺ ←☐—☐—☐—☐—☐→ ☺ Chatty
Shy ☺ ←☐—☐—☐—☐—☐→ ☺ Confident
Disorganised ☺ ←☐—☐—☐—☐—☐→ ☺ Organised
Serious ☺ ←☐—☐—☐—☐—☐→ ☺ Funny

I like …

☐ Writing ☐ Working on my own ☐ Drawing
☐ Playing games ☐ Working with someone else ☐ Colouring

How I feel about English …
Do you like English? Try to explain why or why not.
What are your favourite and least favourite parts?

ENGLISH
YEAR 6

NEEDS ANALYSIS

Our goals

Work together to set small, achievable goals for the year ahead. Make them as positive as you can and don't limit your goals to areas of English – think about personal development too. Together, look back at this list often to see how you are progressing.

Tick off each goal when you've achieved it!

In four weeks' time, I will …

- [ ] ....
- [ ] ....
- [ ] ....
- [ ] ....
- [ ] ....
- [ ] ....

In three months' time, I will …

- [ ] ....
- [ ] ....
- [ ] ....
- [ ] ....
- [ ] ....
- [ ] ....

By the end of Year 6, I will …

- [ ] ....
- [ ] ....
- [ ] ....
- [ ] ....
- [ ] ....
- [ ] ....

ENGLISH
YEAR 6

PROGRESS REPORT

Fill in the boxes below with help from your tutor.

Things I'm really good at include ...
(Which areas of English do you think you've done really well in recently? Think of at least three!)

My favourite English topic is ...
(Which English topic is your favourite? It doesn't have to be one you are really good at!)

because ...

Activities I really enjoy ...
(Which types of activities do you really enjoy? Try to think of at least three!)

Areas of English I need to work on ...
(In which areas of English do you think you need more practice?)

To improve these areas, we are going to ...
(This space is for your tutor to explain how he/she is going to help you become confident in these areas.)

ENGLISH
— YEAR 6 —

END-OF-LESSON REPORT

We have looked at last week's homework and my tutor thinks ...
(This space is for your tutor to explain how you did on last week's homework.)

Today, we have worked on ...
(This space is for you to list all of the topics you and your tutor have worked on today.)

I feel ...
(This space is for you to explain how you feel about today's lesson. Did you enjoy it? Do you feel confident?)

My tutor thinks ...
(This space is for your tutor to explain how the lesson went.)

At home this week, we can ...
(This space is for your tutor to explain what your homework is and give you other ideas for extra learning.)

ENGLISH
— YEAR 6 —

1 Diagnostic lesson

LEARNING OBJECTIVES
- To find out how well the student reads and writes, and to understand their grammar, spelling and punctuation proficiency
- To find out the student's preferences and attitudes

CONTENT DOMAINS
- A mix of reading, writing and GPS objectives

STARTER ACTIVITY
- **This or that?; 5 minutes; page 18**
  This is a fun ice-breaking activity that provides a light-touch insight into the student's preferences and attitudes. Cover the choices on the sheet so that you reveal each pair one at a time. Ensure the student answers as quickly as possible but allow time for discussion/justification.

MAIN ACTIVITIES
- **Grammar, punctuation and spelling; 20 minutes; page 19**
  This activity provides a brief insight into the student's grammar, punctuation and spelling proficiency. Guide and support the student; this should not be administered as a formal test. Read aloud the full text in the spelling question (see answers) and allow time for the student to fill in the gaps. The words are all taken from the national curriculum word-list for Years 5 and 6.
- **Reading and writing; 20 minutes; page 20**
  This activity provides an opportunity to hear how well the student reads. You may wish to carry out a running record or miscue analysis. The writing element will provide an early indication of how well the student can compose a piece of writing following a model. Allow time to discuss the student's ideas before they write.

PLENARY ACTIVITY
- **Rewards; 5 minutes**
  Ask the student what kind of things help or motivate them. Do they like a timed challenge? Do they like stickers? Do they prefer numerical marks or comments or both? What do they consider a reward? Decide on a suitable reward system. You may wish to confirm this approach with the student's parent(s) or guardian(s).

HOMEWORK ACTIVITY
- **The eight-legged recluse; 30 minutes; page 21**
  This activity is a reading comprehension exercise that incorporates some grammar elements too. Review the answers with the student at the next session.

DIFFERENTIATION AND EXTENSION IDEAS
- **Reading and writing** Ask questions to assess the student's comprehension of the story. Support by allowing time for the student to produce a short plan before they start writing.
- **The eight-legged recluse** Ask the student to research and record some further information about octopuses.

PROGRESS AND OBSERVATIONS

ENGLISH
— YEAR 6 —

Starter activity: This or that?

Timing: 5 mins

Learning objectives
- To reveal preferences from a pair of choices

Equipment
- highlighter

Your tutor will now reveal a series of strange choices. For each pair, highlight the one you prefer. Don't think about it for too long; just choose!

white bread		brown bread
loud		quiet
live one life for 1,000 years		live ten lives in 1,000 years
reading		writing
change the past		see into the future
no knees		no elbows
free chocolate		free ice cream
sing in the shower		dance in public
no internet for a week		no washing for a week
dogs		cats
fruit		vegetables
get up early	or	stay up late
be a police officer		be a fire fighter
be invisible		be a mind reader
spelling		grammar
fast		strong
cleverest		most popular
family occasions		friends' birthdays
cook a meal		tidy up after a meal
think about homework		talk about homework
summer		winter
a thick coat in a desert		pyjamas at the north pole
beach		pool
yes		no

18

ENGLISH
— YEAR 6 —

MAIN ACTIVITY: GRAMMAR, PUNCTUATION AND SPELLING   TIMING: 20 MINS

LEARNING OBJECTIVES	EQUIPMENT
• To measure confidence in grammar, punctuation and spelling	none

Your tutor will read you a short piece of text. Fill in the missing words below, spelling them as well as you can.

1. Most experts agree that climate change will have a _____ effect on the _____.
   They say that it will take a _____ effort by everyone to make the _____ changes.
   Evidence shows that the _____ of the world is rising, and _____
   will need to take _____ action. _____ to others, the dangers are being _____.

2. **The following sentences are missing some punctuation. Rewrite them correctly below.**

   a) last saturday i went to visit my aunt who is 67 because it was her birthday

   ----

   ----

   b) "no youre too late said the guard "the train has already left

   ----

   ----

   c) Paresh bought a pair of gloves (it was cold outside some strawberries a tin of tuna and a cola

   ----

   ----

3. **Underline the nouns and circle the adjectives in this sentence.**

   A huge, white dog bounded happily across the lawn and into the neat flowerbed.

4. **Underline the subordinate clause in this sentence.**

   Kerrie loved her pet tortoise although she wished it would move a bit faster.

5. **Circle the modal verbs in this sentence.**

   "Perhaps you could stay a bit longer because I may be able to give you a lift later."

ENGLISH
— YEAR 6 —

MAIN ACTIVITY: READING AND WRITING

TIMING: 20 MINS

LEARNING OBJECTIVES
- To read a text out loud with confidence
- To write a story using a stimulus

EQUIPMENT
none

Read the following passage out loud.

"Where are you going, Finn?" his mum asked. "It's nearly time to go to the restaurant."

Finn was strapping on his bike helmet. "Do I really have to come, Mum?" he protested. "It's gonna be so boring!"

"Yes," insisted his mum. "It's your gran's seventieth birthday."

"But … but," said Finn, searching his mind for excuses, "but you're always telling me to get off my games station and get more fresh air."

His mum rolled her eyes and smiled at him. "Well, okay, ten minutes only. Is that helmet on properly?"

"Uh-huh," he replied and shot out of the door before she could delay him any longer.

Finn was in a desperate hurry. He had to get the object back to Harry. And now he only had five minutes to get there. He leapt onto his bike and pedalled furiously out on to street. He could feel the strange coldness of the object through his coat pocket. He stood up on the pedals to accelerate and powered on. His thigh muscles began to ache.

Four minutes later, he reached the corner of Harry's cul-de-sac. The object in his pocket suddenly dropped in temperature. It felt like ice directly on his skin and it threw him off balance. He swerved and the front wheel of his bike clipped the pavement hard enough to twist the handlebars out of his grip. Before he could regain control, Finn's world turned upside down and he felt a terrible pain shoot through his shoulder.

Now discuss with your tutor what you think might happen next.
On a separate piece of paper, spend ten minutes writing the next part of the story.
Is Finn OK? Does he get the object back to Harry?

ENGLISH — YEAR 6

HOMEWORK ACTIVITY: THE EIGHT-LEGGED RECLUSE

TIMING: 30 MINS

LEARNING OBJECTIVES
- To improve reading comprehension skills

EQUIPMENT
none

Read the following passage.

The eight-legged recluse

In the old days, pubs were full of sailors happy to tell you a terrifying tale for the price of a pint of beer. An old sea dog would often describe his encounter with a vicious sea beast. He would wave his arms around wildly as he told you how his ship had been almost overwhelmed by a huge monster with a thousand arms of enormous strength. The myth of the giant, ship-crunching octopus would strike terror into the hearts of his audience.

The truth about the octopus is a lot less frightening. Whilst very large octopuses do exist around the world, those living in European waters never grow more than a metre long. In fact, the majority are quite small. Despite its monstrous reputation, the octopus is actually a shy, house-proud creature. All it really wants is a nice hole to hide in. It can also hide in plain sight by using a network of pigment cells in its skin to match its background. If threatened, the octopus squirts a cloud of dark ink to mask its escape. It propels itself away rapidly by expelling water through a funnel. With no skeleton, the fleeing octopus can squeeze into impossibly small cracks where a predator cannot follow.

On a separate piece of paper, answer the following questions.

1. Copy out an example of alliteration from the first paragraph.

2. Find a word in the first paragraph that is a synonym of 'destroyed'.

3. How does an octopus camouflage itself?

4. What does the author mean by 'an old sea dog' in the first paragraph?

5. Find and copy two adjectives that describe the octopus's real behaviour.

6. Copy out a fronted adverbial from the second paragraph.

7. What do you think the word 'recluse' means in the title?

8. What word is an antonym of the word 'majority' in the second paragraph?

ENGLISH
— YEAR 6 —

1 ANSWERS

STARTER ACTIVITY: THIS OR THAT?
Student's own answer.

MAIN ACTIVITY: GRAMMAR, PUNCTUATION AND SPELLING
1. Check the student has identified and spelled the missing words correctly:
Most experts agree that climate change will have a <u>disastrous</u> effect on the <u>environment</u>. They say that it will take a <u>determined</u> effort by everyone to make the <u>necessary</u> changes. Evidence shows that the <u>average</u> <u>temperature</u> of the world is rising, and <u>governments</u> will need to take <u>aggressive</u> action. <u>According</u> to others, the dangers are being <u>exaggerated</u>.
2. a) Last Saturday, I went to visit my aunt, who is sixty-seven, because it was her birthday.
   b) "No, you're too late," said the guard. "The train has already left."
   c) Paresh bought a pair of gloves (it was cold outside), some strawberries, a tin of tuna and a cola.
3. A (huge) (white) dog bounded happily across the <u>lawn</u> and into the (neat) flowerbed.
4. Kerrie loved her pet tortoise <u>although she wished it would move a bit faster</u>.
5. "Perhaps you (could) stay a bit longer because I (may) be able to give you a lift later".

MAIN ACTIVITY: READING AND WRITING
Student's own writing. Check the student has written their version of the next part of the story.

HOMEWORK ACTIVITY: THE EIGHT-LEGGED RECLUSE
Answers may vary.
1. 'to tell you a terrifying tale'; 2. overwhelmed; 3. by using a network of pigment cells in its skin to match its background; 4. an old sailor; 5. shy, house-proud; 6. 'despite its monstrous reputation'; 7. something that is shy and hides away; 8. minority

GLOSSARY

Noun
A naming word for a person, place or thing.

Adjective
A word that describes a noun. It can come before or after the noun it describes.

Subordinate clause
A clause that is introduced by a subordinating conjunction and that must contain a subject and a verb. It does not make sense as a sentence on its own. A subordinate clause can be placed before or after a main clause with appropriate punctuation.

Modal verb
A verb, such as *may*, *should* or *must*, that comes before another verb to show how possible, certain or necessary something is.

Synonym
Words that have the same or a very similar meanings, such as *happy* and *cheerful*.

Antonym
Words that have opposite meanings, such as *beautiful* and *ugly*.

Alliteration
When a series of words that start with the same sound or letter are close together, such as *the silly sausage saw a sad salad*.

Fronted adverbial
A fronted adverbial phrase is placed at start of a sentence and separated from the main clause by a comma.

Non fiction text: Report

REPORT:
WHAT ARE ANTIBIOTICS?

Bacteria are microscopic organisms. Some bacteria are harmless, while others are good for us. Antibiotics are used to treat infections caused by bacteria, from sore throats to killer diseases such as tuberculosis (TB).

The first antibiotic was discovered in 1928 by the Scottish scientist, Alexander Fleming. He accidentally discovered that some mould growing in a dish had stopped bacteria growing. He named the active chemical in the mould penicillin. It is estimated that the discovery of penicillin has saved several hundred million lives.

◀ Alexander Fleming discovered the first antibiotic in 1928

Antibiotics work in one of two ways. One type of antibiotic, such as penicillin, kills the bacteria. This type usually attacks the cell walls of the bacteria so that they burst and can no longer harm you.

Another type of antibiotic prevents the bacteria from multiplying, slowing down the infection. This allows your body's own defences (called the immune system) to better fight the infection.

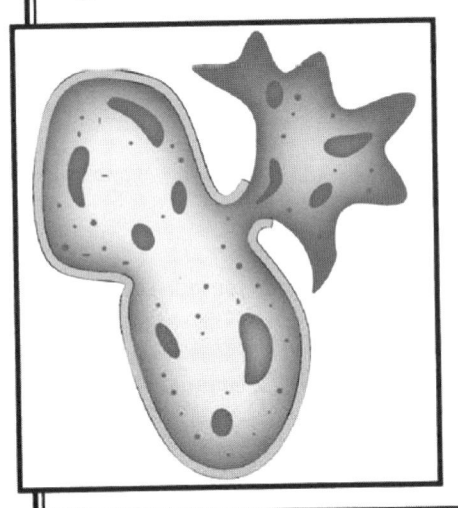

Some antibiotics can fight many types of bacteria in the body, while others are more specific. Penicillin only kills a few types of bacteria. It is known as a narrow-spectrum antibiotic. Tetracycline works against a wide range of bacteria. It is called a broad-spectrum antibiotic.

Antibiotics do not work against viruses and viral infections, such as common colds or flu.

◀ The cell walls of a bacterium bursting because of an antibiotic

NON-FICTION TEXT: NEWS ARTICLE

Science News

No. 1

Forget Zombies! Is the Antibiotic Apocalypse coming?

By Claire Coombes, Health Reporter, 16th March 2016

Imagine if a simple paper cut could kill you.

Scientists are warning that we could be facing an 'antibiotic apocalypse'.

This is because some bacteria are now able to fight off even the strongest antibiotics. The bacteria have become resistant. If bacteria become completely resistant to antibiotics, common infections will become untreatable and as dangerous as they were before the discovery of penicillin.

Pills given out 'like sweets'

So why aren't antibiotics working so well anymore? Research suggests that bacteria have become more and more resistant to antibiotics because we use them too often and in the wrong way.

There is evidence that doctors are giving people too many antibiotics, sometimes when they don't need them at all. Some people accuse doctors of handing them out 'like sweets', even for colds caused by viruses. Also, some patients don't finish all of their pills because they are feeling better, which helps bacteria develop resistance.

It is also claimed that farmers use too many antibiotics on their animals. Resistant bacteria develop on farms.

This resistance can then transfer to bacteria found in our bodies. In Europe, farmers have been banned from giving antibiotics to farm animals to help them grow, but this still happens in other parts of the world.

Whether for humans or animals, scientists stress that antibiotics should now only be used when absolutely necessary.

Nanobots vs Superbugs

It may sound like a rubbish sci-fi movie, but the future of fighting resistant bacteria (so-called superbugs) may be a battle between bugs and machines!

To avoid an antibiotic apocalypse, drug companies are putting lots of effort into developing a new generation of antibiotics. They are also experimenting with other kinds of medicines, some even made from insects!

It may even be possible to fight bacteria using microscopic technology. One day, doctors might inject tiny robots into your body that would fight bacteria in one-on-one combat.

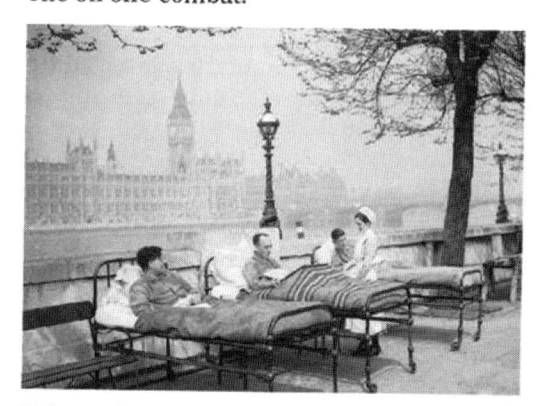

Before antibiotics, the only treatment for killer diseases like tuberculosis was fresh air. Will we see scenes like this on our streets again?

Non-fiction text: Explanation

How do vaccinations work?

Antibiotics fight infections, but vaccinations prevent us from catching dangerous diseases like measles, mumps and whooping cough. Normally, your body's defences (your immune system) find it hard to react quickly enough to fight off such invaders. A vaccination trains your immune system to fight a disease quickly. So, how does it work?

First, scientists make a weakened version of a dangerous bacterium or virus. It is so weak that it cannot actually give you the disease itself. Using this, the scientists make a safe and stable medicine called a vaccine for doctors to give to patients.

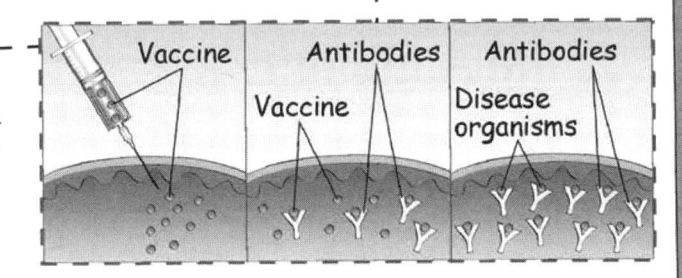

Next, a doctor usually injects a dose of the vaccine into your body. The vaccine triggers a very important and clever reaction because it makes your body produce special Y-shaped molecules called antibodies. You can produce millions of antibodies a day. Your immune system sends these antibodies around your body to fight and destroy the weakened version of the disease organism that was injected into your body.

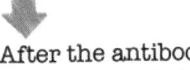

After the antibodies have done their job, most of them break down. But it's as if your immune system has been to school. It has learned an important lesson and remembers it, often for the rest for your life! As a result, your body is now prepared to act quickly.

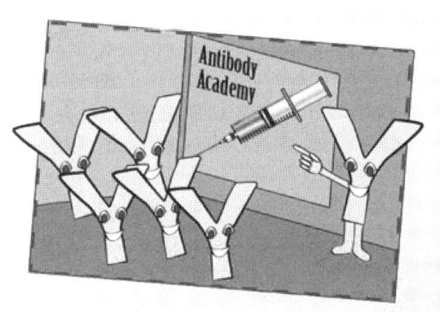

So now, if your body is invaded by the disease – this time the real, full-strength version – then special cells react immediately to produce millions of antibodies before the disease can make you ill.

Vaccines also protect communities. If most people are vaccinated, unvaccinated people are less likely to come in contact with dangerous diseases, so they probably won't get ill either. This means that the more people who are vaccinated in a community, the better.

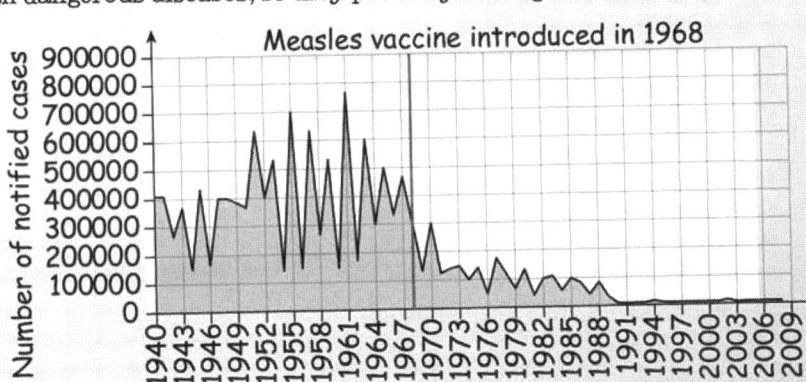

▶ The number of measles cases in the United Kingdom since 1940

ENGLISH
YEAR 6

FICTION TEXT: POEMS

POEM 1

Title: ....

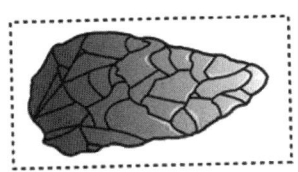

An emerald is as green as grass;
A ruby red as blood;
A sapphire shines as blue as heaven;
A flint lies in the mud.
A diamond is a brilliant stone,
To catch the world's desire;
An opal holds a fiery spark;
But a flint holds fire.

Christina Georgina Rossetti

POEM 2

Title: ....

A silver-scaled Dragon with jaws flaming red
Sits at my elbow and toasts my bread.
I hand him fat slices, and then, one by one,
He hands them back when he sees they are done.

William Jay Smith

POEM 3

Title: ....

The rusty spigot
sputters,
utters
a splutter,
spatters a smattering of drops,
gashes wider;
slash
splatters
scatters
spurts
finally stops sputtering
and plash!
gushes rushes splashes
clear water dashes.

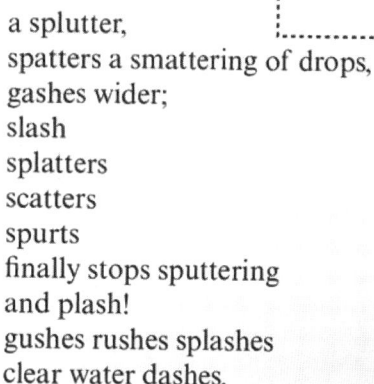

Eve Merriam

POEM 4

Title: ....

To begin to toboggan, first buy a toboggan,
But don't buy too big a toboggan.
(A too big a toboggan is not a toboggan
To buy to begin to toboggan.)

Colin West

ENGLISH — YEAR 6

FICTION TEXT: SHORT STORY

The Treasure Hunter

"Sal, look, there's a light ahead. I think we're nearly there."

"Stop!" whispered Salisbury Smith urgently. "Take it easy. There's something not right."

Several feet ahead in the narrow tunnel, Salisbury's old friend Gunther froze. Gunther knew he should listen to the treasure hunter's warning: it had saved his life a number of times.

"What's up, boss?" Gunther asked quietly. A bead of sweat snaked down his back.
"There's nothing but more walls and cobwebs. But look … the light."

Salisbury peered over his friend's shoulder, casting his experienced eye along the passage. He knew the kinds of dangers that might lay ahead: falling rocks, holes full of bamboo spikes, poisoned darts, fire pits. He knew because he had faced them the last time he had been here.

Gunther was right though. A faint glow – green … or was it blue … no, red – illuminated the bare walls of the tunnel up ahead. Apart from that, there was nothing out of the ordinary. Except, something was making his heart thump a little more firmly. Perhaps it was the weird, colourful light. Or perhaps it was just his own excitement building. Had he found it at last? Was he really nearly there? "Stay focused", he urged himself, although he felt a smile lifting the corners of his mouth.

"Well, Sal?" asked Gunther quietly.

"Swap places," said Salisbury. "I'll go first." Salisbury squeezed his powerful frame past his friend's rounder, softer body. Carefully, Salisbury moved further along the tunnel. Stopping every few paces, he shone his torchlight over the surfaces of the rock to look for any signs of trouble: a crack that might give way underfoot; a gap from which a blade might drop; or a hole from which a spike might thrust. Slowly, very slowly, they drew closer to a low doorway.

"Can you hurry up a bit?" asked Gunther casually. "I'm getting hungry."

Salisbury smiled back over his shoulder at his friend. "You're always hungry," he replied.

Gunther rolled his eyes. "Well, let's tick off some things on today's fun-filled checklist, shall we? Crocodile-infested swamp. Check. Giant falling statue. Check. Cave full of poisonous frogs. Check. Oh, and hour after hour of creeping through gloomy tunnels. Check! All this adventuring gives a man an appetite, you know."

FICTION TEXT: SHORT STORY CONTINUED...

The Treasure Hunter

Salisbury chuckled. "Stop your grumbling, big guy," he said.

"I'm only grumbling cos my stomach's rumbling," quipped Gunther.

"We're here," said Salisbury. He took a long breath in through his nose, bent down and slipped through the doorway.

Salisbury emerged into a small chamber that had been carved roughly out of the white rock. He stood up slowly. He was careful not to step any further yet. His keen eyes took in the room. Light filtered in from a hole in the ceiling and beamed down directly onto a stone pillar. An object sat on top of the pillar at shoulder height. Salisbury realised he still hadn't breathed out.
His fingers trembled as he let out a gasp. The object was more beautiful than he had ever imagined. After all these years, all the frustrations and failures, he had found it: the legendary crown of Azpaticus was suddenly only a few yards away. The light from the ceiling glinted and gleamed off hundreds of precious rubies, emeralds, and sapphires, casting a kaleidoscope of dancing colours across the walls and floor. It was so mesmerising that Salisbury barely noticed Gunther now standing beside him.

"Bingo," said Gunther with a smirk.

"Bingo indeed," replied Salisbury, nodding slowly. He was about to step forward when the hairs on his neck stood up. He frowned. There was something about the coloured lights. They seemed to be moving in a strange way, almost as if they were ...

"C'mon, Sal, grab the thing and let's get out of here," urged Gunther.

"Sure, why not?" Salisbury agreed with a tight smile. As was his habit, he rolled his neck to ease his tension. Something about the moving lights was holding him back. He shook his head.
Surely, it was just his imagination. It was just light reflecting off all those priceless jewels set in that beautiful crown. The crown he had been searching for ever since ...

Searching. That was the word. The lights were moving in a strange way, almost as if they were searching ...

A pinpoint of ruby light traced a path across Salisbury's chest. Half-way across, the spot of light stopped. It began to vibrate on the spot. Almost immediately, another light, this one emerald green, raced up his arm to join the red one. Salisbury watched in fascination as a blue light suddenly arced across the floor and up his leg. At the spot directly above Salisbury's heart, the three coloured dots combined in a brilliant point of excited white light.

The silence was broken by a loud rumble. Salisbury shot a worried glance at Gunther.

"I promise, that wasn't my stomach," Gunther gulped.

ENGLISH
YEAR 6

2 READING: QUESTION TYPES

LEARNING OBJECTIVES
- To become familiar with different types of question used in KS2 English assessments
- To deal with different response types appropriately
- To use textual evidence

CONTENT DOMAINS
- 2a give / explain the meaning of words in context
- 2b retrieve and record information / identify key details from fiction and non-fiction

STARTER ACTIVITY
- **Did you know?; 10 minutes; page 30**
  Discuss the information on the starter activity sheet with the student to familiarise them with the KS2 English testing arrangements.

MAIN ACTIVITIES
- **Selected answers; 10 minutes; page 31**
  This activity focuses on familiarising the student with selected answer questions. Emphasise how such questions do not demand a written response and how care should always be taken to respond in the correct way. For example: *Don't tick two boxes where it asks for only one.*
- **Short answers; 10 minutes; page 32**
  This activity focuses on familiarising the student with short answers, including single-word answers or those requiring a few words only, and inserting punctuation. Again, emphasise the importance of following the instructions, paying particular attention to any words in bold text.
- **Homework preparation; 15 minutes; page 33**
  Read the text on the homework sheet with the student to ensure they understand the content and the task (to write a set of selected and short answer questions about the text). Model an example and guide the student through creating their own question, or questions if you have time, using the question formats from the main activities.

PLENARY ACTIVITY
- **What's in the tests?; 5 minutes**
  Quiz the student on what they can recall about the testing arrangements discussed in the starter activity.

HOMEWORK ACTIVITY
- **Write your own; 45 minutes; page 34**
  This activity asks the student to write some selected or short answer questions about the given text. Model and discuss as outlined in the plenary activity above prior to setting this work. Give the student their completed main activity sheets to use as exemplars for question formats.

DIFFERENTIATION AND EXTENSION IDEAS
- **Did you know?** Update the information on the sheet to reflect any changes in testing arrangements.
- **Write your own** Support by preparing some blank questions using different formats (e.g. a tick box list) for the student to complete. Extend by asking the student to work out their own mark scheme.

PROGRESS AND OBSERVATIONS

ENGLISH
— YEAR 6 —

STARTER ACTIVITY: DID YOU KNOW?

TIMING: 10 MINS

LEARNING OBJECTIVES
- To understand the English SATs tests

EQUIPMENT
none

What do you know about the English tests at the end of Key Stage 2?
What will you have to do exactly?

At the moment, the English Key Stage 2 national curriculum tests include:

1. **An English reading test.**

   This test has one paper only.
   The test lasts 60 minutes, which includes reading time.
   You will be given a reading booklet and a separate answer booklet to write in.
   The reading booklet will have a selection of texts, which may include non-fiction, fiction and poetry.
   The maximum number of marks is 50.

2. **An English grammar, punctuation and spelling test.**

   This test has two papers:

   Paper 1: questions
   The test lasts 45 minutes.
   You will be given a question and answer booklet to write in.
   The maximum number of marks is 50.

   Paper 2: spelling
   The test lasts about 15 minutes.
   You will be given an answer booklet to write in.
   The maximum number of marks is 20.

You will take these tests on set dates with everyone else.
There is no writing test; your writing will be assessed by your teacher.

ENGLISH
YEAR 6

MAIN ACTIVITY: SELECTED ANSWER QUESTIONS **TIMING: 10 MINS**

LEARNING OBJECTIVES
- To measure confidence in grammar, punctuation and spelling

EQUIPMENT
none

For some questions in the reading test, you won't need to write anything.

Instead, you will need to tick, underline, circle or draw lines to show your answer.

Try to answer the questions below:

1. Draw lines to match the first names to the surnames of these famous people:

| David |
| Anne |
| William |
| Malala |

| Shakespeare |
| Yousafzai |
| Beckham |
| Frank |

2. Tick one box in each row to show whether each statement is a fact (f) or an opinion (o).

	f	o
Broccoli is really tasty.		
Barack Obama was the first African American President of the United States.		
Horror films are better than thriller films.		
England shares borders with Scotland and Wales.		

3. Circle the modal verbs in the sentence below.

   It might rain tomorrow, so we should probably cancel the barbecue.

4. Tick one option that describes this phrase: *as cold as ice.*

   ☐ metaphor

   ☐ alliteration

   ☐ simile

   ☐ personification

5. Underline the subordinate clause in the sentence below:

   The young woman, who was scared of flying, won a trip to Italy.

ENGLISH
— YEAR 6 —

MAIN ACTIVITY: SHORT ANSWER QUESTIONS	**TIMING: 10 MINS**

LEARNING OBJECTIVES
- To understand how to answer short answer questions

EQUIPMENT
none

For some questions you might need to write a few words or insert some punctuation.

1. Complete the sentence below by writing the prepositions from the box in the correct place. Use each preposition only once.

    | across | at | from |

    We caught the bus [____] Waterloo to Tower Bridge, walked [____] the bridge and arrived [____] the Tower of London.

2. Replace the underlined words in the sentence below with their expanded forms.

    They're arriving soon so we'd better get ready.

    [____]   [____]

3. Insert a colon in the correct place in the sentence below.

    Sorry we took so long to get here the train was delayed.

4. Rearrange the words in the statement below to make it a question. Use only the given words and remember to punctuate your sentence correctly.

    He should tell them what he did.

5. Answer these questions:

a) Write an explanation of the word *synonym*.

b) Write an antonym of the word *ugly*.

ENGLISH
— YEAR 6 —

HOMEWORK ACTIVITY: WRITE YOUR OWN QUESTIONS!   TIMING: 45 MINS

LEARNING OBJECTIVES
- To write selected answers or short answer questions about a text.

EQUIPMENT
none

Now it's your turn! Write some selected answer questions and some short answer questions in your book about the text below. They can be about the facts in the text or about grammar, punctuation or spelling. Think back to the type of questions you covered with your tutor if you need inspiration.

Famous moments in British history

In 55 BC, the Roman general Julius Caesar tried to invade Britain. He wanted to make Britain part of the Roman Empire. The Celts fought back and Caesar soon went back to Gaul (which is now France). It wasn't until nearly 100 years later that Emperor Claudius successfully conquered the south of Britain.

A great fire spread through central London in September 1666. It started in Pudding Lane in a baker's shop. The heat was so great that the lead roof of a cathedral melted. Amazingly, only five people were killed!

In 1805, Admiral Lord Nelson won a famous sea battle against the French and Spanish off the coast of Spain. The Battle of Trafalgar stopped Napoleon's plans to conquer Europe. During the battle, Nelson was struck by a single musket ball. His dying words were, "Thank God I have done my duty."

The Titanic set sail on its maiden voyage on 10th April 1912 with over 2,200 people on board. Five days later, it struck an iceberg in the Atlantic Ocean and sank. About 1,500 people died because there were not enough lifeboats.

In 1842, the Houses of Parliament voted to stop children under ten from working in mines. Coal was the main source of power, and children as young as five had worked underground for up to 12 hours a day in dangerous, dark conditions.

So far, the one and only time England has won a major football tournament was the 1966 World Cup. The captain was called Bobby Moore and he led his team to a 4-2 victory in the final against West Germany.

The first female prime minister of the United Kingdom was Margaret Thatcher. She was elected into power in 1979.

ENGLISH — YEAR 6

2 ANSWERS

STARTER ACTIVITY: THIS OR THAT?
Discussion with student. Check their understanding.

MAIN ACTIVITY: SELECTED ANSWER QUESTIONS
1. David Beckham; Anne Frank; William Shakespeare; Malala Yousafzai
2. opinion, fact, opinion, fact
3. It (might) rain tomorrow, so we (should) probably cancel the barbeque.
4. simile
5. The young woman, who was scared of flying, won a trip to Italy.

MAIN ACTIVITY: SHORT ANSWER QUESTIONS
1. We caught the bus [from] Waterloo to Tower Bridge, walked [across] the bridge and arrived [at] the Tower of London.
2. they are; we had
3. Sorry we took so long to get here: the train was delayed.
4. Should he tell them what he did?
5. a) a synonym is word with the same meaning as another word; b) pretty

HOMEWORK ACTIVITY: WRITE YOUR OWN QUESTIONS!
Student's own answers. Check they have written selected answer questions and short answer questions based on the homework text.

GLOSSARY

Question type
The format of a question, such as multiple choice, ranking/ordering, matching, labelling, find and copy, short response or open-ended response.

Response type
The type of response expected by a question, such as a selected response or an extended answer. In the cognitive domain, it refers to the complexity of the written responses required and the extent to which the student needs to organise/structure their responses.

Textual evidence
Text quoted directly from an extract as evidence for an answer, such as an exact fact or an inference made.

ENGLISH — YEAR 6

3 READING: NON-FICTION FEATURES

LEARNING OBJECTIVES
- To become familiar with the features of non-fiction texts
- To identify the features of reports, news articles and explanations
- To write a short report

CONTENT DOMAINS
- 2b retrieve and record information and identify key details from fiction and non-fiction
- 2f identify and explain how information and narrative content are related and contribute to meaning as a whole
- 2h make comparisons within the text

STARTER ACTIVITY
- **Fiction or non-fiction?; 5 minutes; page 36**
  Cut out the book titles before starting the session. This activity assesses the student's understanding of the difference between fiction and non-fiction. Explain that the main session involves examining a number of non-fiction texts.

MAIN ACTIVITIES
- **Non-fiction features; 25 minutes; page 37**
  Ask the student to identify the most likely non-fiction features from the cloud on the activity sheet, and discuss any gaps in knowledge depending on their answers. Next, ask the student to read the non-fiction texts (pages 23-25) out loud, and support as appropriate.
- **Find the features; 15 minutes; page 38**
  Ask the student to identify examples of non-fiction features from the three non-fiction texts about diseases. Encourage the student to use their knowledge of how the texts are organised to locate examples.

PLENARY ACTIVITY
- **Make up a book title; 5 minutes**
  On a whiteboard, write a fake book title, such as *A Childhood in Africa*. Ask the student to say whether they think it is a fiction or non-fiction book and what genre it might be, for example *report* or *autobiography*. Repeat or swap roles.

HOMEWORK ACTIVITY
- **Dangerous diseases; 45 minutes; page 39**
  This activity will allow you to assess the student's writing skills. Provide the student with some source material or suggest some websites they can use to complete the task. When you set it, discuss what is involved and help the student to complete the list of organisational features on the sheet.

DIFFERENTIATION AND EXTENSION IDEAS
- **Non-fiction genres** Extend by asking the student to first come up with their own list of non-fiction features.
- **Write a report** Add or remove questions to adjust the difficulty of the research task. Support by completing the list of organisational features or by providing a planning sheet or writing frame.

PROGRESS AND OBSERVATIONS

ENGLISH
— YEAR 6 —

STARTER ACTIVITY: FICTION OR NON-FICTION?   **TIMING: 5 MINS**

LEARNING OBJECTIVES
- To sort book titles into either fiction or non-fiction

EQUIPMENT
- scissors
- glue stick

Stick the book titles to the correct page in the book below. If you haven't heard of the titles, look at the type of words used in the titles to help you.

Fiction | **Non-fiction**

How to Survive in the Wild	Terry the Talking Tadpole
The Fall of the Roman Empire	THE BIG BOOK OF FUNNY FACTS
Weird World Weather	Space Gorillas from Mars
One Hundred Meat-Free Recipes	The Magic Carpet Adventure
REVENGE OF THE DINOSAUR ROBOTS	FISHFACE

ENGLISH
— YEAR 6 —

MAIN ACTIVITY: NON-FICTION FEATURES   **TIMING: 25 MINS**

LEARNING OBJECTIVES
- To identify features in non-fiction texts

EQUIPMENT
- highlighter
- Non-fiction texts from pages 23–25

What features would you expect to find in non-fiction texts?

Look at the cloud below and highlight all the features you think you might find in a non-fiction text.

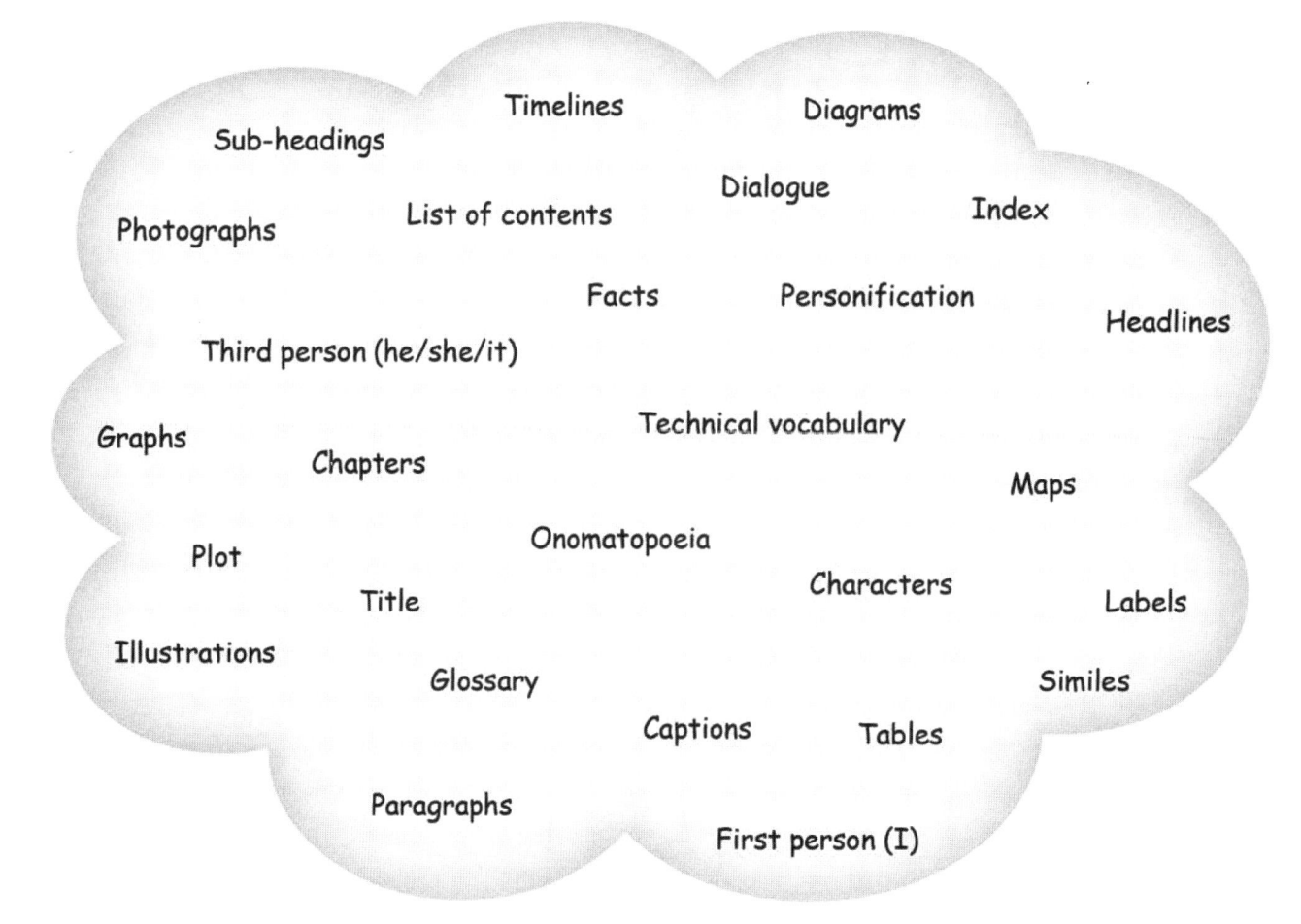

- Timelines
- Diagrams
- Sub-headings
- Dialogue
- Index
- Photographs
- List of contents
- Facts
- Personification
- Headlines
- Third person (he/she/it)
- Technical vocabulary
- Graphs
- Maps
- Chapters
- Onomatopoeia
- Plot
- Characters
- Labels
- Title
- Illustrations
- Similes
- Glossary
- Captions
- Tables
- Paragraphs
- First person (I)

Read out loud the three non-fiction texts your tutor gives you.

ENGLISH
YEAR 6

MAIN ACTIVITY: FIND THE FEATURES **TIMING: 15 MINS**

LEARNING OBJECTIVES
- To identify features in non-fiction texts

EQUIPMENT
none

Complete this table with examples of some of the non-fiction features you identified in the three texts you have just read.

non-fiction feature	which text?	example
title		
headline		
sub-heading		
caption		
fact		
photograph		
label		
graph		
illustration		
third person (he/she/it)		
technical vocabulary		

ENGLISH
— YEAR 6 —

HOMEWORK ACTIVITY: DANGEROUS DISEASES **TIMING: 45 MINS**

LEARNING OBJECTIVES
- To write a short report

EQUIPMENT
- information from books or websites

Your task is to write about a disease of your choice.

Your tutor will suggest some books or websites that you can use for research. Here are some questions you might want to find answers to and include in your report:

- What is the name of the disease?
- What microorganism causes it? Is it a bacteria or a virus?
- Where does it come from? How do you catch it?
- What are the symptoms (signs that you have the disease)?
- What is the treatment?
- How do you protect yourself from it?
- Who does it affect? Everyone or just a group of people?
- What danger rating would you give it?

Before you begin, discuss with your tutor the list of features you will use to organise your work and write them below.

ENGLISH
YEAR 6

3 Answers

STARTER ACTIVITY: FICTION OR NON-FICTION?

Fiction:
Terry the Talking Tadpole
Space Gorillas from Mars
The Magic Carpet Adventure
Revenge of the Dinosaur Robots
Fishface

Non-fiction:
How to Survive in the Wild
The Fall of the Roman Empire
The Big Book of Funny Facts
Weird World Weather
One Hundred Meat-Free Recipes

MAIN ACTIVITY: NON-FICTION FEATURES

Student's own answers. Check that their responses focus on the most likely non-fiction features, such as list of contents, headlines and graphs, rather than the less likely, such as plot, personification and dialogue.

MAIN ACTIVITY: FIND THE FEATURES

Student's own answers. There are many examples of non-fiction features across the three texts. Examples include:
Label = vaccine; Technical vocabulary = nanobot, bacteria.

HOMEWORK ACTIVITY: DANGEROUS DISEASES

Student's own answers. When reviewing the student's report, discuss how successfully they have organised their report and the non-fiction features they have included.

Glossary

Non-fiction
Prose writing that is about facts and real events rather than being fictional.

Report
A non-fiction text full of facts about a particular topic. It describes what something is like. It has a title and an introduction, and information is organised into paragraphs with subheadings. The language is usually formal.

Explanation
A non-fiction text similar to a report which explains how or why something happens. The language is formal and the vocabulary often technical.

Article
A non-fiction text that reports or discusses a particular topic or event, such as a news story. It often contains a headline, subheadings, a range of opinions and captioned images.

4 Reading: Finding answers

Learning objectives
- To scan text to find answers
- To retrieve and record information
- To use Point, Evidence and Explain (PEE) to answer open questions

Content domains
- 2b retrieve and record information / identify key details from fiction and non-fiction texts

Starter activity
- **Scanning skills; 5 minutes; page 42**
  Show the student a copy of the news article *Forget Zombies! Is the Antibiotic Apocalypse Coming?* (page 24). Cover the words on the sheet and then reveal the first one. Ask the student to scan the text for the word and highlight it as quickly as possible. Repeat for each word one at a time.

Main activities
- **Fetch!; 20 minutes; page 43**
  This activity involves the student retrieving and recording pieces of information on a sticky note as quickly as they can from an explanation text placed on the other side of the room. Attach the explanation text *How do Vaccinations Work?* (page 25) to a wall or surface on the other side of the room. Cover the questions on the activity sheet and reveal them to the student one at a time, giving them a sticky note to record each answer on. Reveal the answer when they return with their completed sticky note. Emphasise that the student should retrieve and record exact words from the explanation text each time, rather than paraphrasing or making inferences. Check and discuss each answer the student presents.
- **Point, Evidence, Explain; 20 minutes; page 44**
  This activity encourages the student to practise answering open, multi-mark questions. Provide a clean copy of the news article *Forget Zombies! Is the Antibiotic Apocalypse Coming?* (page 24) and the explanation article *How do Vaccinations Work?* (page 25). Ensure completion of the activity is a collaborative process. Guide and discuss the PEE questions and support the student in finding evidence if they need it. Ensure the student uses evidence from the texts, not from other sources.

Plenary activity
- **Quick scan; 5 minutes**
  Show the student a copy of the news article from the starter activity. Ask the student to highlight and tally all instances of the noun *antibiotics* as quickly as possible (the word occurs 18 times).

Homework activity
- **Report comprehension; 45 minutes; page 45**
  This activity puts the student's scanning, retrieving and recording and PEE skills into practice. Discuss their answers when you review it together at the lesson.

Differentiation and extension ideas
- **Scanning skills** Add or remove words from the list. Extend by asking the student to scan for words that occur in the text more than once (see answers).
- **Point, Evidence, Explain** Extend by removing the scaffolding phrases in the answer box or add more to further support the student in framing an answer.

Progress and observations

ENGLISH
YEAR 6

STARTER ACTIVITY: SCANNING SKILLS

TIMING: 5 MINS

LEARNING OBJECTIVES
- To scan the text for particular words

EQUIPMENT
- highlighter

Your tutor will reveal the words in the table below one at a time. Scan the news article to find each word as quickly as you can, highlighting it when you find it.

bacteria
resistant
tuberculosis
Europe
microscopic
evidence
scientists

ENGLISH
YEAR 6

MAIN ACTIVITY: FETCH! **TIMING: 20 MINS**

LEARNING OBJECTIVES
- To find and record information from a text quickly and accurately

EQUIPMENT
- sticky notes
- stopwatch

This is a golden retriever. This type of dog is brilliant at fetching and bringing things back. In this activity, you are going to become an 'information retriever'.

Your tutor has placed a text on the other side of the room and will reveal the questions in the table below one-by-one. Find each answer in the text as quickly as possible, writing the exact words you need for your answer on a sticky note. Return to your tutor and check your answer. Remember, you must record the information accurately.

What is the proper name for your body's defences?
the immune system
When was the measles vaccine introduced in the United Kingdom?
1968
What are antibodies?
special Y-shaped molecules
How are vaccines usually given to patients?
a doctor usually injects a dose of vaccine into your body
What happens to antibodies after an infection?
most of them break down
Why do scientists use a weakened organism for vaccines?
so that it cannot actually give you the disease itself
What are the names of three diseases you can be vaccinated against?
measles, mumps and whooping cough
How do vaccines help communities?
unvaccinated people are less likely to come into contact with dangerous diseases

ENGLISH
— YEAR 6 —

MAIN ACTIVITY: POINT, EVIDENCE, EXPLAIN　　　　**TIMING: 20 MINS**

LEARNING OBJECTIVES
- To write a longer answer that uses evidence from the text

EQUIPMENT
- highlighter

This is an example of an open question:
Why are antibiotics and vaccines both important to human health?

To answer this open question, you will need to look at the news article and the explanation text.

Before you write your answer below, discuss these questions with your tutor.

What general POINT would you make first?

What EVIDENCE can you find for this in the texts? Highlight it.

Can you EXPLAIN how this evidence proves your point?

Now write your answer in full sentences below.

Antibiotics and vaccines are important because ...

This means that ...

ENGLISH
— YEAR 6 —

HOMEWORK ACTIVITY: REPORT COMPREHENSION

TIMING: 45 MINS

LEARNING OBJECTIVES
- To use your answer-finding skills
- To scan, retrieve and record and use PEE

EQUIPMENT
- highlighter
- report text

Read the report text about antibiotics and answer the following questions on a separate piece of paper.

Use one- or two-word answers for these questions:

1. Who discovered penicillin?

2. What is the name of a broad-spectrum antibiotic?

3. What is the full name of the disease TB?

4. When was penicillin discovered?

5. Antibiotics are useful to treat common colds. True or false?

6. Are all bacteria dangerous?

7. What are bacteria?

Use a longer phrase or sentence for these questions:

8. What happens to some bacteria when they come into contact with penicillin?

9. In what two ways do antibiotics work?

Try to use Point, Evidence, Explain (PEE) for this question:

10. Why was the discovery of penicillin so important?

4 Answers

Starter activity: Scanning skills

Student's own answers. Three words occur more than once in the text (bacteria 10; resistant 5; scientists 2).

Main activity: Fetch!

1. the immune system
2. 1968
3. special Y-shaped molecules
4. a doctor usually injects a dose of vaccine into your body
5. most of them break down
6. so that it cannot actually give you the disease itself
7. measles, mumps and whooping cough
8. unvaccinated people are less likely to come into contact with dangerous diseases

Main activity: Point, Evidence, Explain

Student's own answer. Check the student has used PEE to answer the question, for example:

Antibiotics and vaccines are important because they protect us from dangerous diseases. Before antibiotics, treatment for tuberculosis (TB) was "fresh air". Without antibiotics, common infections would become "untreatable and dangerous again." Vaccines prevent people "from catching dangerous diseases" by training "your immune system to fight a disease quickly." This means that antibiotics and vaccines are both important for keeping us healthy and fighting diseases.

Homework activity: Report comprehension

1. Alexander Fleming
2. Tetracycline
3. Tuberculosis
4. 1928
5. False
6. No
7. Microscopic organisms
8. Their cell walls burst and they can no longer harm you.
9. One type of antibiotic kills the bacteria. Another type of antibiotic prevents the bacteria from multiplying.
10. Student's own answer. Check they have used PEE to answer the question, for example:
    The discovery of penicillin was important because it was the first antibiotic to be discovered. Bacteria can cause "killer diseases such as tuberculosis" and antibiotics can kill the bacteria or stop them from multiplying. Antibiotics can work "against a wide range of bacteria". This means that millions of lives have been saved from dangerous infections.

Glossary

Scanning
Looking for a particular word or phrase in a text, such as a name, date, or word in a dictionary in order to retrieve information.

Skimming
Looking through the whole text quickly to get the general idea and pick up the main points without close reading.

PEE
PEE stands for Point, Evidence, Explain. It is a response technique for answering open questions. It involves stating a point, providing textual evidence for that point and explaining how that evidence proves that point.

5 Reading: Character, theme and language

Learning objectives

- To understand how writers portray characters in a story
- To look for sequences of events and patterns of ideas
- To explain the main theme or message of a text
- To explain the effect and meaning of the author's choice of language

Content domains

- 2b retrieve and record information / identify key details from fiction and non-fiction texts
- 2d make inferences from the text / explain and justify inferences with evidence from the text
- 2f identify / explain how information and narrative content are related and contribute to meaning as a whole
- 2g identify / explain how meaning is enhanced through choice of words and phrases

Starter activity

- **The Treasure Hunter; 10 minutes**
  Provide a copy of the story *The Treasure Hunter* (pages 27-28). Ask the student to read it out loud to you.

Main activities

- **What are the characters like?; 15 minutes; page 48**
  This activity focuses on describing characters using textual evidence. Discuss the two characters first. Guide the student in locating evidence and encourage them to use direct quotes from the text or paraphrasing.
- **Story themes; 10 minutes; page 49**
  This activity focuses on finding evidence of the theme of a story (Salisbury Smith's ambition). Briefly discuss the meaning of the word *ambition* if required. Guide the student in deciding how relevant each statement is in providing evidence. Ask the student to justify their choices.
- **Author's language; 10 minutes; page 50**
  This matching activity asks the student to link statements to the mood the author is trying to create. Encourage the student to match each statement to more than one mood word and to justify their choices.

Plenary activity

- **What happens next?; 5 minutes**
  Reread the final few paragraphs of the story together. Ask the student what they think happens next. Discuss possible plot lines.

Homework activity

- **Continue the adventure; 45 minutes; page 51**
  Provide a copy of the story *The Treasure Hunter* (pages 27-28). Ask the student to write a continuation of the story, trying to match the author's style, characterisation and themes of adventure, risk, ambition, friendship and danger. A planning frame is provided.

Differentiation and extension ideas

- **What are the characters like?** Support by highlighting evidence of character in the text and ask the student to identify what the evidence tells them about the character.
- **Story themes** Shorten the activity by removing some of the statements.
- **Continue the story** Support by providing a writing frame, including a basic plot to follow, some possible dialogue or a new character biography. You could also provide a list of connective phrases to link paragraphs and ideas.

Progress and observations

ENGLISH
— YEAR 6 —

MAIN ACTIVITY: WHAT ARE THE CHARACTERS LIKE? **TIMING: 15 MINS**

LEARNING OBJECTIVES
- To use evidence from the text to say what a character is like

EQUIPMENT
- highlighter

There are two characters in the story: Salisbury Smith and Gunther. What can you tell about these characters from the text? Write your ideas in the boxes below.

Salisbury Smith	Gunther
Example: • brave – had faced the dangers before and had come back	Example: • sensible – listened to Sal's warning about stopping

ENGLISH
YEAR 6

MAIN ACTIVITY: STORY THEMES   **TIMING: 10 MINS**

LEARNING OBJECTIVES
- To identify the theme in a fiction text

EQUIPMENT
- green, orange and red pencils

"Daa da da daa, da da daa". Like a movie theme tune, the theme of a story is the main message or idea that runs throughout. The main theme of *The Treasure Hunter* story is Salisbury Smith's ambition.

The statements below are taken from the text. Which ones provide evidence for this theme? Colour in the best evidence in green, weaker evidence in orange and irrelevant statements in red.

Gunther knew he should listen to the treasure hunter's warning: it had saved his life a number of times.	Salisbury peered over his friend's shoulder, casting his experienced eye along the passage.
Salisbury squeezed his powerful frame past his friend's rounder, softer body.	"Stop your grumbling," said Salisbury.
He took a long breath in through his nose, bent down and slipped through the doorway.	As was his habit, he rolled his neck to ease his tension.
"Sure, why not?" Salisbury agreed with a tight smile.	He knew because he had faced them (the dangers) the last time he had been here.
Or perhaps it was just his own excitement building.	The object was more beautiful than he had ever imagined.
"Bingo indeed," replied Salisbury, nodding slowly.	Salisbury watched in fascination as a blue light suddenly arced across the floor and up his leg.
His fingers trembled as he let out a gasp.	The crown he had been searching for ever since ...
After all these years, all the frustrations and failures, he had found it:	It was so mesmerising that Salisbury barely noticed Gunther now standing beside him.
Salisbury shot a worried glance at Gunther.	His keen eyes took in the room.

ENGLISH
YEAR 6

MAIN ACTIVITY: AUTHOR'S LANGUAGE

TIMING: 10 MINS

LEARNING OBJECTIVES
- To understand how the words an author chooses create an effect

EQUIPMENT
none

Authors think carefully about the words they use, because they often want to create a particular mood or feeling.

Match each statement to the mood you think the author is trying to create. You can link each statement to more than one mood. One has been started for you.

statement
Something about the moving lights was holding him back.
"Stop!" whispered Salisbury Smith urgently.
Searching. That was the word. The lights were moving in a strange way, almost as if they were searching …
It was so mesmerising that Salisbury barely noticed Gunther now standing beside him.
At the spot directly above Salisbury's heart, the three coloured dots combined in a brilliant point of excited white light.
"Take it easy. There's something not right."
"Can you hurry up a bit?" asked Gunther casually. "I'm getting hungry."
Salisbury realised he still hadn't breathed out.
Except, something was making his heart thump a little more firmly.
Had he found it at last? Was he really nearly there?

mood
tense
mysterious
exciting
dangerous
humorous
breaks the tension

The second statement is linked to "tense" with an arrow.

ENGLISH
— YEAR 6 —

HOMEWORK ACTIVITY: CONTINUE THE ADVENTURE   TIMING: 45 MINS

LEARNING OBJECTIVES   EQUIPMENT
- To write the next part of a story in a similar style   none

Continue the story of Sal and Gunther from the point the text finished. What happens next? Use the questions below to help you plan.

- What is making the strange rumbling noise?
- Are the lights dangerous?
- Have they triggered a trap? What type of trap is it?
- Do they have time to grab the crown? How do they escape?
- How does Sal's ambition affect his decisions? What risks does he take?
- Does one of them get stuck or hurt? How does the other help? Does one of them have to make a difficult decision? How does their friendship affect events?
- Does another character appear? Why? Do they help or to attack them?

Write your notes in the box below.

Now, continue the story on a separate sheet of paper. Try to write in a similar style to the text. The mood should be exciting, dangerous, tense and maybe funny too!

You do not need to finish the story. You could leave it with another exciting cliff-hanger. Discuss with your tutor how much you should write.

ENGLISH
YEAR 6

5 ANSWERS

MAIN ACTIVITY: WHAT ARE THE CHARACTERS LIKE?
Student's own answers. These could include: **Salisbury Smith**: ambitious – after all these years … he had found it; experienced – he knew the kinds of dangers that might lay ahead; instinctive – something about the coloured lights was holding him back; careful – he shone his torchlight over the surface of the rock for any signs of trouble; strong – squeezed his powerful frame past. **Gunther**: trusting – knew he should listen to Sal; large – Sal has to squeeze past his rounder, softer body; humorous – makes jokes about his stomach rumbling; sarcastic – rolls his eyes and lists all the dangers they've faced.

MAIN ACTIVITY: STORY THEMES
Green: He knew because he had faced them (the dangers) the last time he had been here; The object was more beautiful than he had ever imagined; After all these years, all the frustrations and failures, he had found it; The crown he had been searching for ever since …
Orange: Gunther knew he should listen to the treasure hunter's warning: it had saved his life a number of times; Salisbury peered over his friend's shoulder, casting his experienced eye along the passage; He took a long breath in through his nose, bent down and slipped through the doorway; Or perhaps it was just his own excitement building; "Bingo indeed," replied Salisbury, nodding slowly; His fingers trembled as he let out a gasp; It was so mesmerising that Salisbury barely noticed Gunther now standing beside him; His keen eyes took in the room.
Red: Salisbury squeezed his powerful frame past his friend's rounder, softer body; "Stop your grumbling," said Salisbury; As was his habit, he rolled his neck to ease his tension; "Sure, why not?" Salisbury agreed with a tight smile; Salisbury watched in fascination as a blue light suddenly arced across the floor and up his leg; Salisbury shot a worried glance at Gunther.

MAIN ACTIVITY: AUTHOR'S LANGUAGE
Something about the moving lights was holding him back. (tense, mysterious)
"Stop!" whispered Salisbury Smith urgently. (tense, dangerous)
Searching. That was the word. The lights were moving in a strange way, almost as if they were searching … (mysterious, dangerous)
It was so mesmerising that Salisbury barely noticed Gunther now standing beside him. (mysterious, exciting)
At the spot directly above Salisbury's heart, the three coloured dots combined in a brilliant point of excited white light. (mysterious, dangerous)
"Take it easy. There's something not right." (mysterious, dangerous)
"Can you hurry up a bit?" asked Gunther casually. "I'm getting hungry." (humorous, breaks the tension)
Salisbury realised he still hadn't breathed out. (tense, exciting)
Except, something was making his heart thump a little more firmly. (mysterious, exciting)
Had he found it at last? Was he really nearly there? (tense, exciting)

HOMEWORK ACTIVITY: CONTINUE THE ADVENTURE
Student's own answers. Check for consistency of style, mood and characterisation with the original story text.

GLOSSARY

Character
A person in a novel, play or film. It may also refer to a person's individual personality.

Theme
The main message or idea that runs through a story. The theme can often be inferred from the sequence of events or pattern of ideas in the story.

Author's choice of language
This refers to how the words chosen by an author can create a particular effect and meaning. For example, an author may describe something in an unusual way using personification or a metaphor.

6 READING: MEANING

LEARNING OBJECTIVES

- To make predictions using the text
- To determine the meaning of single words from their context and explain them using synonyms
- To make inferences using evidence from the text

CONTENT DOMAINS

- 2a give / explain the meaning of words in context
- 2d make inferences from the text / explain and justify inferences with evidence from the text
- 2e predict what might happen from details stated and implied

STARTER ACTIVITY

- **The cliff-top conundrum; 5 minutes; page 54**
  Encourage the student to make predictions based on a text. Cover the word grid and reveal one row at a time. Ask the student to repeat the exercise and discuss how their prediction is altered.

MAIN ACTIVITIES

- **The siege of Synonym City; 20 minutes; page 55**
  Ask the student to read the first sentence on the parchment image and discuss the possible meaning of the underlined word. Ask the student to highlight the synonym on the castle map (sufficient = enough). All the words in this activity are taken from the National Curriculum word-list for Years 5 and 6.
- **Reading between the lines; 20 minutes; page 56**
  Read the story with the student and discuss each question or ask the student to write their answer on a separate piece of paper. Ask the student to highlight their evidence to practise finding textual evidence to justify inferences.

PLENARY ACTIVITY

- **Yes/No game; 5 minutes**
  Ask questions such as: *Do you like the colour purple?* The student may answer in any way they choose except by saying *yes* or *no*. This is good preparation for the homework activity.

HOMEWORK ACTIVITY

- **Banned!; 45 minutes; page 57**
  This activity encourages the student to extend their understanding and use of inference, and use it in writing. Check the student understands that they cannot use the banned word in their answers.

DIFFERENTIATION AND EXTENSION IDEAS

- **The cliff-top conundrum** Extend by asking the student to think of synonyms for some of the words in the grid.
- **The siege of Synonym City** Extend by discussing the meaning of other words on the castle map and ask the student to write sentences that use them in an appropriate context.
- **Reading between the lines** Remind the student of the skills they used in the starter activity.
- **Banned!** Support by reducing the required length of answers or providing a bank of useful words. Extend by increasing the number of banned words.

PROGRESS AND OBSERVATIONS

ENGLISH
— YEAR 6 —

STARTER ACTIVITY: THE CLIFF-TOP CONUNDRUM   **TIMING: 5 MINS**

LEARNING OBJECTIVES
- To make a prediction from the text

EQUIPMENT
- rubber

Here is a story with some words missing. Look at the small number next to each gap and choose a word from the numbered rows in the table below. Write your answers in pencil.

The two [1] .... stood by the edge of the cliff. They both [2] ....
[3] .... over the edge down towards the [4] ....

"It's a long way down," one said with a [5] ....

"Are you [6] ....?" asked the other.

Suddenly, they heard a [7] .... from below. [8] "..............................!" a
[9] .... voice cried.

1	boys	old women	climbers
2	peeked	glanced	stared
3	thoughtfully	nervously	confidently
4	rocks	beach	waves
5	frown	smile	giggle
6	ready	hungry	scared
7	scream	shout	laugh
8	Hi	Help	Stop
9	panicked	furious	friendly

Now answer these questions.

1. What do you think happens next in the story? Explain why.

2. Rub out the answers you put in each gap and this time, choose different words to fill them.

3. Now what do you think happens next in the story? How has your prediction changed now that the words in the gaps are different?

ENGLISH
YEAR 6

MAIN ACTIVITY: THE SIEGE OF SYNONYM CITY　　　　**TIMING: 20 MINS**

LEARNING OBJECTIVES
- To work out the meaning of words using the surrounding words (context) and words with similar meanings (synonyms)

EQUIPMENT
none

You are the commander of an army surrounding the city of Synonym. You need to work out how to get to the castle inside the city walls.

Your spies have brought you a piece of parchment showing a list of clues to the passwords that will open the eight gates of the castle on the map below. Work out the meaning of each underlined word by looking at the surrounding words (the context) in each clue. Circle the right synonym for each gate on the map to enter the castle and overthrow your enemy!

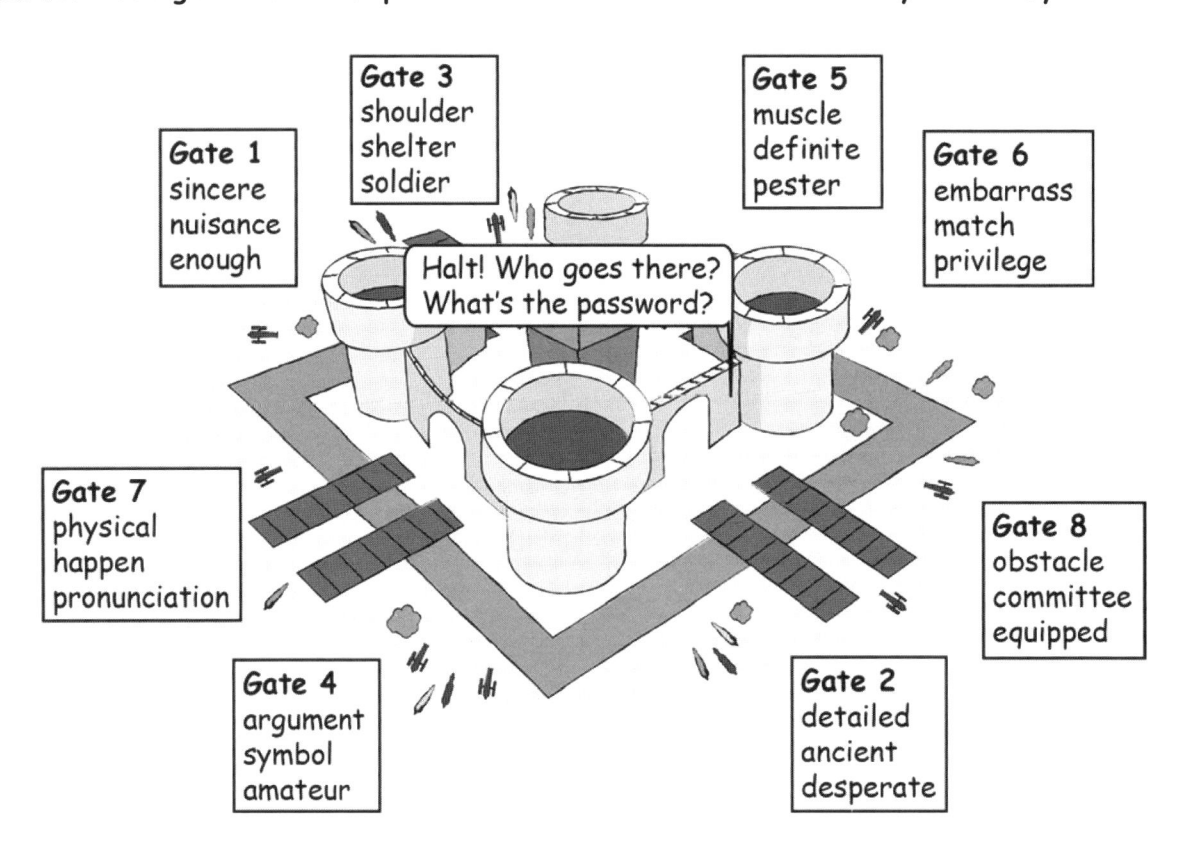

Gate 1
sincere
nuisance
enough

Gate 2
detailed
ancient
desperate

Gate 3
shoulder
shelter
soldier

Gate 4
argument
symbol
amateur

Gate 5
muscle
definite
pester

Gate 6
embarrass
match
privilege

Gate 7
physical
happen
pronunciation

Gate 8
obstacle
committee
equipped

Halt! Who goes there? What's the password?

Top Secret: Ye Olde Password Reminders

Gate 1 There's one doughnut each. That should be <u>sufficient</u> unless our guests are greedy.

Gate 2 The police will carry out a <u>thorough</u> search of the area.

Gate 3 I'm sorry but the hotel is full. We cannot <u>accommodate</u> you tonight.

Gate 4 The rock star's behaviour caused a real <u>controversy</u> in the newspapers.

Gate 5 Denny decided to <u>harass</u> his parents about his pocket money until they gave in.

Gate 6 The design of the T-shirts that have just been delivered does not <u>correspond</u> with what I ordered online.

Gate 7 Strange events <u>occur</u> at that old house every year.

Gate 8 The man's sore knee was a <u>hindrance</u> to him on his hiking trip.

ENGLISH
— YEAR 6 —

MAIN ACTIVITY: READING BETWEEN THE LINES　　　**TIMING: 20 MINS**

LEARNING OBJECTIVES
- To use clues in the text to understand it more deeply
- To understand what making inferences means

EQUIPMENT
- highlighter pens

Sometimes writers don't tell you everything, but you can work out what they mean from clues in the text. This is called reading between the lines. Try to read between the lines of this short story.

Kemal fell flat on his face again and slid clumsily across the grass. "Not again," he thought. His bulging shirt was smeared with mud. He looked up and saw his opponent – his talented, super fit, athletic opponent called George – smiling down at him.

"Hey, guys, it's true what they say: hippos do love the mud," George called out. A couple of the other boys laughed. Kemal felt his cheeks burning and his eyes pricking.

"That's enough, George," said Mr Harrison. He blew his whistle and announced, "Free kick to Blues."

"What? You blind, Sir?" protested George. "I can't help it if this cake-destroyer falls over every time I even breathe near him."

Kemal clenched his jaw. "I'll take it," he shouted. All the other boys stopped talking and looked at him in astonishment. Mr Harrison raised an eyebrow. The silence was broken by George bursting into laughter. "Come on then, Hippo, let's see you hoof it!"

One of Kemal's team mates approached him, put a hand on his shoulder and said quietly, "Hey, mate, don't you think Freddie should take this?"

Kemal shrugged his friend's hand away and repeated, "I'll take it." George was leading a chant of "Hippo! Hippo!" Kemal took all of his anger and channelled it down his chunky leg into his foot. He swung his leg and struck the ball as hard as he could. On its way into the top corner of the goal, the ball struck George on the shoulder, sending him spinning sideways and down into the greasy mud.

Answer the questions below on a separate piece of paper, highlighting the parts of the text that help you decide on your answer. Use a different colour for each question and highlight the square to show which colour you have used.

☐ 1. What sport are the boys playing?

☐ 2. What can you tell about Kemal's appearance?

☐ 3. How would you describe George's character?

☐ 4. How do Kemal's feelings change?

☐ 5. What do the others think of Kemal's sporting ability?

ENGLISH
— YEAR 6 —

HOMEWORK ACTIVITY: BANNED!

TIMING: 45 MINS

LEARNING OBJECTIVES
- To write three short paragraphs without using the banned words
- To write so that a reader has to make inferences

EQUIPMENT
none

Read the sentences below and then write a short paragraph about each one.
There's only one rule: you must not use the words that are banned.

Example sentence	Banned words
Write about meeting a big, scary monster.	BIG, SCARY, FRIGHTENING, MONSTER
Example paragraph	
The cave suddenly became much darker: something enormous was blocking the light at the entrance. I looked up, higher and higher, until I was almost leaning backwards. I wished I hadn't. My hands started shaking and my legs felt like jelly. I could almost hear my heart beating in my chest. Suddenly, the cave was filled with a deafening roar. A thick dollop of stinky saliva dropped down in front of me and splattered onto my shoes.	

Now it's your turn. On a separate piece of paper, write a short paragraph for each of the sentences below.

	Banned words
Write a description of a very cold morning.	COLD, WINTER
Write about meeting a scary witch.	WITCH, SCARY
Write a conversation between a mum and a dad who are angry with their child.	ANGRY

6 ANSWERS

STARTER ACTIVITY: THE CLIFF-TOP CONUNDRUM
Answers will vary. Ensure that the student bases their prediction on the text and can justify it with reference to the text.

MAIN ACTIVITY: THE SIEGE OF SYNONYM CITY
1. sufficient = enough
2. thorough = detailed
3. accommodate = shelter
4. controversy = argument
5. harass = pester
6. correspond = match
7. occur = happen
8. hindrance = obstacle

MAIN ACTIVITY: READING BETWEEN THE LINES
Answers will vary, but look for the following points:
1. The boys are playing football (highlighted words might include *grass, opponent, whistle, ball, goal*).
2. Kemal is overweight (highlighted words might include *bulging shirt, hippo, cake-destroyer, chunky leg*).
3. George is unkind, rude and disrespectful. He might be a bully (highlighted words might include *"Hippo! Hippo!", "You blind, Sir?", bursting into laughter*).
4. Kemal is upset, then angry and determined (highlighted words might include *his cheeks burning, his eyes pricking, clenched his jaw*).
5. The others think Kemal is bad at football (highlighted words might include *looked at him in astonishment, raised an eyebrow, "don't you think Freddie should take this?"*).

HOMEWORK ACTIVITY: BANNED!
Student's own answers. Check the student has not used any of the banned words and discuss their use of synonyms and how successfully they have caused you to make inferences when reading the paragraphs.

GLOSSARY

Inference
You make an inference when you interpret clues in the text to discover something that is not written explicitly. This is sometimes known as *reading between the lines*.

Synonym
A word that has the same meaning or a very similar meaning to another word.

Context
The words surrounding another word.

ENGLISH — YEAR 6

7 READING: MAKING COMPARISONS

LEARNING OBJECTIVES
- To make comparisons within the text
- To explain how narrative content is related and how it contributes to meaning as a whole
- To summarise main ideas from more than one paragraph

CONTENT DOMAINS
- 2c summarise main ideas from more than one paragraph
- 2f identify / explain how information and narrative content are related and contribute to meaning as a whole
- 2h make comparisons within the text

STARTER ACTIVITY
- **Making comparisons; 5 minutes; page 60**
  Give the student a copy of the poems (page 26). Read poems 3 and 4. Ask the student to write brief notes in a Venn diagram about the similarities and differences between the two poems.

MAIN ACTIVITIES
- **Sal's mood; 25 minutes; page 61**
  Give the student a copy of the story *The Treasure Hunter* (pages 27-28). Guide the student in ordering the cards and then describing Sal's mood for each one. Discuss how Sal's mood changes in general. For example: at first, he is wary and worried, then he relaxes and jokes with Gunther, then he is happy and relieved, before becoming wary and worried again.
- **The main message (summary); 15 minutes; page 62**
  Provide a copy of the news article *Forget Zombies! Is the Antibiotic Apocalypse Coming?* (page 24). Guide the student in identifying relevant points and rejecting irrelevant detail. Discuss how to choose three main points and guide them in paraphrasing if required. Emphasise the importance of thinking about the whole text when answering questions 2 and 3.

PLENARY ACTIVITY
- **Comparative words; 5 minutes**
  On a whiteboard, write an adjective (e.g. *big*). Challenge the student to write the comparative form (*bigger*) and the superlative form (*biggest*). Repeat for a variety of adjectives including irregular formations (*good, better, best*).

HOMEWORK ACTIVITY
- **Sum it up; 45 minutes; page 63**
  This activity puts the student's learning about summarising into practice. Provide a list of suitable source news material or websites.

DIFFERENTIATION AND EXTENSION IDEAS
- **Making comparisons** Extend by covering or removing the word bank to increase difficulty.
- **Sal's mood** Extend by asking the student: *What effect does Sal's mood have on the reader?* How does it fit with the adventure story/hero genre?
- **Sum it up** Support by narrowing the choice to three set articles suited to the needs of the student.

PROGRESS AND OBSERVATIONS

ENGLISH
— YEAR 6 —

STARTER ACTIVITY: MAKING COMPARISONS　　　　**TIMING: 5 MINS**

LEARNING OBJECTIVES
- To identify the similarities and differences between two poems

EQUIPMENT
- poems from page 26

Read poems 3 and 4. What are the differences between them? What do they have in common (their similarities)? Use the words from the word bank to complete the Venn diagram below.

alliteration	free verse	rhyme
rhythm	humour	usual punctuation
tongue twister	onomatopoeia	creates an image

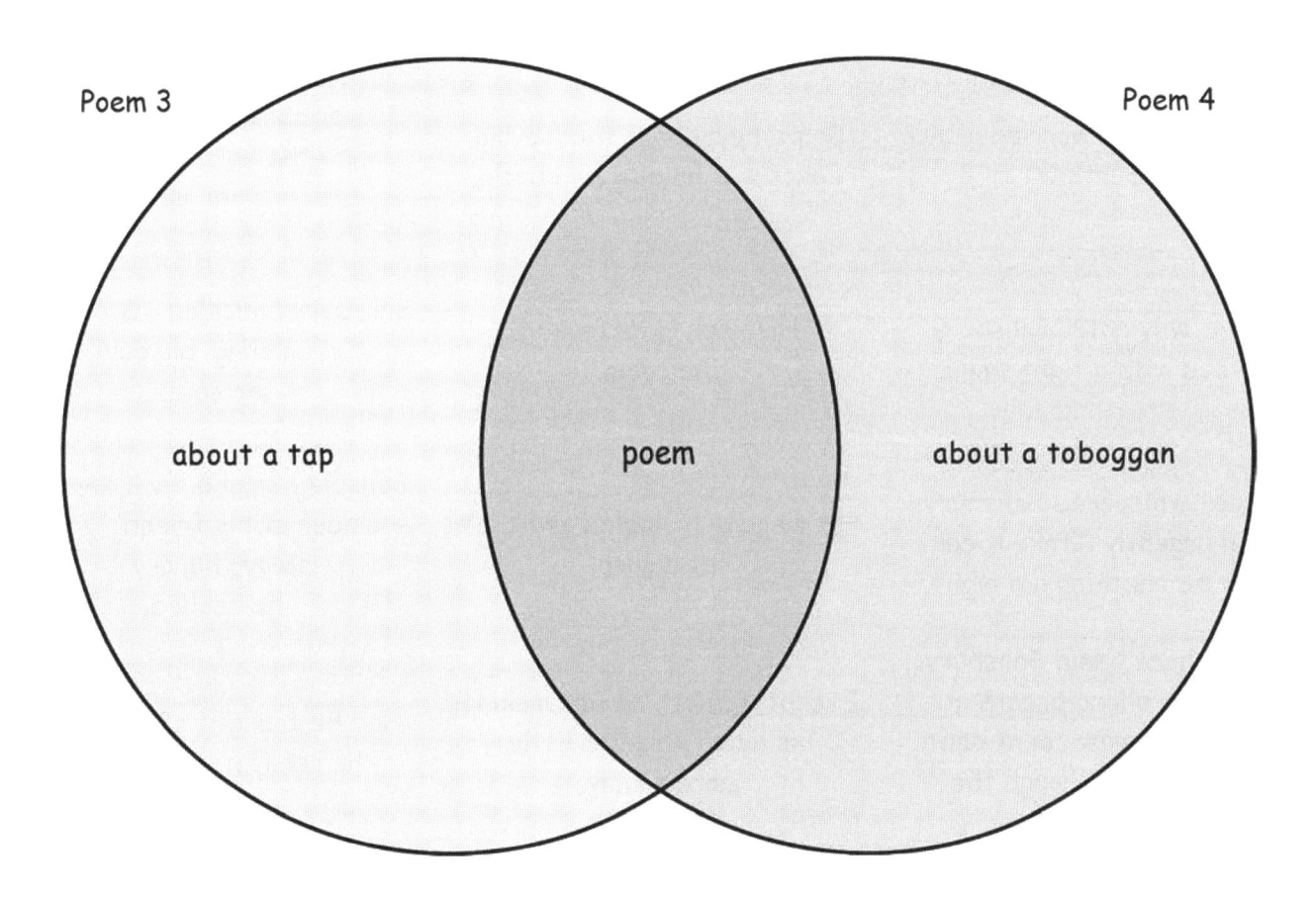

Poem 3 — about a tap

Common — poem

Poem 4 — about a toboggan

ENGLISH
— YEAR 6 —

MAIN ACTIVITY: SAL'S MOOD

TIMING: 25 MINS

LEARNING OBJECTIVES
- To make comparisons within a text

EQUIPMENT
- scissors

How does Salisbury's Smith mood change during his adventure? There are lots of clues about how Salisbury is feeling.

Cut out the cards below and put them in the same order as the story.

After all these years, all the frustrations and failures, he had found it.	He knew because he had faced them the last time he had been here.	Stay focused, he urged himself, although he felt a smile lifting the corners of his mouth.
Salisbury shot a worried glance at Gunther.	Something about the moving lights was holding him back.	He was about to step forward when the hairs on his neck stood up.
"Sure, why not?" Salisbury agreed with a tight smile.	His keen eyes took in the room.	Salisbury chuckled. "Stop your grumbling, big guy," he said.
"Stop!" whispered Salisbury Smith urgently. "Take it easy. There's something not right."	His fingers trembled as he let out a gasp.	Salisbury smiled back over his shoulder at his friend. "You're always hungry," he replied.
"We're here," said Salisbury. He took a long breath in through his nose, bent down and slipped through the doorway.	Except, something was making his heart thump a little more firmly.	Had he found it at last? Was he really nearly there?

On a separate piece of paper, use adjectives to describe Sal's changing mood in the extract on each card.

Example:

"Stop!" whispered Salisbury Smith urgently. "Take it easy. There's something not right."	=	nervous, wary, on edge

ENGLISH
— YEAR 6 —

MAIN ACTIVITY: THE MAIN MESSAGE (SUMMARY)　　　　**TIMING: 15 MINS**

LEARNING OBJECTIVES
- To identify the main message of a piece of writing

EQUIPMENT
- highlighter
- news article from page 24

A summary gathers together the main points in a piece of writing.

Highlight the main points of the news article *Forget Zombies! Is the Antibiotic Apocalypse coming?*

1. Choose your top three points and write them below. These points should summarise everything the article says.

_____
_____
_____
_____
_____
_____
_____
_____

2. What is the main message of the news article? Tick one box.

☐ Bacteria are becoming resistant to antibiotics.

☐ Doctors give out antibiotics too easily.

☐ There is a need to develop new ways to fight bacteria.

☐ Tuberculosis may become untreatable.

3. Thinking about the text as a whole, tick one box to show whether each statement is true or false.

statement	true	false
People need to be educated about taking antibiotics.		
Scientists are worried about how people are using antibiotics.		
It will take a lot of work to find new ways of fighting diseases.		
Antibiotics will become useless in the future.		

ENGLISH
— YEAR 6 —

HOMEWORK ACTIVITY: SUM IT UP **TIMING: 45 MINS**

LEARNING OBJECTIVES
- To summarise some news articles

EQUIPMENT
- newspapers and websites

Find and read some interesting news articles in a newspaper or online. For each article, copy the headline and write a short summary (maximum of two sentences). Remember, your summary must cover the main points in each article.

Headline:
Summary:

Headline:
Summary:

Headline:
Summary:

ENGLISH
YEAR 6

7 ANSWERS

STARTER ACTIVITY: MAKING COMPARISONS
Poem 3: about a tap, onomatopoeia, usual punctuation, creates an image
Poem 4: about a toboggan, rhythm, humour, tongue twister
Both: poem, alliteration, free verse

MAIN ACTIVITY: SAL'S MOOD
Answers may vary. Examples of possible answers:
"Stop!" whispered Salisbury Smith urgently. (*nervous, wary, on edge*)
"Take it easy. There's something not right." (*worried, sensing danger*)
He knew because he had faced them the last time he had been here. (*concerned about risks*)
Except, something was making his heart thump a little more firmly. (*excited, nervous*)
Had he found it at last? Was he really nearly there? (*excited, looking forward to something*)
Stay focused, he urged himself, although he felt a smile lifting the corners of his mouth. (*happier, relaxing*)
Salisbury smiled back over his shoulder at his friend. "You're always hungry," he replied. (*happy, jokey*)
Salisbury chuckled. "Stop your grumbling, big guy," he said. (*happy, jokey, more relaxed*)
"We're here," said Salisbury. He took a long breath in through his nose, bent down and slipped through the doorway. (*excited, looking forward to something*)
His keen eyes took in the room. (*excited*)
His fingers trembled as he let out a gasp. (*excited, happy, relieved*)
After all these years, all the frustrations and failures, he had found it: (*happy, relieved*)
He was about to step forward when the hairs on his neck stood up. (*concerned, worried, sensing danger*)
"Sure, why not?" Salisbury agreed with a tight smile. (*nervous, unsure*)
Something about the moving lights was holding him back. (*nervous, unsure*)
Salisbury shot a worried glance at Gunther. (*worried, sensing danger*)

MAIN ACTIVITY: THE MAIN MESSAGE (SUMMARY)
1. Answers may vary. Examples of possible answers: bacteria are becoming resistant to antibiotics; new medicines need to be developed; antibiotics should only be used when absolutely necessary.
2. There is a need to develop new ways to fight bacteria.
3. People need to be educated about taking antibiotics (true); Scientists are worried about how people are using antibiotics (true); It will take a lot of work to find new ways of fighting diseases (true); Antibiotics will become useless in the future (false).

HOMEWORK ACTIVITY: SUM IT UP
Student's own answers. Check they have completed the tables correctly and have covered the main points in each summary.

GLOSSARY

Summary
The main points of a text. Summarising involves identifying the main message across more than one paragraph or the whole text.

ENGLISH — YEAR 6

8 Reading: Poetry (similes and metaphors)

LEARNING OBJECTIVES
- To become familiar with poetic forms
- To become familiar with a range of figurative language
- To recognise and write similes and metaphors

CONTENT DOMAINS
- 2a give / explain the meaning of words in context
- 2f identify / explain how information and narrative content are related and contribute to meaning as a whole
- 2g identify / explain how meaning is enhanced through choice of words and phrases

STARTER ACTIVITY
- **What is a poem?; 5 minutes; page 66**
  Discuss features of poetry with the student, especially form and figurative language. Address the misconception that conventions such as rhythm and rhyme are necessary (the poems in this lesson are free verse).

MAIN ACTIVITIES
- **Free verse; 20 minutes; page 67**
  Give the student a copy of the four poems (page 26). Ask the student to read each poem out loud. Discuss what each one is about and identify and highlight poetic features (similes, metaphors, onomatopoeia, alliteration). Ask the student to guess the title for each poem. Write the titles in the space provided above each poem (see answers). Emphasise the lack of rhyme and rhythm in free verse and how poetic features allow writers to play with language and meaning.
- **Similes and metaphors; 20 minutes; page 68**
  This activity assesses the student's ability to recognise the difference between similes and metaphors and to write some of their own.

PLENARY ACTIVITY
- **What am I?; 5 minutes**
  Ask the student the following metaphorical riddles:
  I lose my head in the morning and get it back at night (a pillow); *Feed me food, I will live. Feed me water, I will die* (fire); *You can catch me but you can't throw me* (a cold); *I go up but never come down* (your age).

HOMEWORK ACTIVITY
- **Poetry writing 1; 45 minutes; page 69**
  This activity gives the student the opportunity to write some free verse using similes and metaphors. Provide the student with a copy of the poems (page 26).

DIFFERENTIATION AND EXTENSION IDEAS
- **Free verse** Extend by providing a list of key poetic terms for the student to highlight.
- **Similes and metaphors** Support by providing full examples of similes and metaphors as models for writing.
- **Poetry writing 1** Support by providing a writing frame of half-completed similes (e.g. *the sun hits me like …*) or possible metaphors that can be expanded (e.g. oven = a dark cave; microwave = a silver spaceship).

PROGRESS AND OBSERVATIONS

ENGLISH
— YEAR 6 —

STARTER ACTIVITY: WHAT IS A POEM?　　　　　　**TIMING: 5 MINS**

LEARNING OBJECTIVES
- To discuss what makes a poem different to other writing

EQUIPMENT
none

Think about what makes a poem a poem. How do you know when you come across one?

Discuss these questions with your tutor and write your ideas in the bubbles below.

ENGLISH
— YEAR 6 —

MAIN ACTIVITY: FREE VERSE **TIMING: 20 MINS**

LEARNING OBJECTIVES
- To read some free verse poems
- To discuss their features and meaning

EQUIPMENT
- highlighter

Read the four poems your tutor gives you. Make sure you read them out loud too.

What are these poems about? What features can you find in them? What do you think the title of each poem is? Your tutor will reveal the answer.

Poem 1 What is it about? • Features? • Title •	**Poem 2** What is it about? • Features? • Title •
Poem 3 What is it about? • Features? • Title •	**Poem 4** What is it about? • Features? • Title •

ENGLISH
— YEAR 6 —

MAIN ACTIVITY: SIMILES AND METAPHORS   **TIMING: 20 MINS**

LEARNING OBJECTIVES
- To recognise and write similes
- To recognise and write metaphors

EQUIPMENT
- highlighter

A simile says something is *like* something else.

Example:
An emerald is as green as grass.

A metaphor says something *is* something else.

Example:
(A toaster is) a silver-scaled Dragon with jaws flaming red.

1. Identify each sentence below as either a simile or a metaphor. Highlight the two things in each sentence that are being compared.

sentence	simile or metaphor?
a) Life is a journey.	
b) He is as brave as a lion.	
c) You are such a couch potato.	
d) My toes are as cold as ice.	
e) Sarah can swim like a fish.	
f) My little sister is a pain in the neck.	
g) Granny is now as blind as a bat.	
h) He is like a volcano ready to erupt.	
i) You are a star.	
j) My piano teacher is an old dragon.	

On a separate piece of paper, describe yourself, someone or something else using similes and metaphors.

Example:

similes	metaphors
I am as …	My sister is a …
My brother eats like …	The moon is a …

Homework activity: Poetry writing 1

Timing: 45 mins

Learning objectives
- To write two poems using similes and metaphors

Equipment
none

Your tutor will give you a copy of the four poems.

On a separate piece of paper draft two free verse poems of your own.

1. A poem about something in the natural world such as water, wind, a tree or the sun. Use similes, like the ones in *Flint*.

2. A poem about a household object such as a kettle, microwave or oven. Use a metaphor, like the one in *The Toaster*.

When you are happy with your poems, write them out neatly in the spaces below and add an illustration if you like.

8 Answers

STARTER ACTIVITY: WHAT IS A POEM?
Answers may vary, but might include: rhythm, rhyme, shape, form, similes, metaphors, alliteration, onomatopoeia, personification, imagery, narrative

MAIN ACTIVITY: FREE VERSE
Student's own answers. Poem titles and examples of answers:
Poem 1: About: don't judge a book by its cover; Features: similes, personification; Title: *Flint*
Poem 2: About: metaphor for a toaster; Features: metaphor, personification; Title: *The Toaster*
Poem 3: About: an old tap being turned on; Features: onomatopoeia; Title: *The Rusty Spigot*
Poem 4: About: a tongue twister about buying a suitable toboggan; Features: alliteration; Title: *Toboggan*

MAIN ACTIVITY: SIMILES AND METAPHORS
1. a) metaphor; b) simile; c) metaphor; d) simile; e) simile; f) metaphor; g) simile; h) simile; i) metaphor; j) metaphor
2. Student's own answers. Examples could include:
I am as slow as a snail; My brother eats like a pig; My sister is a cheeky monkey; The moon is a white plate.

HOMEWORK ACTIVITY: POETRY WRITING 1
Student's own answers. Check for appropriate construction of similes (using *as* or *like*) and of metaphors.

GLOSSARY

Poetic form
The form of a poem means its rhythm, rhyme, repetitions and shape. The form of a poem is often related to its meaning.

Figurative language
The use of words to express meaning in a non-literal way. In other words, whenever you describe something by comparing it with something else, you are using figurative language. Examples of figurative language include similes, metaphors and personification.

Simile
Describes something by saying how it is 'like' something else. The word *as* is also used in similes. For example, *the sun was like a giant, orange ball*.

Metaphor
Describes something by saying it is something else. For example, *the sun was a giant, orange ball*.

9 READING: POETRY (OTHER FIGURATIVE LANGUAGE)

LEARNING OBJECTIVES

- To become familiar with poetic forms
- To become familiar with a range of figurative language
- To recognise and use personification, alliteration and onomatopoeia

CONTENT DOMAINS

- 2a give / explain the meaning of words in context
- 2f identify / explain how information and narrative content are related and contribute to meaning as a whole
- 2g identify / explain how meaning is enhanced through choice of words and phrases

STARTER ACTIVITY

- **Tongue twisters; 5 minutes; page 72**
  Discuss reasons the tongue twisters are difficult to say (rapid repetition of the same or similar sounds). Introduce the term *alliteration* if not already known.

MAIN ACTIVITIES

- **A day at the beach (personification); 20 minutes; page 73**
  This activity focuses on identifying how personification works and writing some examples. Make sure the student understands that the personified object can be non-human or not even alive, including abstract nouns (e.g. *guilt gnawed at my conscience*).
- **Alliteration and onomatopoeia; 20 minutes; page 74**
  Recall with the student the starter activity on alliteration. Give them the four poems on page 26 and focus on *The Rusty Spigot* and *Toboggan*. Make sure the student understands that only the same initial letters or sounds are classed as alliteration (e.g. *gushes rushes splashes*: the repeated *sh* is consonance not alliteration; the repeated *u* is assonance).

PLENARY ACTIVITY

- **Silly sentences; 5 minutes**
  Start a sentence with a word (e.g. *Big …*). Ask the student to add a word that starts with the same sound that makes sense (e.g. *Big bunnies …*). Continue to build the sentence word by word using as many alliterative words as possible (e.g. *Big bunnies bounce on brilliant beds*).

HOMEWORK ACTIVITY

- **Poetry writing 2; 45 minutes; page 75**
  This activity gives the student the opportunity to write a free verse poem using alliteration and onomatopoeia. Provide the student with a copy of the poems on page 26 for inspiration.

DIFFERENTIATION AND EXTENSION IDEAS

- **A day at the beach (personification)** Support writing by adding further words to the table.
- **Alliteration and onomatopoeia** Extend by discussing consonance and assonance, highlighting examples in the poem *The Rusty Spigot*.
- **Poetry writing 2** Support writing by agreeing a topic for the poem and discussing possible content. Alternatively, provide a writing frame using generic wording, such as: *Down underground I saw … , Down below the city, I heard …*

PROGRESS AND OBSERVATIONS

ENGLISH
— YEAR 6 —

TUTORS GUILD

Starter activity: Tongue Twisters

Timing: 5 mins

Learning objectives
- To try to say some tongue twisters

Equipment
none

Here are some famous tongue twisters. Say them out loud slowly first, then try speeding up! Why do you think they are difficult to say?

1. Peter Piper picked a peck of pickled peppers
   A peck of pickled peppers Peter Piper picked
   If Peter Piper picked a peck of pickled peppers
   Where's the peck of pickled peppers Peter Piper picked?

2. Four fine fresh fish for you.

3. Betty Botter bought some butter
   But she said, "The butter's bitter.
   If I put it in my batter, it will make the batter bitter.
   But a bit of better butter will make my batter better."
   So 'twas better Betty Botter bought a bit of better butter.

4. She sells seas shells on the seashore.

5. Fred fed Ted bread and Ted fed Fred bread.

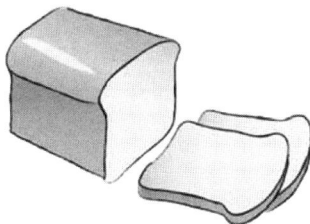

ENGLISH
— YEAR 6 —

MAIN ACTIVITY: A DAY AT THE BEACH (PERSONIFICATION)   **TIMING: 20 MINS**

LEARNING OBJECTIVES
- To understand personification
- To write some examples of personification

EQUIPMENT
- highlighter

A writer can make a non-human thing sound human by giving it human characteristics.

1. Look at the sentences below and highlight the object being personified. For each, explain which human characteristic is being given to the object.

a) On the beach, the sun beat down on me.

....

b) As I lay on my towel, the sea breeze whispered gently through my hair.

....

c) Time seemed to crawl as I waited for my mum to come back with the ice creams.

....

d) I listened to the waves licking the shore.

....

e) Suddenly, my beach ball squealed and wheezed as a dog sank its teeth in to it.

....

2. Now imagine a huge storm arrives and you see a ship in trouble out at sea. What objects can you see? What can you hear? What can you smell? Write your ideas below.

e.g. wind ....
....
....
....

3. What human characteristics could you give to these objects?

e.g. screaming ....
....
....
....

4. Now write a few sentences describing this stormy scene using personification.

Example:
The wind screamed through the yacht's flapping sails.

ENGLISH
— YEAR 6 —

MAIN ACTIVITY: ALLITERATION AND ONOMATOPOEIA **TIMING: 20 MINS**

LEARNING OBJECTIVES
- To understand what alliteration and onomatopoeia are
- To write some examples of your own

EQUIPMENT
- highlighters

Remember the alliteration from the tongue twisters?

1. Have a look at the poems *The Rusty Spigot* and *Toboggan*. Highlight any examples of alliteration you can find.

2. Try some alliterations of your own by completing these sentence starters following the alliterative pattern.

a) Toby's tortoise ....

b) The lazy llama ....

c) Silly Sunil ....

d) Barry the baker ....

e) The extraordinary expert ....

3. Next, underline any words in *The Rusty Spigot* that sound the same as the thing they are describing, for example: *a loud bang*.

4. Now write a sentence using each of the onomatopoeic words below.

a) pop: ....

b) snap: ....

c) knock: ....

d) zoom: ....

e) flutter: ....

5. Can you write a sentence that uses both alliteration and onomatopoeia?
Example:
The sizzling sausages spat hot fat in the saucepan.

ENGLISH
— YEAR 6 —

HOMEWORK ACTIVITY: POETRY WRITING 2   **TIMING: 45 MINS**

LEARNING OBJECTIVES
- To write a poem using alliteration and onomatopoeia

EQUIPMENT
none

On a separate piece of paper, draft a free verse poem about a trip somewhere, such as a visit to a wildlife park, a journey on the underground or a walk by a river.

Use alliteration and onomatopoeia in your poem. Here is a list of some onomatopoeic words to help you.

> screech, slam, chatter, boom, crunch, zap, pow, gasp, roar, splat, sob, click, buzz, whoosh, ring, squish, chirp, crash, crack, rattle, squeak, squelch, chug, plop, whistle, twang, groan

Write your poem neatly in the space below and add an illustration if you like.

ENGLISH
YEAR 6

9 ANSWERS

STARTER ACTIVITY: TONGUE TWISTERS
Check the student understands that rapid repetition of the same or similar sounds make tongue twisters difficult to say.

MAIN ACTIVITY: A DAY AT THE BEACH (PERSONIFICATION)
1. a) On the beach, the sun beat down on me. (ability to beat)
   b) As I lay on my towel, the sea breeze whispered gently through my hair. (ability to whisper)
   c) Time seemed to crawl as I waited for my mum to come back with the ice creams. (ability to crawl)
   d) I listened to the waves licking the shore. (ability to lick)
   e) Suddenly, my beach ball squealed and wheezed as a dog sank its teeth in to it. (ability to squeal and wheeze)
2. Student's own answers. 3. Student's own answers.

MAIN ACTIVITY: ALLITERATION AND ONOMATOPOEIA
1. The rusty spigot sputters, utters a splutter, spatters a smattering of drops, gashes wider; slash splatters scatters spurts finally stops sputtering and splash! gushes rushes splashes clear water dashes.
To begin to toboggan, first buy a toboggan, But don't buy too big a toboggan. (A too big a toboggan is not a toboggan To buy to begin to toboggan.)
2. Student's own answers. Examples could include:
   a) Toby's tortoise took too long to turn round.
   b) The lazy llama loved lying in leaves.
   c) Silly Sunil sat sloppily in Sam's soft seat.
   d) Barry the baker baked a billion buns.
   e) The extraordinary expert expected the exact answer in the exam.
3. Sputters, splutter, spatters, slash, splatters, scatters, spurts, sputtering, plash, gushes, rushes, splashes, dashes.
4. Student's own answers. Examples could include:
   a) The red balloon drifted into the thorn bush and popped.
   b) The angry man snapped his head round to stare at me.
   c) At midnight, there was a loud knock at the door.
   d) A sliver fighter jet zoomed directly over our heads.
   e) The brown autumn leaves fluttered down to the damp earth.
5. Student's own answers.

HOMEWORK ACTIVITY: POETRY WRITING 2
Student's own answers. Check they have used alliteration and onomatopoeia in their poem.

GLOSSARY

Poetic form
The rhythm, rhyme, repetitions and shape of a poem. The form of a poem is often related to its meaning.

Figurative language
Using words to express meaning in a non-literal way. In other words, whenever you describe something by comparing it with something else, you are using figurative language. Examples of figurative language include similes, metaphors and personification.

Personification
When a writer attributes human characteristics to something non-human or that is not alive. For example: *The table groaned under the weight of the books*.

Alliteration
When a series of words that start with the same sound or letter are close together. For example: *The silly sausage saw a sad salad*.

Onomatopoeia
When a word mimics the sound of the thing it is describing. For example: *Bang, sizzle, slam*.

ENGLISH — YEAR 6

10 Writing: Audience and purpose

Learning objectives

- To understand the terms *audience* and *purpose* in relation to composition
- To recognise the intended audience and purpose of texts
- To write for a particular audience and purpose

Statutory NC requirements

Pupils should be taught to:
- plan their writing by identifying the audience for, and the purpose of the writing, selecting the appropriate form and using other similar writing as models for their own.

Starter activity

- **Who and what?; 5 minutes; page 78**
  This activity introduces the terms *audience* and *purpose* by asking the student to identify the most likely audience and purpose for each text title.

Main activities

- **Audience and purpose; 20 minutes; page 79**
  This activity focuses on identifying the audience and purpose of some short texts by using textual clues. Guide the student in locating, highlighting and recording evidence from the texts for their choices.
- **Planning for a purpose; 20 minutes; page 80**
  This activity focuses on planning a short piece of persuasive writing (an advert). Discuss ideas fully before the student begins, providing support and prompts as appropriate. Emphasise the need to think about the audience and purpose at each stage of planning.

Plenary activity

- **Appealing language; 5 minutes**
  On a whiteboard, write a phrase (e.g. *A healthy sandwich*). Challenge the student to make it sound more appealing by adding further detail and using comparative adjectives (e.g. *A mouth-watering, fresh, healthy sandwich for busy people*). Repeat with different phrases as time allows.

Homework activity

- **Write an advert; 45 minutes; page 81**
  Ask the student to use their plan from the main activity to draft and then write their advert text. Explain that you will focus on how well their advert addresses the chosen audience and purpose when you review it.

Differentiation and extension ideas

- **Planning for a purpose** Support by providing examples of similar adverts or an exemplar to act as a model.
- **Write an advert** Support by including a more detailed writing frame or a list of appealing features to include. Increase or decrease the number of quick tips.

Progress and observations

ENGLISH
— YEAR 6 —

STARTER ACTIVITY: WHO AND WHAT?   **TIMING: 5 MINS**

LEARNING OBJECTIVES
- To understand the terms *audience* and *purpose*

EQUIPMENT
- colouring pencils

The title of a text can give you a clue about who the writing is for (audience) and what the writer is trying to do (purpose).

Use different colours to match each title to its likely audience and purpose. One has been done for you.

title	audience	purpose
Modern Problems: How to Use Modern Technology	children	to entertain
Volcano Adventure	adults	to explain
1001 Jokes About Grown Ups	grandparents	to instruct
Sick Wheels: Customise your Car in Ten Easy Steps	adults	to entertain
Bad Doggy, Good Kitty	6-year-old children	to argue
My Vampire BFF	adults	to educate
The History of Ancient Roman Winemaking	18-20-year-olds	to persuade
You Can Change your Life!	8-year-old children	to entertain
Should Prisoners be Locked Up for Life?	teenage girls	to amuse

ENGLISH
— YEAR 6 —

MAIN ACTIVITY: AUDIENCE AND PURPOSE	TIMING: 20 MINS

LEARNING OBJECTIVES
- To use text clues to work out the audience and purpose

EQUIPMENT
- highlighter

Read the following short texts. For each one, decide who you think the text is for and what its purpose is. Provide evidence for your answers.

1. Place your cake on a cake plate. Measure across the top and sides using a length of string. This will guide you when rolling out your icing later. Cover the cake with a generous amount of buttercream icing by placing it on top and easing it across the top and down the sides. Create smooth edges by rotating the cake on the turntable and simultaneously using a palette knife to smooth the buttercream into any gaps.

Audience: ....
Purpose: ....
Evidence: ....
....

2. Crunchy, munchy, choccy, rocky, crispy, biscuity, moreish! Fat-free Mini Bites. The healthy way to keep you going. Only 99 calories a bag. Try some today!

Audience: ....
Purpose: ....
Evidence: ....
....

3. Tag said, "Hello Tig."
   Tig said, "Hello Tag."
   "Have you seen Zog?" asked Tag. But Tig hadn't seen Zog.
   "Have you seen Zug?" asked Tag. But Tig hadn't seen Zog or Zug.
   "Have you seen Zeg?" asked Tag. But Tig hadn't seen Zog or Zug or Zeg.
   "I haven't seen Zog, Zug or Zeg, only you Tag," said Tig.

Audience: ....
Purpose: ....
Evidence: ....
....

ENGLISH
— YEAR 6 —

MAIN ACTIVITY: PLANNING FOR A PURPOSE

TIMING: 20 MINS

LEARNING OBJECTIVES
- To plan a persuasive piece of writing

EQUIPMENT
none

Write some text for an advert. It's your choice what you write about. It could be for a new toy, item of clothing or drink.

Who is your audience?
....

What is the purpose of your advert?
....

For each of the features below, keep asking yourself: *"Who is the audience? What is the purpose?"* Continue on a separate piece of paper if you need to.

What is your product called? ....

What are its benefits? ....

How is it different/better? ....

Memorable slogan ....

An intriguing question to draw the reader in ....

Appealing adjectives ....

Bossy imperative verbs ....

Word play or a joke ....

Exaggeration ....

Product details (price, size, colour, features) ....

Special offers ....

How / where to buy it ....

ENGLISH — YEAR 6

Homework Activity: Write an Advert

Timing: 45 mins

Learning Objectives
- To write an advert from your plan for a particular audience and purpose

Equipment
none

Use your plan to write a draft of your advert in the box below. When you are happy with your draft, write your finished text on a separate piece of paper and add an illustration if you wish.

Quick Tips:

- Remember your audience and purpose at all times.
- Start with a question or a slogan.
- Repeat the name of your product a few times.
- Use short, snappy sentences or phrases.
- Use lots of appealing and exaggerated language.
- Describe all the benefits that make your product better or different.
- Make sure you include the price (including special offers!) and how and where to buy it.

10 Answers

STARTER ACTIVITY: WHO AND WHAT?

Answers may vary. Suggested answers may include:

Modern Problems: How to Use Modern Technology → grandparents → to explain
Volcano Adventure → 8-year-old children → to entertain
1001 Jokes About Grown Ups → children → to amuse
Sick Wheels: Customise your Car in Ten Easy Steps → 18–25-year-olds → to instruct
Bad Doggy, Good Kitty → 6-year-old children → to entertain
My Vampire BFF → teenage girls → to entertain
The History of Ancient Roman Winemaking → adults → to educate
You Can Change your Life! → adults → to persuade
Should Prisoners be Locked Up for Life? → adults → to argue

MAIN ACTIVITY: AUDIENCE AND PURPOSE

Answers may vary. Suggested answers might include:

1. Audience: adult cooks; Purpose: to instruct; Evidence: bossy verbs (*place, create*); technical, complicated vocabulary (*simultaneously using a palette knife*).
2. Audience: adult dieters; Purpose: to persuade; Evidence: appealing language (*crunchy, munchy*); benefits for audience (*only 99 calories a bag*).
3. Audience: young children learning to read; Purpose: to entertain; Evidence: repetition of vowels (*Tag, Zeg, Tig, Zog, Zug*); simple sentence construction (*Tag said, "Hello Tig."*).

MAIN ACTIVITY: PLANNING FOR A PURPOSE

Student's own answers. Check they have thought about audience and purpose in their planning.

HOMEWORK ACTIVITY: WRITE AN ADVERT

Student's own answers. Check for how well the final advert addresses chosen audience and purpose.

Glossary

Audience
Who a piece of writing is for. The form, tone and sophistication of structure and vocabulary should be guided by the intended audience.

Purpose
What you are trying to say and how you want readers to react to it. The purpose affects the genre chosen for the writing.

11 Writing: The writing process

Learning objectives
- To plan a piece of non-fiction writing
- To organise ideas into paragraphs
- To draft non-fiction writing from an organised plan

Statutory NC requirements
Pupils should be taught to:
- plan their writing by noting and developing initial ideas, drawing on reading and research where necessary
- draft and write by using a wide range of devices to build cohesion within and across paragraphs

Starter activity
- **A review; 10 minutes; page 84**
  This activity is a discussion. Discuss all four sections on the sheet and encourage the student to expand on their answers.

Main activities
- **Get your ideas down; 15 minutes; page 85**
  This activity requires the student to make short, quick notes of their ideas for a review. Guide them with questions, prompts and reminders to encourage ideas covering all features of a review text. Discuss or suggest ways of paraphrasing or reducing word count to make note taking efficient.
- **Now get organised; 20 minutes; page 86**
  This activity helps the student to organise their initial ideas into cohesive paragraphs. Support the student in sorting their notes into relevant sections. Encourage the student to discriminate between relevant and irrelevant material using their notes, and to add further detail where necessary.

Plenary activity
- **Conjunctions; 5 minutes**
  On a separate sheet of paper, write a conjunction or adverbial phrase that could be used to link ideas or paragraphs in a review (e.g. *To start off ...*). Ask the student to think of another example. Repeat as time allows. Remind the student of the importance of using such conjunctions in their review.

Homework activity
- **Draft your review; 45 minutes; page 87**
  Ensure the student knows to write an unedited first draft of their review. When they have written the review, they should use the checklist and discuss successes/omissions when you review it together next time.

Differentiation and extension ideas
- **A review** If the student has no recent experience of any of the suggested topics, try a fictional TV programme / drama or a favourite website.
- **Get your ideas down** Extend by asking the student to highlight their strongest ideas.
- **Now get organised** Support by adding scaffolding text to the plan (e.g. *Last week I watched ... starring ...*).

Progress and observations

ENGLISH
— YEAR 6 —

STARTER ACTIVITY: A REVIEW

TIMING: 10 MINS

LEARNING OBJECTIVES
- To discuss a recent film, book, game or play

EQUIPMENT
none

What was the latest film you saw? Did you enjoy it? Which actors were in it? What was it about?

Have you read a book recently? What genre was it? What score would you give it out of ten?

Have you watched any matches or sport recently? What was the score? Were there any stand-out performances or bad decisions?

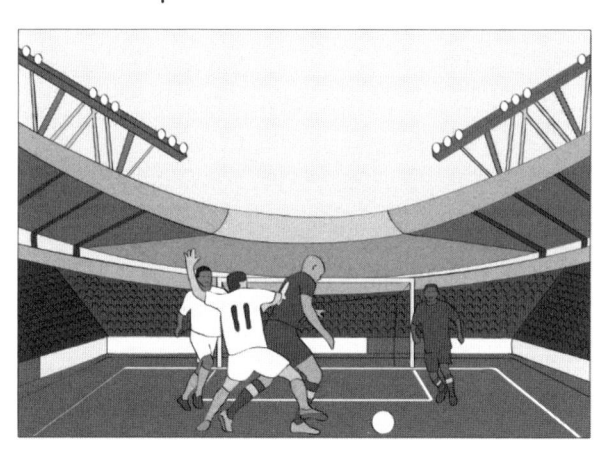

Have you seen a show or play? Would you recommend it? Why?

ENGLISH
— YEAR 6 —

MAIN ACTIVITY: GET YOUR IDEAS DOWN **TIMING: 15 MINS**

LEARNING OBJECTIVES
- To note down your initial ideas

EQUIPMENT
none

You are going to plan and draft a review of a fictional film, TV programme or play you have seen recently. Start by thinking of as many ideas as you can and write them as quick, short notes.

Follow these rules:
- Write anything that comes to mind – you can always leave it out later.
- Record your ideas quickly as single words, spider diagrams, bullet points, sketches – just enough to remind you of your ideas.
- Don't try to organise your ideas at this point. It doesn't matter if it looks messy.
- Don't write in detail.
- Keep going until you have noted down all your ideas. Then think of some more!

Write your notes in the box below:

ENGLISH
— YEAR 6 —

MAIN ACTIVITY: NOW GET ORGANISED **TIMING: 20 MINS**

LEARNING OBJECTIVES
- To organise your notes into a plan

EQUIPMENT
none

Now you can organise your notes so that your review is logical and easy to follow. Copy your notes into the relevant sections of the planning frame below. You can change what you include as you go along.

paragraph theme	should contain	notes
basic information	name, genre, length, suitable age	
plot	brief outline of the story	
characters	brief details of the main characters	
effects	my opinion of sound, music and visual effects	
likes	what I particularly liked	
dislikes	anything I didn't like	
conclusion	my overall opinion	

ENGLISH
YEAR 6

HOMEWORK ACTIVITY: DRAFT YOUR REVIEW **TIMING: 45 MINS**

LEARNING OBJECTIVES
- To write a draft of your review

EQUIPMENT
none

On a separate sheet of paper, write a draft of your review from your plan.

Once you have finished, use this checklist to make sure you have included everything you need:

☐ I have mentioned the title.

☐ I have used a strong sentence to hook the reader.

☐ I have stated who the film is targeted at or suitable for (audience).

☐ I have included the genre.

☐ I have mentioned some of the actors by name.

☐ I have summarised the plot without giving away the ending.

☐ I have mentioned strengths and weakness of the plot, acting, effects, etc.

☐ I have given my opinion or recommendation.

☐ I have organised my review into paragraphs.

☐ I have used conjunctions to link ideas or paragraphs.

ENGLISH
YEAR 6

11 Answers

Starter activity: A review
Discussion with student.

Main activity: Get your ideas down
Student's own answer. Check they have written short, quick notes.

Main activity: Now get organised
Student's own answer. Check they have completed the planning frame.

Homework activity: Draft your review
Student's own answer. Check they have ticked items in the checklist.

Glossary

Non-fiction
Writing that is about facts and real events rather than being fictional.

Paragraph
A distinct section of a piece of writing often shown by a new line, indentation or number. Paragraphs are used to group together related material within a longer text.

Cohesion
A cohesive device is a word or phrase used to link ideas within and across paragraphs. It is used to show how parts of the text fit together, creating cohesion. For example, the use of adverbials such as: *on the one hand* and *in contrast*.

Genre
The style or category of a piece of writing.

ENGLISH — YEAR 6

12 Writing: The editing process

Learning objectives
- To edit a draft piece of writing
- To check writing against a plan
- To proof-read to check spelling and punctuation

Statutory NC requirements
Pupils should be taught to:
- evaluate and edit by assessing the effectiveness of their own and others' writing
- propose changes to vocabulary, grammar and punctuation to enhance effects and clarify meaning
- proof-read for spelling and punctuation errors

Starter activity
- **Checking drafts and plans; 10 minutes; page 90**
  Ask the student to think about how well or not the writer has followed a well-structured plan by comparing it with a poor first draft. As indicated, the student should highlight the plan rather than the draft.

Main activities
- **Editing and improving; 20 minutes; page 91**
  This activity focuses on improving a first draft by including missing elements from the plan and making the writing clearer. Show the student how to make and mark up any changes in the spaces between the text. Encourage the student to read back their improvements to check for improved clarity and content.
- **Proof-reading; 15 minutes; page 92**
  This activity focuses on checking for spelling and punctuation mistakes. Ask the student to mark-up errors and changes on the text on the activity sheet.

Plenary activity
- **How to improve your writing; 5 minutes**
  Discuss the different ways the student can improve their work (check against a plan, edit and improve, proof-read) and ask them to define what is meant by each stage.

Homework activity
- **Editing and proof-reading; 20 minutes; page 93**
  This activity puts the student's learning into practice. Discuss any areas of weakness/misconceptions when you review it together next lesson.

Differentiation and extension ideas
- **Editing and improving** Support or extend by decreasing or increasing the amount of text to edit and improve using the first draft text from the starter activity.
- **Proof-reading** Support or extend by decreasing or increasing the number of errors in the text.
- **Proof-reading** Support by removing the first three questions or extend by adding three further proof-reading questions.

Progress and observations

ENGLISH
— YEAR 6 —

Starter activity: Checking drafts and plans

Timing: 10 mins

Learning objectives
- To check a draft piece of writing matches up with a plan

Equipment
- green and pink highlighters

Magdalena has written a news article about cyberbullying. Here is the plan she wrote, followed by her first draft.

Audience: 10–11-year-old children
Genre: News article
Headline: Online bullying
Byline: Magdalena Dubicki
First paragraph   **What?** growing problem, children using technology to bully / threaten / insult / tease someone   **How?** texts, instant messaging, email, social networks, online gaming   **Where?** in children's online worlds, away from people who can help
Second paragraph   **Why?** Easy to do online because it's safer / not face to face. Bullies might have own problems / be unhappy. Anonymous.   **Who?** people picking on individual, sometimes ganging up   **When?** any time of day, no escape
Third paragraph   **Details:** example of someone, Lily aged 11, depressed, low confidence, ended up ringing a helpline   **Quotes:** from Lily about her experience – felt lonely, started with jokes, insulted my looks, friends joined in thinking it was a bit of fun, as if everyone is against you, deleted posts, felt embarrassed calling a helpline but it helped

Online bullying – first draft of news article

Cyberbullying is a problem that is getting bad. Tons of children are being hurt by other children on the internet. Bullies send them horrible texts and messages and emails. Cyberbullying can take place on mobiles and games consoles. It happens any time and victims can't escape. It's easy for bullies to do because they are unhappy and have problems. Lily lost her confidence when she was bullied by cyberbullies. She said, "I felt lonely. It started with a few jokes. People who I thought were my friends even joined in, probably thinking it was just a bit of fun. I tried to ignore it by deleting posts and comments but it got worse"

Colour each part of the plan in the following way:
- Green = draft follows plan;
- Pink = some improvement needed/missing from draft.

Give the first draft a mark out of ten.

ENGLISH
YEAR 6

MAIN ACTIVITY: EDITING AND IMPROVING	TIMING: 20 MINS

LEARNING OBJECTIVES	EQUIPMENT
• To edit a text to improve it	none

Here is the first part of Magdalena's draft again.

Look over her plan and make some improvements to her writing in the spaces between the lines below. The aim is to make the draft clearer and more organised, and to include all the information from her plan. You can delete things, add things, reword things and reorder things.

Online bullying

Cyberbullying is a problem that is getting bad. Tons of

children are being hurt by other children on the internet.

Bullies send them horrible texts and messages and emails.

Cyberbullying can take place on mobiles and games consoles.

ENGLISH
— YEAR 6 —

MAIN ACTIVITY: PROOF-READING　　　　　　　　　　**TIMING: 15 MINS**

LEARNING OBJECTIVES
- To check for spelling and punctuation mistakes

EQUIPMENT
- highlighter

Here is Magdalena's own improved draft. The last things you need to check for are spelling and punctuation mistakes. This is called proof-reading.

Proof-read the draft below, highlighting any mistakes and writing corrections as close as possible to the mistakes.

Online bullying

By Madgalena Dubicki

Cyberbullying is a growing problem Every day, many Children are being teased or even threatened buy others online. Cyberbullying takes place in childrens online lives when they use social networks on their mobiles and during online gameing. cyberbullies often send insulting texts, instent messages or emails. Unfortunatly, that means the bullying takes place out off site of people who can help.

Cyberbullies find it easy too pick on there victims online They are not face to face with them, they can gang up with others and they can send anonymous messages. the bullies themselfes may be unhappy or have their own problems. But for the victims, cyberbullying often feals as if theres no escape any time of day or night.

Lily, aged 11, became depressed and lost her confidance when she was cyberbullied. She said, I felt lonely. It started with a few Jokes about my looks. people who I thought were my friends even joined in, probably thinking it was just abit of fun. It feels as if everyone is against you. I tryed to ignore it by deleting posts but it got wurse. in the end, even though it felt imbarasing, I called a helpline They helpt me so much"

ENGLISH
— YEAR 6 —

HOMEWORK ACTIVITY: EDITING AND PROOF-READING **TIMING: 20 MINS**

LEARNING OBJECTIVES	EQUIPMENT
• To rewrite sentences to make them clearer • To proof-read sentences for spelling and punctuation mistakes	none

The following sentences are a bit clumsy or contain mistakes. On a separate piece of paper, rewrite each one to make the meaning clearer.

Example:
It was decided by the teacher that break time would be cancelled.
The teacher decided to cancel break time.

1. He should have not left no sweets for everyone else.

2. I tried to tidy my room, but I watched TV instead because it's so boring.

3. The best students are students who study hard and students who learn from their mistakes.

The following sentences contain spelling and punctuation mistakes. Rewrite each one correcting the mistakes.

4. do you no what Riley did this Morning or we're You still asleep

5. Erica would of bean lait if she had mist the last Bus

6. Witch way is it too the shopping Centre.

7. their are plenty off things to do before its time to leaf.

8. Wat a terrible peace of righting!

9. Talvinder took hi's dads motorbike but he was stoped buy The police

10. i wonder weather the whether will bee quiet nice today.

12 Answers

Starter activity: Checking drafts and plans

Answers may vary. Highlighting indicates areas for improvement/missing elements from first draft.

Audience: 10-11 year old children
Genre: news article
Headline: Online bullying
Byline: Magdalena Dubicki
First paragraph: What? growing problem, children using technology to bully / threaten / insult / tease someone How? texts, instant messaging, email, social networks, online gaming Where? in children's online worlds, away from people who can help
Second paragraph: Why? Easy to do online because it's safer / not face to face. Bullies might have own problems/be unhappy. Anonymous. Who? people picking on individual, sometimes ganging up When? any time of day, no escape
Third paragraph: Details: example of someone, Lily aged 11, depressed, low confidence, ended up ringing a helpline Quotes: from Lily about her experience – felt lonely, started with jokes, insulted my looks, friends joined in thinking it was a bit of fun, as if everyone is against you, deleted posts, felt embarrassed calling a helpline but it helped

Main activity: Editing and improving

Answers may vary. Example answer: Cyberbullying is a growing problem. Every day, many children are being teased or even threatened by others online. Cyberbullying takes place in children's online lives when they use social networks on their mobiles and during online gaming. Cyberbullies often send insulting texts, instant messages or emails. Unfortunately, that means the bullying takes place out of sight of people who can help.

Main activity: Proof-reading

Cyberbullying is a growing problem. Every day, many children are being teased or even threatened by others online. Cyberbullying takes place in children's online lives when they use social networks on their mobiles and during online gaming. Cyberbullies often send insulting texts, instant messages or emails. Unfortunately, that means the bullying takes place out of sight of people who can help.

Cyberbullies find it easy to pick on their victims online. They are not face to face with them, they can gang up with others and they can send anonymous messages. The bullies themselves may be unhappy or have their own problems. But for the victims, cyberbullying often feels as if there's no escape any time of day or night.

Lily, aged 11, became depressed and lost her confidence when she was cyberbullied. She said, "I felt lonely. It started with a few jokes about my looks. People who I thought were my friends even joined in, probably thinking it was just a bit of fun. It feels as if everyone is against you. I tried to ignore it by deleting the posts but it got worse. In the end, even though it felt embarrassing, I called a helpline. They helped me so much."

Homework activity: Editing and proof-reading

1. He should have left sweets for everyone else. 2. I tried to tidy my room, but because it's so boring, I watched TV instead. 3. The best students are students who study hard and learn from their mistakes. 4. Do you know what Riley did this morning, or were you still asleep? 5. Erica would have been late if she had missed the last bus. 6. Which way is it to the shopping centre? 7. There are plenty of things to do before it's time to leave. 8. What a terrible piece of writing! 9. Talvinder took his dad's motorbike but he was stopped by the police. 10. I wonder whether the weather will be quite nice today.

Glossary

Editing

Editing (also known as copy editing) involves improving the content, style, organisation and grammar of a piece of writing in order to enhance its effect and clarify meaning.

ENGLISH — YEAR 6

13 WRITING: ARTICLES

LEARNING OBJECTIVES
- To revise the features of articles
- To plan a news article from source material
- To write a news article

STATUTORY NC REQUIREMENTS
Pupils should be taught to:
- plan their writing by selecting the appropriate form and use other similar writing as models for their own
- note and develop initial ideas, drawing on reading and research where necessary
- draft and write using a wide range of devices to build cohesion within and across paragraphs

STARTER ACTIVITY
- **Features of articles; 5 minutes; page 96**
Provide a copy of the news article *Forget Zombies! Is the Antibiotic Apocalypse Coming?* (page 24). Guide the student in locating evidence of typical genre features.

MAIN ACTIVITIES
- **Crime scene reporter; 15 minutes; page 97**
Introduce the student to the partial evidence collected from the crime scene by the reporter. Discuss what they think happened and encourage imaginative responses. Ask the student to complete missing details from the reporter's notes. Pretend to be two different witnesses offering different opinions (suggestions in answers). Ask the student to interview you and record your quotes.
- **Draft your article; 25 minutes; page 98**
Guide the student in completing the plan by transcribing ideas from the reporter's notes. Encourage the student to add further detail to 'flesh out' their ideas fully.

PLENARY ACTIVITY
- **Time conjunctions; 5 minutes**
Remind the student that some conjunctions are useful for expressing chronological order. On a whiteboard, write a time conjunction (e.g. *after, next,* etc.) and ask the student to write one of their own. Repeat as time allows. Remind the student to use time conjunctions in their article.

HOMEWORK ACTIVITY
- **Read all about it!; 45 minutes; page 99**
If possible, provide an A3 photocopy of the sheet to provide adequate space for writing. Tell the student to set their report out within the suggested framework. Discuss how well the student has used the features of an article when you review it together at the next session.

DIFFERENTIATION AND EXTENSION IDEAS
- **Crime scene reporter** Extend or support by adding or removing details from the reporter's notes.
- **Read all about it** Support the student's writing by providing a more detailed writing frame (e.g. *One witness … said, "…"*).

PROGRESS AND OBSERVATIONS

ENGLISH
— YEAR 6 —

STARTER ACTIVITY: FEATURES OF ARTICLES **TIMING: 5 MINS**

LEARNING OBJECTIVES
- To revise the features of news articles

EQUIPMENT
none

Have a look at the news article about an 'antibiotic apocalypse'. Which of these typical features can you find?

Tick	Feature
☐	Headline
☐	Byline (name of the writer)
☐	Date
☐	Snappy start to grab your attention
☐	Subheadings
☐	Who?
☐	What?
☐	Where?
☐	When?
☐	Why?
☐	How?
☐	Photo or illustration
☐	Captions or labels
☐	Third person
☐	Past tense
☐	Present tense
☐	Facts
☐	Opinions
☐	Quotes
☐	Data or figures
☐	Final paragraph stating what is going to happen as a result

ENGLISH — YEAR 6

MAIN ACTIVITY: CRIME SCENE REPORTER

TIMING: 15 MINS

LEARNING OBJECTIVES
- To use pronouns to replace nouns

EQUIPMENT
none

BREAKING NEWS! BREAKING NEWS!

Humpty Dumpty sat on a wall.

Humpty Dumpty had a great fall.

All the king's horses and all the king's men

Couldn't put Humpty together again.

There has been a terrible incident! You have been sent to the scene of an awful crime. Here are your notes so far. **Fill in the rest of the notes.**

Who? *Victim = Mr H Dumpty*
Age: ....
Address: ....

What? *HD found injured bottom of high wall. Received medical help from king's men who arrived on horses. Too late to save him.*

Where? ....

When? ....

How? *Evidence = ladder on other side of wall. Pushed?* ....
....

Why? *Possible revenge. Who by? What for?* ....
....
....

Witness statements: ....
....
....
....

ENGLISH
— YEAR 6 —

MAIN ACTIVITY: PLAN YOUR ARTICLE

TIMING: 25 MINS

LEARNING OBJECTIVES
- To draft a news article

EQUIPMENT
none

Now it's time to shape your notes into a news article.

Headline:

Byline, date: ....

....

Opening paragraph summarising story: ....

....

....

....

Subheading? What happened? Who? ....

....

....

....

Subheading? When and where? ....

....

....

....

How and why? ....

....

....

....

Subheading? Quote from a witness: ....

....

....

....

Quote (a different opinion): ....

....

....

....

What is going to happen as a result? ....

....

....

....

ENGLISH
— YEAR 6 —

HOMEWORK ACTIVITY: READ ALL ABOUT IT!　　　**TIMING: 45 MINS**

LEARNING OBJECTIVES
- To write a news article

EQUIPMENT
- A3 photocopy of this sheet

Use the plan below to write your own news article. It could be completely fictional or based on something you've seen or done.

Headline

Opening paragraph

Witness quotes

Who, what, where, when, how, why?

What will happen as a result?

13 Answers

STARTER ACTIVITY: FEATURES OF ARTICLES

There is evidence in the text for all of the features to be ticked, except quotes.

MAIN ACTIVITY: CRIME SCENE REPORTER

Answers may vary. Suggestions for witnesses role play:
Witness 1: Dr Foster from Gloucester. Passing on his way treat a boy called Jack who had fallen down a hill. Quote: "I heard a sudden scream and a crack. I think he just slipped and fell, poor fellow."
Witness 2: Little Bo Peep. Herding her sheep to the shed. Quote: "It was Miss Muffet, I swear. She blamed Humpty for putting that spider next to her. This was revenge, pure and simple."

MAIN ACTIVITY: DRAFT YOUR ARTICLE

Student's own answers.

HOMEWORK ACTIVITY: READ ALL ABOUT IT

Student's own answers.

Glossary

Article
A non-fiction text that reports or discusses a particular topic or event, such as a news story. It often contains a headline, a byline, subheadings, a range of opinions and captioned images.

Cohesion
A cohesive device is a word or phrase used to link ideas within and across paragraphs. It is used to show how parts of the text fit together, creating cohesion. For example, the use of adverbials such as *on the one hand* and *in contrast*.

Organisational devices
Organisational devices, such as heading, subheading, columns, bullets and tables are used to structure and present text.

14 Writing: Explanations

Learning objectives
- To revise the features of explanations
- To plan an explanation
- To write and evaluate explanations

Statutory NC requirements
Pupils should be taught to:
- plan their writing by selecting the appropriate form and using other similar writing as models for their own
- evaluate and edit by assessing the effectiveness of their own and others' writing

Starter activity
- **What is an explanation text?; 5 minutes; page 102**
  Provide a copy of the explanation text *How Do Vaccinations Work?* (page 25). Guide the student in locating evidence of features. To save time, the student could highlight any large sections of text instead of copying them out.

Main activities
- **The electric kettle; 15 minutes; page 103**
  You will need access to an electric kettle. Using both the kettle and the picture on the sheet, discuss the labelled parts of the kettle. Demonstrate how to boil water and explain what is happening and why (see answer to homework activity for an explanation). Answer any resulting questions and address any misconceptions.
- **Explanation plan; 25 minutes; page 104**
  Before starting the plan, ask the student to explain in detail the answer to the question *How does a kettle boil water?* Guide the student in completing the plan. Encourage the student to use words from the conjunctions bank and refer to the other features listed in the starter activity to aid them.

Plenary activity
- **Explain quickly; 5 minutes**
  Ask the student to explain in detail how they brush their teeth. Encourage them to use time and causal conjunctions to explain the exact order they do it in.

Homework activity
- **How a kettle boils water; 45 minutes; page 105**
  Provide a copy of the kettle activity sheet for reference. Explain to the student how to evaluate their own work. Discuss how much you agree with their evaluation and go over their sentence improvement when you review their explanation at the next session.

Differentiation and extension ideas
- **What is an explanation text?** Support by highlighting evidence in the text beforehand so the student focuses on sorting material rather than searching for it.
- **Explanation plan** Support by including scaffolding guidance for each section of the flowchart (e.g. *how* or *what* questioning in first section).

Progress and observations

ENGLISH
— YEAR 6 —

STARTER ACTIVITY: WHAT IS AN EXPLANATION TEXT?   **TIMING: 5 MINS**

LEARNING OBJECTIVES
- To revise the features of explanations

EQUIPMENT
none

Have a look at the explanation text about vaccines. Below, write one or more examples of the following typical features in the text.

feature	example from text
how or *why* question	
statement about what is being explained	
a series of events in time order	
time conjunctions (e.g. *first*)	
causal conjunctions (e.g. *so*)	
technical vocabulary	
present tense verbs	
third person	
diagrams to add information	

ENGLISH
— YEAR 6 —

MAIN ACTIVITY: THE ELECTRIC KETTLE

TIMING: 15 MINS

LEARNING OBJECTIVES
- To understand how a kettle boils water

EQUIPMENT
- kettle

Labelled diagram of an electric kettle:
- steam
- spout
- lid
- thermostat
- on/off switch
- handle
- socket
- plug
- boiling water
- heating element
- stainless steel or plastic body

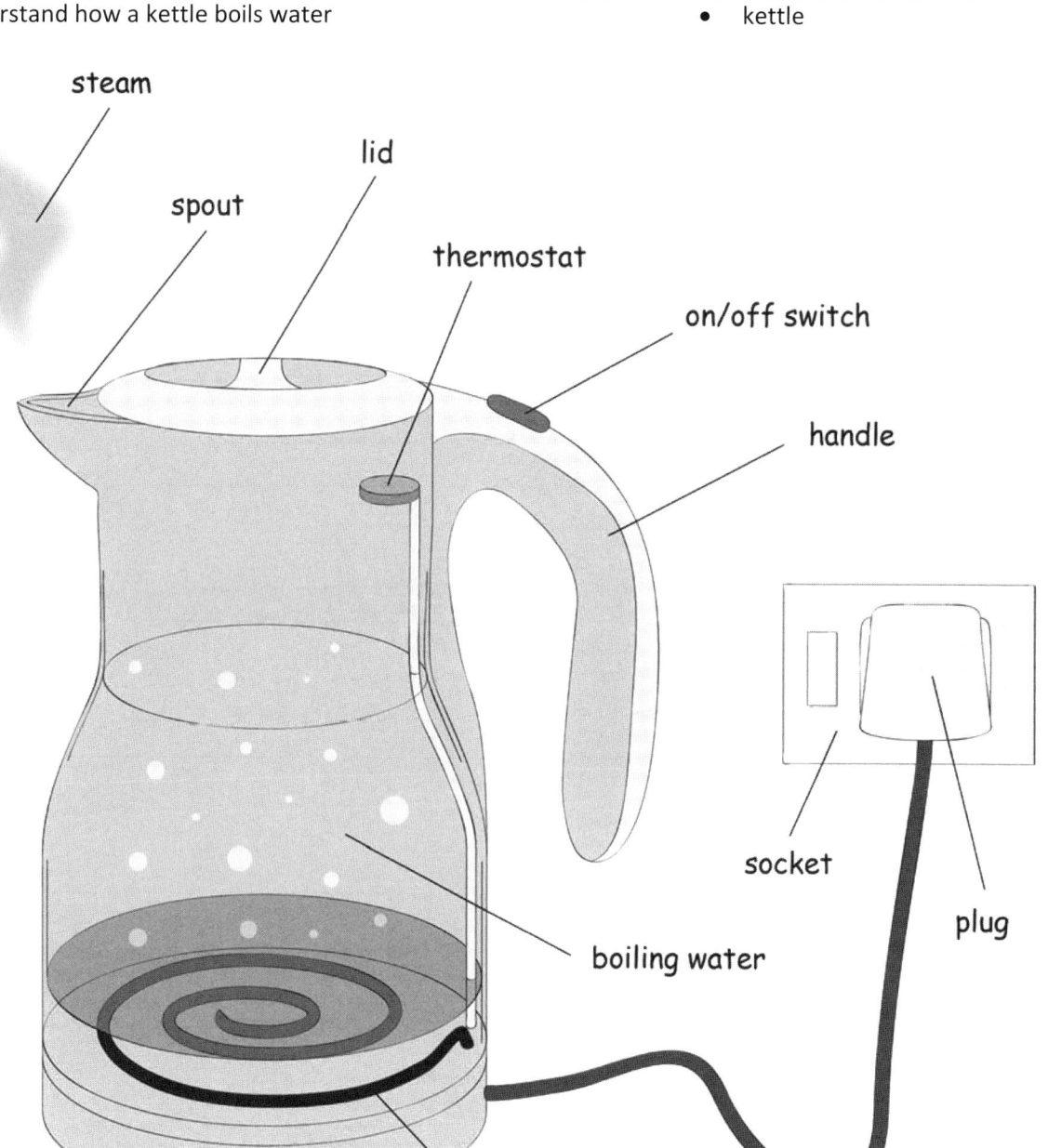

ENGLISH
— YEAR 6 —

MAIN ACTIVITY: EXPLANATION PLAN

TIMING: 25 MINS

LEARNING OBJECTIVES
- To draft an explanation text

EQUIPMENT
none

Use the flowchart below to write a step-by-step plan of how a kettle boils water. Use words from the conjunctions bank below to help you.

Conjunctions bank

first	next	then
while	when	after
so	because	as soon as
immediately	consequently	finally
	before	as a result

ENGLISH
YEAR 6

HOMEWORK ACTIVITY: HOW A KETTLE BOILS WATER **TIMING: 45 MINS**

LEARNING OBJECTIVES
- To write an explanation of how a kettle boils water

EQUIPMENT
- pink and green pencils

On a separate piece of paper, use your plan to help you write an explanation of how a kettle boils water. You can use the kettle sheet to help you with the technical vocabulary.

Once you have finished writing, evaluate your own work in the following way:

Colour a statement **green** for 'I have achieved this'.
Colour a statement **pink** for 'I could improve this'.

I have included ...
a *how* or *why* title
an opening statement about what is being explained
clear steps to explain what happens and why
a few time conjunctions (e.g. *first*)
a few causal conjunctions (e.g. *so*)
a series of events in time order
technical vocabulary
present tense verbs
third person

Choose a statement you have coloured pink. In the space below, rewrite one sentence from your explanation to improve it so that you can say 'I have achieved this'.

----

14 ANSWERS

STARTER ACTIVITY: WHAT IS AN EXPLANATION TEXT?

Answers may vary. Examples might include:
How or why question: How do vaccinations work?
Statement about what is being explained: A vaccination trains your immune system to fight a disease quickly.
Organised as a series of events: yes (vaccine made, vaccine injected, antibodies made, immune system ready)
Time conjunctions (e.g. first): next, after, now
Causal conjunctions (e.g. so): because, as a result
Technical vocabulary: vaccine, antibodies, molecules, immune system
Present tense verbs: fight, prevent, make, injects, react
Third person: a doctor usually injects a dose of the vaccine
Diagrams to add information: yes (chart showing number of measles cases)

MAIN ACTIVITY: THE ELECTRIC KETTLE

Discussion with student.

MAIN ACTIVITY: EXPLANATION PLAN

Student's own answers. Check they have used some of the conjunctions from the conjunctions bank.

HOMEWORK ACTIVITY: HOW A KETTLE BOILS WATER

Student's own answers.
How does a kettle boil water? It seems easy to 'stick the kettle on', but an electric kettle is more complicated than it looks. Here is what happens in those few moments a kettle takes to boil the water for your cup of tea.
First, the kettle's plug is plugged into the power socket to provide electricity. When the on / off switch is turned on, electricity flows to a metal ring called the heating element at the bottom of the kettle. As a result, the element becomes very hot and it begins to heat up the water inside the body of the kettle. The element continues to heat the water until the water becomes so hot, it begins to bubble. When the water is boiling rapidly, steam is produced, which may escape from the spout. The steam also hits a thermostat inside the kettle. The thermostat recognises that the water is boiling and it triggers the on / off switch to return to the off position automatically. The heating element immediately begins to cool and the boiled water is ready for use.

GLOSSARY

Explanation
A text that explains how something works or why something happens. The purpose is to describe a process clearly, usually in time order. It often contains time and causal conjunctions.

Conjunction
A word that links words, phrases and clauses together inside a sentence. Time conjunctions connect actions or events to a point in time. Causal conjunctions introduce a statement about the cause of something.

ENGLISH — YEAR 6

15 Writing: Persuasive letters

Learning objectives
- To recognise formal language
- To use persuasive language
- To plan and write a formal letter

Statutory NC requirements
Pupils should be taught to:
- plan their writing by selecting the appropriate form and using other similar writing as models for their own
- develop their understanding of concepts by recognising vocabulary and structures that are appropriate for formal speech and writing, including subjunctive forms

Starter activities
- **Recognising formal writing; 5 minutes; page 108**
  Show the student the formal letter on the starter activity sheet. Guide them in locating formal language and explain the conventional layout of a formal letter. Ask the student what they think the purpose of the letter is (to persuade someone to do something by setting out a case).

Main activities
- **A new sidekick; 15 minutes; page 109**
  Start by talking through heroes and sidekicks, and ask the student about others they may know. Discuss persuasive reasons and guide the student in using sentence starters to articulate such reasons.
- **Planning a persuasive letter; 25 minutes; page 110**
  Guide the student in completing the plan. Encourage them to use words from the conjunctions and adverbials bank to connect and reinforce their persuasive reasons (generated in the previous activity).

Plenary activities
- **Persuade me; 5 minutes**
  Ask the student to persuade you: 1. to buy them a present; 2. that winter is better than summer; 3. that money is not important to make you happy.

Homework activities
- **Dear Mr / Mrs Hero; 45 minutes; page 111**
  Provide a copy of the formal letter for reference. Explain to the student that their letter should include formal language and follow the conventional layout, and that this will be reviewed at their next session.

Differentiation and extension ideas
- **Recognising formal writing** Extend by expanding the discussion to the conventions of choosing titles (Mr, Mrs, Miss, Ms) and signing off (yours sincerely / yours faithfully).
- **A new sidekick** Support by reducing the number of sentence starters. Extend by leaving a couple of the rows blank for the student to suggest their own. Allow the student to change characters if it helps generate ideas.

Progress and observations

ENGLISH
— YEAR 6 —

STARTER ACTIVITY: RECOGNISING FORMAL WRITING

TIMING: 5 MINS

LEARNING OBJECTIVES
- To revise the features of a formal letter

EQUIPMENT
- highlighter

In the letter below, highlight the language and layout features that show you this is a formal letter.

4 Oxford Lane
Upton Abbots
NF3 6EF

13th July 2016

Simon Vega
Managing Director
Smarter Phone
101 Maybury Avenue
London
LC14 9QX

Dear Mr Vega,

Re: Faulty smartphone screen

I am writing to request a refund and to complain about the poor service that I have received.

Four days ago, I purchased a phone (Model Wave X) from your online store. The product arrived promptly but there is a major problem with the touch screen: it only works occasionally and even then it misreads where I am pressing, so it opens a different app from another part of the display.

I immediately telephoned your helpline. It took over an hour to get through and then a grumpy individual (who refused to give me his name) told me it was a known fault when the weather is cold. To my surprise, he suggested I should "give it 20 minutes to warm up" each time I used it. He also suggested I might try sitting in a room with all the radiators on! I told him I wished to return the phone immediately and receive a refund, but I was told this wouldn't be possible because "Janet's off sick 'til September".

This is not acceptable. The product is obviously faulty and your customer service is completely inadequate. I would be grateful if you would arrange an immediate refund. I look forward to hearing from you soon.

Yours sincerely,

Sasheika Powell

Mrs Sasheika Powell

ENGLISH
— YEAR 6 —

MAIN ACTIVITY: A NEW SIDEKICK　　　　　　　　　　**TIMING: 15 MINS**

LEARNING OBJECTIVES
- To use persuasive language

EQUIPMENT
none

Lots of heroes have sidekicks, don't they?
How would you persuade a hero that you should be their new sidekick?

You can choose to persuade an existing hero character and pretend to be another one yourself or you can make up your own.

Here are some persuasive sentence starters. Complete each one with a reason why the hero should choose you to be a sidekick.

Be your best with me at your side!

Everyone knows that … ....

I really feel that … ....

You must agree that … ....

Of course … ....

I am absolutely certain that … ....

Clearly … ....

Without doubt … ....

The fact is … ....

Surely … ....

It is so important that … ....

The time has come … ....

ENGLISH
— YEAR 6 —

TUTORS' GUILD

MAIN ACTIVITY: PLANNING A PERSUASIVE LETTER   **TIMING: 25 MINS**

LEARNING OBJECTIVES
- To plan a persuasive, formal letter

EQUIPMENT
none

You are going to write a formal letter to your hero to persuade them that you should be their new sidekick. Use the writing frame below to plan and organise your letter. Use words from the conjunctions and adverbials bank below to help you.

Your address:
Their name, title and address:
Paragraph 1 (explain why you are writing)
Paragraph 2 (persuasive reasons and language)
Paragraph 3 (summarise your main points and say what you hope will happen next)
Paragraph 4 (sign off with your name)

Conjunctions and adverbials bank				
firstly	secondly	furthermore	in addition	moreover
similarly	likewise	if …	then …	for example
in fact	for these reasons	as you can see	overall	without a doubt
in short	finally	for instance		on the whole

110

ENGLISH
YEAR 6

HOMEWORK ACTIVITY: DEAR MR / MRS HERO   **TIMING: 45 MINS**

LEARNING OBJECTIVES
- To write a formal, persuasive letter

EQUIPMENT
none

On a separate piece of paper, write a persuasive letter to convince a hero character that you should be his or her new sidekick. Your letter should be formal. Your tutor will supply a copy of the example letter to help you.

Once you have finished writing, use the checklist below to evaluate your work.

Tick I have included …

☐ My address

☐ Date under address

☐ Name, title and address of person to whom I am writing

☐ What the letter is about

☐ A logical sequence of paragraphs joined by conjunctions

☐ Persuasive reasons and language

☐ What I hope will happen next

☐ Yours sincerely,

☐ My signature

☐ My title and full name

☐ No contractions, slang or use of a 'chatty' style

ENGLISH
YEAR 6

15 ANSWERS

STARTER ACTIVITY: RECOGNISING FORMAL WRITING

Answers may vary. Examples might include:

Language: *Dear, Re:, I am writing to request, I purchased, the product arrived promptly, receive a refund, this is not acceptable, your customer service is completely inadequate, I look forward to hearing from you soon, yours sincerely*

Layout features: *positioning of addresses, appropriate salutation, reference line, sign off (yours sincerely, signature, full name)*

MAIN ACTIVITY: A NEW SIDEKICK

Answers may vary. Examples might include:

I believe that your powers and my fighting skills would make an unbeatable combination.

In my opinion, the evil ruler cannot be stopped without us joining up to defeat him together.

The time has come for use to join forces and fight crime as a team.

MAIN ACTIVITY: PLANNING A PERSUASIVE LETTER

Student's own answers. Check they have used some of the words from the conjunctions and adverbials bank.

HOMEWORK ACTIVITY: DEAR MR / MRS HERO

Student's own answers. Assess for correct use of layout conventions and inclusion of formal language. Provide the student with feedback on how well they have used persuasive language and how well such sentiments are linked by conjunctions and adverbials within and across paragraphs.

GLOSSARY

Formal language

Grammatically correct language that avoids contractions, slang and dialect words. It is often used in serious situations or when communicating with unfamiliar people.

Conjunction

A word that links words, phrases and clauses together inside a sentence.

Adverbial phrase

A group of words that acts as an adverb. It can tell you how, where and when something is happening.

ENGLISH — YEAR 6

16 Writing: Balanced arguments

Learning objectives

- To examine different sides of an argument
- To plan and write a balanced argument text
- To use cohesive devices to structure and develop arguments

Statutory NC requirements

Pupils should be taught to:

- draft and write by using a wide range of devices to build cohesion within and across paragraphs
- evaluate and edit by proposing changes to vocabulary, grammar and punctuation to enhance effects and clarify meaning

Starter activity

- **For and against; 5 minutes; page 114**
  Cover the table on the starter activity sheet and reveal each statement one at a time. Ensure the student answers as quickly as possible, but allow time for a simple discussion / justification if you wish.

Main activities

- **Fast food ban; 15 minutes; page 115**
  Ask the student to sort the statements into arguments for and arguments against. Remind the student that they might not agree with each point personally, but that should not influence how they sort the cards. Do not elaborate on each point but provide further explanation if required.
- **Planning a balanced argument; 25 minutes; page 116**
  Guide the student in completing the plan. Encourage them to narrow down their choices and choose the strongest arguments from the previous activity as the basis for their paragraphs for and against. Encourage the student to use the conjunctions to link the points within and across paragraphs.

Plenary activity

- **On balance; 5 minutes**
  Show the student the statements from the completed starter activity. Ask them to give their brief opinion on why they chose for or against. Encourage the student to summarise and to use sentence starters such as: *On balance, I believe …* or *In my opinion … .*

Homework activity

- **Writing a balanced argument; 45 minutes; page 117**
  Explain to the student how they should find and suggest an improvement after they have finished writing. Explain that feedback will be given on how effectively the student has structured their writing and how well they have used cohesive devices.

Differentiation and extension ideas

- **Fast food ban** Extend by asking the student to include three more points of their own in the blank boxes. Support by reducing the number of points for and against.
- **Writing a balanced argument** Support by providing a more detailed writing frame, including suggested conjunctions in order.

Progress and observations

ENGLISH
YEAR 6

STARTER ACTIVITY: FOR AND AGAINST   **TIMING: 5 MINS**

LEARNING OBJECTIVES
- To examine whether you are for or against some ideas
- To use the terms *for* and *against*

EQUIPMENT
- highlighter

Your tutor will reveal a list of statements people could disagree about.

Highlight *for* if you agree with the statement and highlight *against* if you disagree with it. You don't have to say your reasons why!

1.	Children shouldn't have to go to school.	for	against
2.	Children should be allowed to drive from age 12.	for	against
3.	Everyone should learn another language.	for	against
4.	Children shouldn't be allowed to use social networks.	for	against
5.	School lunches should be compulsory.	for	against
6.	You should be fined for dropping litter.	for	against
7.	We shouldn't bother to learn anything because we have the internet.	for	against
8.	Footballers shouldn't be paid so much.	for	against
9.	Fast food should be banned.	for	against

Ban burgers!

One now and again is okay – just not every day.

ENGLISH
— YEAR 6 —

MAIN ACTIVITY: FAST FOOD BAN | **TIMING: 15 MINS**

LEARNING OBJECTIVES
- To examine two sides of an argument
- To sort points into for and against categories

EQUIPMENT
- scissors
- glue stick

Some people think fast food should be banned. Below are some reasons for and against the argument.

Cut out the squares below. Sort them into arguments for and arguments against fast food being banned.
When you have sorted the arguments stick them to a separate sheet of paper.

It is important to eat a balance of different foods.	People can control how much fast food they eat.	Fast food contains large amounts of salt and sugar.
Fast food tastes better than healthy food.	A poor diet can lead to health problems such as diabetes and heart disease.	Banning things often makes people want them more.
Fast food restaurants provide jobs for millions of people around the world.	Burgers contain lots of calories but not many nutrients.	Fast food may increase the risk of depression in teenagers.
It should be your choice what you eat.	Buying fast food saves time.	Lots of vitamins are destroyed when food is fried.
Fast food is cheap and convenient.	Experts keep changing their minds about what is good or bad for us.	Eating fast food is linked to being overweight or obese.

ENGLISH
YEAR 6

MAIN ACTIVITY: PLANNING A BALANCED ARGUMENT **TIMING: 25 MINS**

LEARNING OBJECTIVES
- To plan a balanced argument

EQUIPMENT
none

You are going to write a balanced argument. The title is *Should fast food be banned?* Use the writing frame below to plan and organise your writing.

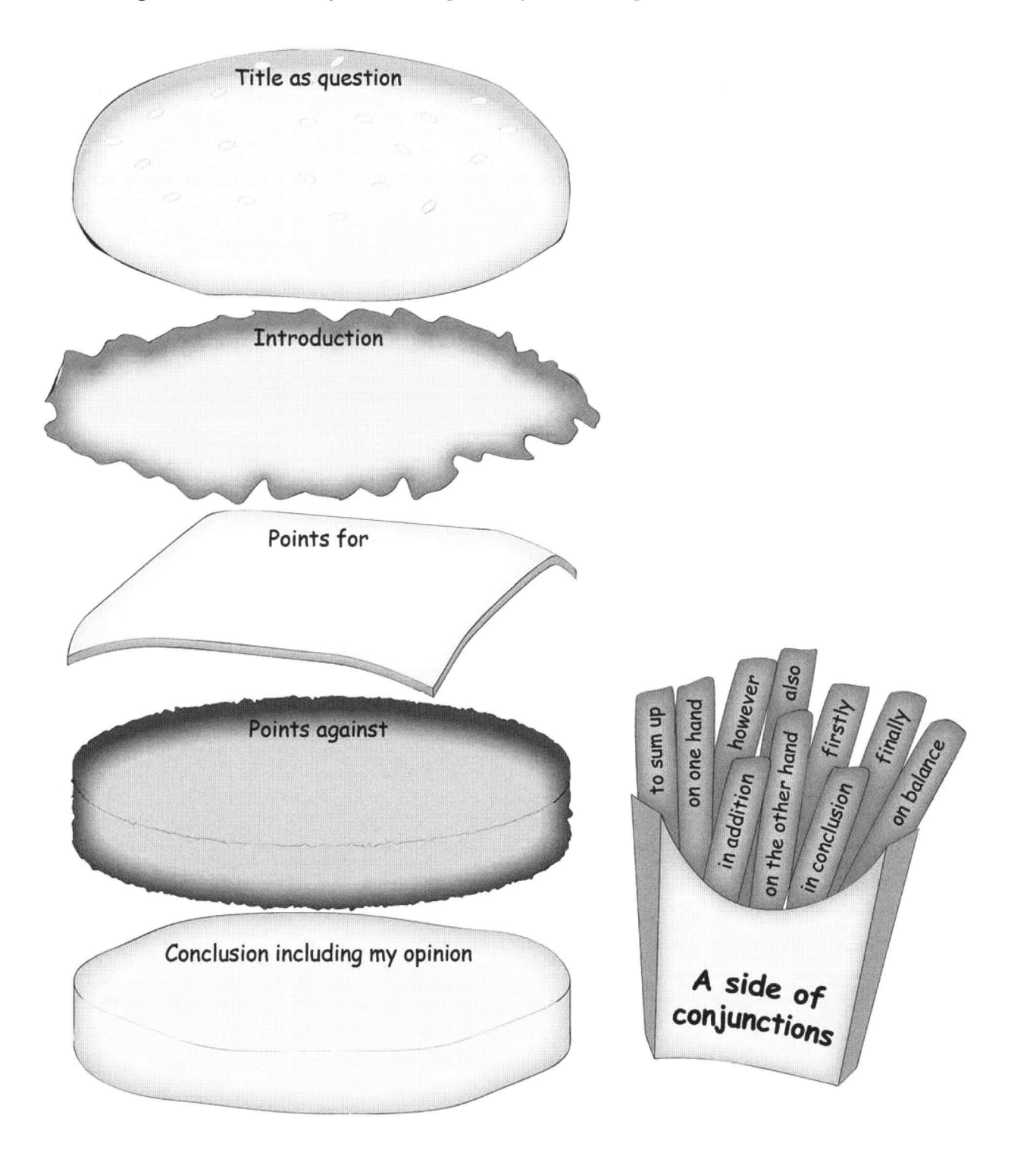

- Title as question
- Introduction
- Points for
- Points against
- Conclusion including my opinion

A side of conjunctions: to sum up, on one hand, however, also, firstly, in addition, on the other hand, in conclusion, finally, on balance

ENGLISH
YEAR 6

HOMEWORK ACTIVITY: WRITING A BALANCED ARGUMENT   **TIMING: 45 MINS**

LEARNING OBJECTIVES
- To write a balanced argument

EQUIPMENT
none

On a separate piece of paper, write your balanced argument about fast food using your plan. Once you have finished writing, underline all of the conjunctions you have used. Find sentences where you haven't used any conjunctions to link them.

Example:
Burgers contain lots of calories but not many nutrients. Lots of vitamins are destroyed when food is fried.

Now rewrite your sentences in the box below to include a conjunction or adverbial that links them together.

Example:
Burgers contain lots of calories but not many nutrients. Furthermore, lots of vitamins are destroyed when food is fried.

16 Answers

Starter activity: Fast food ban
Answers may vary.

Main activity: Planning a balanced argument
For: *It is important to eat a balance of different foods; Fast food contains large amounts of salt and sugar; A poor diet can lead to health problems such as diabetes and heart disease; Burgers contain lots of calories but not many nutrients; Fast food may increase the risk of depression in teenagers; Lots of vitamins are destroyed when food is fried; Eating fast food is linked to being overweight or obese.*

Against: *People can control how much fast food they eat; Fast food tastes better than healthy food; Banning things often makes people want them more; Fast food restaurants provide jobs for millions of people around the world; It should be your choice what you eat; Buying fast food saves time; Fast food is cheap and convenient; Experts keep changing their minds about what is good or bad for us.*

Main activity: Writing a balanced argument
Student's own answers. Check they have used the conjunctions to link their points within and across paragraphs.

Homework activity: Writing a balanced argument
Student's own answers. Assess the organisation and structure of their writing and how well the student has used cohesive devices such as conjunctions to link ideas within and across paragraphs. Feed back on how well the student has improved their sentences on the homework sheet.

Glossary

Conjunction
Links words, phrases and clauses together to express the where, when and how.

Paragraph
A distinct section of a piece of writing often shown by a new line, indentation or number. Paragraphs are used to group together related material within a longer text.

Cohesion
A cohesive device is a word or phrase used to link ideas within and across paragraphs. It is used to show how parts of the text fit together, creating cohesion. For example, the use of adverbials such *as on the one hand* and *in contrast*.

Adverbial phrase
A group of words that acts as an adverb. It can tell you how, where and when something is happening.

17 Writing: Writing Fiction

Learning Objectives

- To use a stimulus to plan a piece of fiction
- To organise ideas into paragraphs
- To use dialogue
- To write a short story

Statutory NC Requirements

Pupils should be taught to:

- plan their writing by noting and developing initial ideas, drawing on reading and research where necessary
- draft and write by describing settings, characters and atmosphere and integrating dialogue to convey character and advance the action

Starter Activity

- **A box of superpowers; 5 minutes; page 120**
  This starter activity is designed to stimulate the student's imagination. There are no right or wrong responses and the student should be encouraged to use their imagination. Ask the student to verbalise and discuss their ideas before writing anything down.

Main Activities

- **A day of disasters; 20 minutes; page 121**
  This activity focuses on further stimulating ideas for a short story. The student can either think of their own superhero name or generate one. It is important that the student is given opportunity to verbalise and discuss lots of ideas using the picture stimulus. Do not ask the student to write anything at this stage.
- **Story plan; 20 minutes; page 122**
  This activity focuses on turning the student's ideas into a problem-solving short story plot. Again, allow time for the student to express their thoughts out loud before committing their ideas to paper. Encourage the student to note down cohesive devices to help structure and organise their ideas. In particular, encourage planning of any dialogue exchanges appropriate to the genre (e.g. *Never fear, Marvellous Man is here!*).

Plenary Activity

- **First paragraph; 5 minutes**
  Ask the student to put themselves in the shoes of their superhero and imagine they have just woken up. Where are they? What do they see, hear or smell? What is the first thing they do? (e.g. *Put on their cape*). What are their plans for the day?

Homework Activity

- **Short story writing; 45 minutes; page 123**
  Talk through the checklist with the student to make sure they understand it. Encourage the student to write on every other line to leave space for editing, improving and proof-reading.

Differentiation and Extension Ideas

- **Story plan** Support the student in fully expressing their imagination by writing down their ideas for them.
- **Short story writing** Support by removing items from the checklist to narrow the focus.

Progress and Observations

ENGLISH
— YEAR 6 —

STARTER ACTIVITY: A BOX OF SUPERPOWERS

TIMING: 5 MINS

LEARNING OBJECTIVES
- To play with thoughts and ideas

EQUIPMENT
none

Below is a special magic box. It contains lots of different superpowers, but it's closed. Imagine what superpowers might be hidden inside!

Write your suggestions for the superpowers around the outside of the box. Which one would you choose?

ENGLISH
YEAR 6

MAIN ACTIVITY: A DAY OF DISASTERS **TIMING: 20 MINS**

LEARNING OBJECTIVES
- To create a character and some ideas for a short story plot

EQUIPMENT
- a dice

First, you need to name your very own superhero. You can think of a name or roll a dice twice and use the below table to generate one. For example, rolling 4 and a 1 makes *Marvellous Man!*

1st roll	superhero description	2nd roll	superhero type
1	Amazing	1	Man
2	Incredible	2	Girl
3	Wonderful	3	Woman
4	Marvellous	4	Boy
5	Dynamic	5	Guy
6	Mighty	6	Kid

Your superhero is having a difficult day. Look at the scene in this picture. Discuss all the things that are going wrong at the same time.

What would your superhero do to help? What superpower(s) would help them? In what order would your hero help? Talk through what happens from start to finish with your tutor.

ENGLISH
YEAR 6

MAIN ACTIVITY: STORY PLAN　　　　　　　　　　**TIMING: 20 MINS**

LEARNING OBJECTIVES
- To plan a short story

EQUIPMENT
none

Use this planning frame to help you plan your story about your superhero's difficult day.

Opening (introduce the character and setting)

Build-up (describe what the character does and sees before the problem)

Problem (describe the problem that the character is faced with)

Solution (describe how the character solves the problem)

Ending (describe where the character is at the end, and how they feel)

ENGLISH
— YEAR 6 —

HOMEWORK ACTIVITY: SHORT STORY WRITING **TIMING: 45 MINS**

LEARNING OBJECTIVES
- To write a short story using your plan

EQUIPMENT
none

First write your superhero story on a separate piece of paper. When you have finished, use the checklist below to evaluate your work. Be honest!

- ☐ I have written an imaginative story!
- ☐ My story has a problem and a solution.
- ☐ I have used an attention-grabbing story opening.
- ☐ The reader finds out who, when and where in the first paragraph.
- ☐ I have used paragraphs to organise the plot.
- ☐ I have used conjunctions to link ideas and paragraphs (cohesion).
- ☐ I have used a mix of sentence types (simple, compound, complex).
- ☐ I have included some dialogue.
- ☐ My descriptions are clear so readers can see them in their minds.
- ☐ I have used the correct tenses.
- ☐ I have used some figurative language (similes, metaphors, alliteration, onomatopoeia).
- ☐ I have used a range of punctuation.

Now look at the boxes you haven't ticked. Do you think you could improve your story? Try to edit and improve your story using the checklist as a guide.

Finally, proof-read your work (check your spelling and punctuation).

ENGLISH
YEAR 6

17 Answers

Starter activity: A box of superpowers
Answers may vary. Examples might include: invisibility, flight, x-ray vision, ability to manipulate objects, super speed, strength, etc.

Main activity: A day of disasters
Discussion with student.

Main activity: Story plan
Student's own answers. Check they have completed the planning frame.

Homework activity: Short story writing
Student's own answers. Compare the checklist to final story and feedback on the effectiveness of the student's editing, improvement and proof-reading.

Glossary

Fiction
Prose writing that describes imaginary events and characters.

Paragraph
A distinct section of a piece of writing often shown by a new line, indentation or number. Paragraphs are used to group together related material within a longer text.

Cohesion
A cohesive device is a word or phrase used to link ideas within and across paragraphs. It is used to show how parts of the text fit together, creating cohesion. For example, the use of adverbials such as *on the one hand* and *in contrast*.

ENGLISH
YEAR 6

18 GRAMMAR: NOUNS

LEARNING OBJECTIVES

- To differentiate between common and proper nouns and know when to use a capital letter
- To recognise what makes a noun phrase or expanded noun phrase
- To write a variety of expanded noun phrases in context, using capital letters where appropriate

CONTENT DOMAINS

- G1.1 nouns
- G1.3 adjectives
- G3.2 noun phrases
- G5.1 capital letters

STARTER ACTIVITY

- **Capital or not?; 5 minutes; page 126**
  Cut out the cards on the sheet before the lesson. Use them to assess the student's understanding of common and proper nouns. Address the misconception that common nouns need capital letters because they work like a person's name (some students will write *a Dog*).

MAIN ACTIVITIES

- **Katie's diary: a holiday on Mars; 20 minutes; page 127**
  This activity uses common and proper nouns in context. Read out the extract with the nouns in place (see answers on page 130) and follow the instructions on the sheet. Ensure that the student uses a capital letter when copying proper nouns into the gaps.
- **The new teacher; 15 minutes; page 128**
  Discuss exactly which words have been added to each noun in bold to make each noun phrase. Make sure the student highlights every part of each noun phrase, not just the adjectives.
- **Power up your noun phrases; 5 minutes; page 128**
  This activity could be done as a time trial to see how many noun phrases the student can write in five minutes. It may help if you model an example with a plural noun. Encourage the student to use their own adjectives and remind them that phrases do not include verbs.

PLENARY ACTIVITY

- **Quick-fire noun spotting; 5 minutes**
  Consolidate the student's ability to spot the noun in a noun phrase. Provide an example of an expanded noun phrase (e.g. *my oldest friend* or *the star of the show*). Ask the student to identify the main noun (head word) in each phrase.

HOMEWORK ACTIVITY

- **The new teacher (continued); 45 minutes; page 129**
  This activity puts the student's learning into practice. Emphasise the importance of correct capitalisation of nouns and the use of interesting expanded noun phrases and that these will be reviewed together at the next session.

DIFFERENTIATION AND EXTENSION IDEAS

- **Capital or not?** Support by playing a game with the cards. Ask the student to guess whether there is a common, proper, collective or abstract noun on each card before they turn it over. If they are right, they win the word. Extend by asking the student to think of some nouns that can double as other word types: e.g. *lift*, *promise* and *smell* can be verbs as well as nouns.
- **Katie's diary: a holiday on Mars** Support by reducing the number of gaps and words.
- **Power up your noun phrases** Support by discussing the word classes of the modifying words (e.g. determiners, adjectives, etc.) Extend by including noun phrases in which modifying words also come after the noun (e.g. *A huge painting of her mother*).

PROGRESS AND OBSERVATIONS

ENGLISH
YEAR 6

STARTER ACTIVITY: CAPITAL OR NOT?

TIMING: 5 MINS

LEARNING OBJECTIVES
- To understand when a noun needs a capital letter

EQUIPMENT
- scissors

Some of these nouns (naming words) need capital letters and some of them don't.

Sort them into two groups: *needs a capital letter* and *doesn't need a capital letter*.
Then explain to your tutor how you decided where to place each word.

cat	anger	july	flock
london	stanley	truck	ella
jokes	germany	password	city
sister	wednesday	pacific ocean	happiness
spanish	regret	christmas	sherlock holmes

ENGLISH
— YEAR 6 —

MAIN ACTIVITY: KATIE'S DIARY: A HOLIDAY ON MARS   **TIMING: 20 MINS**

LEARNING OBJECTIVES

- To use common and proper nouns with confidence

EQUIPMENT

none

This diary entry from the future has lots of common nouns and proper nouns missing. The missing words are in the word bank below.

1. Your task is to find the word that makes sense for each gap. Remember to give the proper nouns capital letters.

15th April 2216

Dear Diary,

This _____, _____ went to _____ with my _____ for the _____ holidays. We set off on a _____ night. We travelled by drone to a spaceport in _____. Our huge _____ was called _____. It was amazing when we flew past the _____ but my dad, _____ was a bit space-sick. Our _____ had more than 500 rooms. It had a giant _____ with a wave _____. We went on space safari and I took my _____, called _____. I spotted a _____ of wild moondogs and an _____ called a _____. Our cool guide spoke lots of _____ including _____ and _____. Overall, I think our _____ was a great _____.

Bye, Katie

success	april	martian	family	machine	galaxy spirit
languages	i	english	mars	james	pool
pack	holiday	dust beetle	friday	easter	moon
book	scotland	space wildlife	spaceship	insect	hotel

2. Some of the nouns in the word bank are collective nouns, and some are abstract nouns. Read the diary entry again and look out for these special nouns. When you've found them, write them on the answer lines below.

Collective nouns: _____

Abstract nouns: _____

ENGLISH
— YEAR 6 —

MAIN ACTIVITY: THE NEW TEACHER   TIMING: 15 MINS

LEARNING OBJECTIVES
- To recognise a noun phrase
- To write expanded noun phrases

EQUIPMENT
- highlighter pen

If you add words to nouns to make them more specific, you make a noun phrase.

Example:
elephant (noun) → my pink elephant (noun phrase).

Read the text below and highlight all the noun phrases you find.

The new teacher was a very strange-looking person. He had a few wonky teeth and a mop of curly hair. His thick glasses were covered in smudgy fingerprints. His yellow tie was splattered with some greasy food stains. Abi put her hand up. The strange little man peered over the top of his dirty specs and nodded.

"Sir, are you really our new maths teacher?" Abi asked.

"Why, yes, I suppose I am," he replied cautiously. "My name is Mr Cauliflower."

Several children giggled.

POWER UP YOUR NOUN PHRASES!   TIMING: 5 MINS

LEARNING OBJECTIVES
- To write expanded noun phrases

EQUIPMENT
none

You can make your writing more interesting by expanding your noun phrases and using adjectives.

On a separate piece of paper, take it in turns with your tutor to write expanded noun phrases using the words in the table below. Who can come up with the most interesting noun phrase?

Example:
Shell (noun) → a huge, handsome, rosy shell (noun phrase)

common nouns (Use the plurals of these nouns too!)					words to describe nouns				
river	dog	stone	mask	writer	our	the	gold	beautiful	pink
road	evening	leg	person	plate	large	funny	best	several	no
shell	journey	shoe	bag	house	their	little	weird	mysterious	an
door	actor	hair	day	child	brown	very	red	favourite	any
					its	one	young	broken	long
					some	my	three	a	your
					big	bumpy	slow	fat	ugly

ENGLISH
YEAR 6

HOMEWORK ACTIVITY: THE NEW TEACHER (CONTINUED) **TIMING: 45 MINS**

LEARNING OBJECTIVES	EQUIPMENT
• To write a story using a stimulus • To use capital letters for proper nouns • To include expanded noun phrases in fiction writing • To include ambitious adjectives in fiction writing	none

Here is the start of the story about Mr Cauliflower, the new maths teacher.

The new teacher was a very strange-looking person. He had a few wonky teeth and a mop of curly hair. His thick glasses were covered in smudgy fingerprints. His yellow tie was splattered with some greasy food stains. Abi put her hand up. The strange little man peered over the top of his dirty specs and nodded.

"Sir, are you really our new maths teacher?" Abi asked.

"Why, yes, I suppose I am," he replied cautiously. "My name is Mr Cauliflower."

Several children giggled.

On a separate piece of paper, write what happens next. Here are some ideas to get you started.

- What day of the week is it?
- Where does Mr Cauliflower come from? Does he speak another language?
- Introduce another character (the character's name should have a capital letter).
- Imagine the head teacher comes in to see how Mr Cauliflower is getting on.
- Describe the head teacher and what happens.

When you have written your story, complete the checklist below.

Tick I have included …

☐ capital letters on any proper nouns

☐ expanded noun phrases

☐ adjectives to make my writing more interesting.

ENGLISH
— YEAR 6 —

18 ANSWERS

STARTER ACTIVITY: CAPITAL OR NOT?

Needs a capital: *July; London; Stanley; Ella; Germany; Wednesday; Pacific Ocean; Spanish; Christmas; Sherlock Holmes*
Doesn't need a capital: *cat; anger; flock; truck; jokes; password; city; sister; happiness; regret*

MAIN ACTIVITY: KATE'S DIARY: A HOLIDAY ON MARS

1. Dear Diary,
   This <u>April</u>, <u>I</u> went to <u>Mars</u> with my <u>family</u> for the <u>Easter</u> holidays. We set off on a <u>Friday</u> night. We travelled by drone to a spaceport in <u>Scotland</u>. Our huge <u>spaceship</u> was called <u>Galaxy Spirit</u>. It was amazing when we flew past the <u>Moon</u> but my dad, <u>James,</u> was a bit space-sick. Our <u>hotel</u> had more than 500 rooms. It had a giant <u>pool</u> with a wave <u>machine</u>. We went on space safari and I took my <u>book,</u> called <u>Space Wildlife</u>. I spotted a <u>pack</u> of wild moondogs and an <u>insect</u> called a <u>dust beetle</u>. Our cool guide spoke lots of <u>languages</u> including <u>English</u> and <u>Martian</u>. Overall, I think our <u>holiday</u> was a great <u>success</u>. Bye, Katie.
2. Collective nouns: pack; family. Abstract nouns: success; holiday

MAIN ACTIVITY: THE NEW TEACHER

The new teacher was a very strange-looking person. He had a few wonky teeth and a mop of curly hair. His thick glasses were covered in smudgy fingerprints. His yellow tie was splattered with some greasy food stains. Abi put her hand up. The strange little man peered over the top of his dirty specs and nodded.
'Sir, are you really our new maths teacher?' Abi asked.
'Why, yes, I suppose I am,' he replied cautiously. 'My name is Mr Cauliflower.'
Several children giggled.

HOMEWORK ACTIVITY: THE NEW TEACHER CONTINUED

Check the student's answer for correct use of capital letters in proper nouns. Provide feedback on the use of expanded noun phrases.

GLOSSARY

Common noun
A word that refers to people or things. Some common nouns, called abstract nouns, name ideas or feelings that you can't see or touch. Other common nouns, called collective nouns, name groups of things. A common noun only needs a capital letter at the start of a sentence.

Proper noun
A word that names a particular person, place or thing. It always begins with a capital letter. Proper nouns are also used for days, months, languages, special times like Christmas, companies like Pearson and titles like *Alice in Wonderland*.

Collective noun
A noun that describes a collection or group of people or things.

Abstract noun
A noun that describes an idea, quality, state or feeling, rather than a concrete object.

Adjective
A word that adds detail to a noun and can come before or after a noun. Using more than one adjective to describe a noun makes your writing more interesting.

Noun phrase
A group of words that work together like a noun. The noun is the main word in the phrase. An example of a noun phrase is *my car*.

Expanded noun phrase
A noun phrase with more precise or interesting details. The simplest way to expand a noun phrase is to add adjectives. An example of an expanded noun phrase is *my favourite blue car*.

ENGLISH — YEAR 6

19 GRAMMAR: PRONOUNS AND DETERMINERS

LEARNING OBJECTIVES

- To identify and use a range of determiners
- To select pronouns to replace nouns appropriately for clarity and cohesion
- To use pronouns to indicate possession

CONTENT DOMAINS

- G1.5 pronouns
- G1.5a possessive pronouns
- G1.8 determiners

STARTER ACTIVITY

- **Determiners; 5 minutes; page 132**
  Guide the student to use a wide range of determiners from the word bank. Discuss which must go with plural nouns and check for correct spelling of irregular plurals such as: *boxes*.

MAIN ACTIVITIES

- **Replacing nouns; 20 minutes; page 133**
  This activity focuses on using pronouns to replace nouns and noun phrases. Discuss how pronouns are used to reduce repetition. Ensure the student understands that pronouns refer back to nouns already mentioned and how sense can be lost if it is unclear to whom or what a pronoun is referring.
- **Snap!; 20 minutes; page 134**
  This matching game focuses on pairing up possessive pronouns. Whilst it may take time for all the pairs to be matched, the game intrinsically familiarises the student with the full range of pronouns and then calls for the student to use them in context.

PLENARY ACTIVITY

- **Pronoun for noun; 5 minutes**
  On a whiteboard, write a noun or noun phrase (e.g. *My brother and I*) and ask the student to write a suitable pronoun to replace it (e.g. *We*). Repeat or swap roles as time allows.

HOMEWORK ACTIVITY

- **Endangered species; 45 minutes; page 135**
  This activity puts the student's learning into practice. As this is unsupported work, the activity focuses on a narrower range of pronouns (third person). Review and discuss the remaining areas of weakness or misconceptions in the next session.

DIFFERENTIATION AND EXTENSION IDEAS

- **Determiners** Extend or support by adding or removing words from the table. For example, add extra nouns to focus on a particular spelling pattern. Extend by removing the word bank.
- **Mine!** Extend by asking the student to write some short sentences using the possessive pronoun pairs, for example: *Our car is blue. The blue car is ours.*
- **Endangered species** Extend by asking the student to rewrite the five sentences to include a wider range of pronouns, for example: *Mum and I saw an orangutan at the zoo. We thought the orangutan looked sad.* Provide a list of websites or reference books suited to the student's ability.

PROGRESS AND OBSERVATIONS

ENGLISH
YEAR 6

STARTER ACTIVITY: DETERMINERS **TIMING: 5 MINS**

LEARNING OBJECTIVES
- To use a range of determiners with nouns

EQUIPMENT
none

A determiner comes before a noun and tells you more about it.

noun	determiner			
hat	<u>the</u> hat	<u>that</u> hat	<u>some</u> hats	<u>my</u> hat

Complete the table below by adding determiners from the word bank below and some nouns of your own. You can use a determiner more than once but try to use each of them at least once.

noun	determiner			
apple	*an*		*another*	
box		*these*		*our*
leaf			*a lot of*	

a	an	the	this	that	my
those	three	some	any	every	your
another	other	no	a lot of	all	his
her		its		our	their

132

ENGLISH
— YEAR 6 —

MAIN ACTIVITY: REPLACING NOUNS **TIMING: 20 MINS**

LEARNING OBJECTIVES
- To use pronouns to replace nouns

EQUIPMENT
none

Pronouns can replace nouns and noun phrases.

Example:
Mum bought some delicious chocolates for Dad. → She gave them to him on his birthday.

1. Highlight all the nouns and noun phrases in the sentences below. How do they sound to you?

a) Scarlett and Mia went to a new Chinese restaurant.
b) Scarlett and Mia went to the restaurant without Alice.
c) Alice was very upset with Scarlett and Mia.

Now rewrite the second and third sentences, using pronouns to replace the nouns and noun phrases.

------

2. Here is another set of sentences. Rewrite the second, third and fourth sentences using pronouns to replace the nouns and noun pronouns.

a) Noah and I have twelve pet lizards.
b) Noah and I keep our pet lizards in our bedroom.
c) Noah and I feed fresh leaves and dead mice to our pet lizards.
d) Noah's friends Archie and Logan think our pet lizards are cool.

------

3. On a separate piece of paper, write two sentences that follow on from the starter sentence below, using one or more of these pronouns.

My family and I love fish and chips

i	you	he	she
it	we	they	him
her	me	us	them

ENGLISH
— YEAR 6 —

MAIN ACTIVITY: SNAP! **TIMING: 20 MINS**

LEARNING OBJECTIVES
- To recognise pronouns that show who owns something

EQUIPMENT
- scissors

Possessive pronouns show who or what owns something.

Example:
That is my book. It is mine. It is not your book. It is not yours.

Cut out the cards below. Play a matching pairs games against your tutor, shouting "snap!" to claim each pair of pronouns that are in the same person.

Example:
my and mine   your and yours

When you find a pair, you then have five seconds to think up a sentence using one of the pronouns.

Example:
Have you seen my dog?

If you run out of time, your opponent can shout "snap!" and you must give both cards to your opponent. Keep playing until all the pairs have been matched.

my	mine	your	yours
his	his	her	hers
its	its	our	ours
their	theirs		

ENGLISH
— YEAR 6 —

HOMEWORK ACTIVITY: ENDANGERED SPECIES **TIMING: 45 MINS**

LEARNING OBJECTIVES
- To use a range of determiners with nouns

EQUIPMENT
none

Read the five pairs of sentences below about endangered species.

Underline the noun or noun phrase in the first sentence then highlight the pronoun that replaces it in the second sentence.

Example:
<u>Giant pandas</u> live in a few mountain ranges in China. **They** mostly eat bamboo.

1. European settlers in Africa used to kill black rhinos. The settlers regarded them as pests.

2. The high forests of central Africa are home to the mountain gorilla. It has thick fur.

3. Tigers live in a disappearing jungle habitat. They now search for food in villages.

4. The African wild dog is a predator. Its prey includes gazelles.

5. The Yangtze river used to be home to the Baiji dolphin. Human activity has made it extinct.

**Find out more about other endangered species.
Write your own similar pairs of sentences below.**

ENGLISH
YEAR 6

19 ANSWERS

STARTER ACTIVITY: DETERMINERS

Answers may vary. Examples for the first three rows might include the following. Check the student has completed subsequent rows correctly.

apple	an apple	this apple	another apple	your apple
boxes	the box	these boxes	seven boxes	our boxes
leaf	a leaf	that leaf	a lot of leaves	its leaves

MAIN ACTIVITY: REPLACING NOUNS

1. Answers may vary.
a) Scarlett and Mia went to a new Chinese restaurant. → They went to a new Chinese restaurant.
b) Scarlett and Mia went to the restaurant without Alice. → They went to it without Alice.
c) Alice was very upset with Scarlett and Mia. → She was very upset with them.
2. Answers may vary.
a) Noah and I have twelve pet lizards.
b) Noah and I keep our pet lizards in our bedroom. → We keep them in our bedroom.
c) Noah and I feed fresh leaves and dead mice to our pet lizard. → We feed fresh leaves and dead mice to them.
d) Noah's friends Archie and Logan think our pet lizards are cool. → His friends Archie and Logan think they are cool.
3. Student's own answer. Check they have written two sentences using one or more pronouns from the word bank.

MAIN ACTIVITY: SNAP!

Answers may vary.

HOMEWORK ACTIVITY: ENDANGERED SPECIES

1. European settlers in Africa used to kill black rhinos. The settlers regarded them as pests.
2. The high forests of central Africa are home to the mountain gorilla. It has thick fur.
3. Tigers live in a disappearing jungle habitat. They now search for food in villages.
4. The African wild dog is a predator. Its prey includes gazelles.
5. The Yangtze river used to be home to the Baiji dolphin. Human activity has made it extinct.

GLOSSARY

Pronoun
A word that shows ownership (possessive) or refers back to nouns (relative).

Personal pronoun
A word that replaces a noun or noun phrase, such as *I, me, him,* or *they*.

Possessive pronoun
A word that replaces a noun and a possessive apostrophe to show who or what owns something. It can be used with a noun as a determiner such as *my*, or can be used on its own to replace a noun such as *mine*.

Relative pronoun
A word that is used to introduce a relative clause (a subordinate clause that adds detail to a noun), such as *who, whose, that* and *which*.

Determiner
A word that comes before a noun and makes the noun more specific or general, such as *the, some, her* or *two*.

20 Grammar: Adjectives and Adverbs

Learning Objectives

- To use adjectives to add detail to nouns
- To use comparative adjectives to compare nouns
- To use adverbs and adverbial phrases to add detail to verbs
- To use fronted adverbials

Content Domains

- G1.3 adjectives
- G1.6 adverbs
- G1.6a adverbials

Starter Activity

- **Added detail; 10 minutes; page 138**
  Assess the student's knowledge of adjectives and adverbs. Encourage the student to identify the suffix *–ly*. No adverbials are included in the activity although one non *–ly* adverb is included (*very* modifying the adjective *gentle*). Reinforce the difference between adjectives and adverbs.

Main Activities

- **Boastful Bella; 15 minutes; page 139**
  This activity focuses on writing adjectives and comparative adjectives in context. Discuss with the student how to use *–er* and *–est* suffixes and how adjectives with three or more syllables use *more* and *most*. Encourage the student to use irregular comparatives such as *bad* → *worse* → *worst*.
- **Adverbs and adverbials; 20 minutes; page 140**
  This activity focuses on expanding sentences by adding fronted adverbials as well as adverbs and other adverbials (prepositional phrases) elsewhere. For simplicity, follow the structure of the model sentence. The student will need to add some detail of their own. Reinforce the difference between adverbs and adverbials.

Plenary Activity

- **Guess my adverb; 5 minutes**
  Mime an action (waving) in a certain way (slowly). Ask the student to identify both the verb (*wave*) and the adverb (*slowly*) to describe your actions. Swap roles and repeat as time allows.

Homework Activity

- **The discovery; 45 minutes; page 141**
  This activity puts the student's learning into practice. Remind them that not every sentence needs lots of adjectives, adverbs and adverbials, but that including some can add interest. Review and discuss any remaining areas of weakness and misconceptions together in the next session.

Differentiation and Extension Ideas

- **Added detail** Extend by including some adverb-modifying adverbs such as *really soon* or adverbial phrases.
- **Boastful Bella** Extend by challenging the student to write some statements that are modest rather than boastful in tone.
- **Adverbs and adverbials** Extend by exploring how changing the positions of the adverbs and adverbials within the student's sentences does or doesn't affect the meaning.
- **The discovery** Support by including a scaffolding model to guide the student's rewriting of the text.

Progress and Observations

ENGLISH
— YEAR 6 —

STARTER ACTIVITY: ADDED DETAIL   **TIMING: 10 MINS**

LEARNING OBJECTIVES
- To recognise adjectives and adverbs

EQUIPMENT
- two highlighters

The text below is a description of insects you might find in your local park.
The writer has added detail about the nouns and verbs by using adjectives and adverbs.

Highlight the adjectives in one colour and the adverbs in a different colour.

If you look closely, you will see lots of different insects in your local park. In the summer, you will find them scuttling quickly across the grass and hiding by day under logs. They climb up long stems, shelter in cracks in walls, munch continuously on huge leaves and buzz around flowers. Some seem kind and very gentle: female earwigs lay their pearly eggs in spring. They lick their eggs carefully to stop them going mouldy. Others sound really ferocious: the devil's coach-horse beetle hunts tiny caterpillars by night. It squirts a nasty liquid from its arched tail to defend itself.

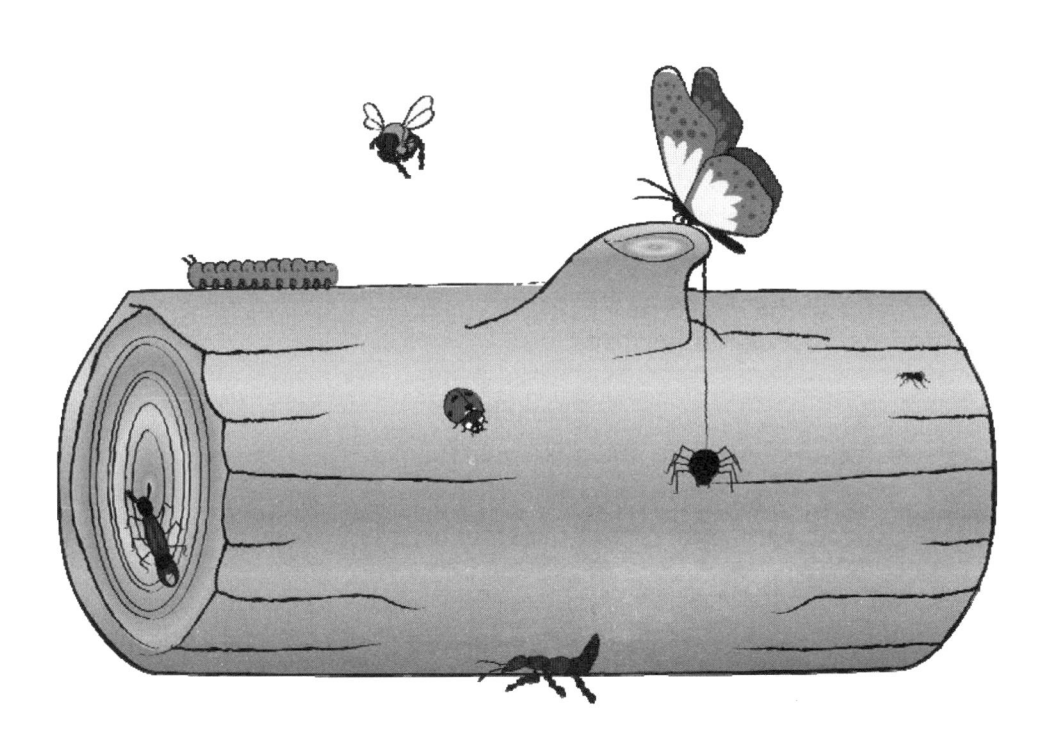

ENGLISH
YEAR 6

MAIN ACTIVITY: BOASTFUL BELLA   **TIMING: 15 MINS**

LEARNING OBJECTIVES
- To use adjectives to add detail to nouns
- To use adjectives to compare nouns

EQUIPMENT
none

Bella thinks she is the best. She thinks everything she owns is the best.
She loves to boast about it too!

> My dad just bought me this *cool* car.
> My dad is *richer* than your dad.
> My *new* sports car is the *best* car!

The words *cool, richer, new* and *best* are adjectives.
Cool and *new* describe her car and *richer* and *best* compare things.

1. **Bella boasts about everything. Complete these sentences with adjectives you think Bella would use.**

a) Your _____ coat is _____ than mine.
b) My _____ house is much _____ than your _____ place.
c) Your mobile is so _____ and _____.
d) We went on the most _____ holiday in the _____ Caribbean last week.
e) Our friends have a _____ yacht that has all the _____ technology on board.

2. **What adjective would you use to describe Bella?**
   Write three sentences for your adjective.

Example:
Bella is boastful.
Bella is more boastful than anyone I know.
Bella is the most boastful person I know.

139

ENGLISH
— YEAR 6 —

MAIN ACTIVITY: ADVERBS AND ADVERBIALS   **TIMING: 20 MINS**

LEARNING OBJECTIVES
- To use adverbs and adverbials to add detail to verbs
- To use fronted adverbials

EQUIPMENT
- a dice

Here is a sentence with some adverbs and adverbials.

<u>In the morning,</u>   Cassie woke up   <u>slowly</u>   <u>in her bedroom</u>.

Fronted adverbial describes when Cassie woke up.   Adverb describes how Cassie woke up.   Adverbial describes where Cassie woke up.

You are going to write some similar sentences. Roll a dice to choose a main clause.

first roll	main clause
1	my friend Rameel walked
2	old Mrs Violet Bloom set off
3	the old security guard spoke
4	a small, brown dog searched
5	some scary-looking bikers rode
6	a group of children swam

Roll three more times to choose two adverbials and an adverb to add to it.

second roll	fronted adverbial (when)	third roll	adverb (how)	fourth roll	adverbial (where)
1	the day before yesterday	1	angrily	1	near ...
2	soon afterwards	2	quickly	2	under ...
3	just at that moment	3	cheerfully	3	next to ...
4	during the night	4	slowly	4	behind ...
5	a week later	5	carefully	5	in front of ...
6	after a while	6	noisily	6	opposite ...

Example:
Your first roll is 3 (*the old security guard spoke*); then 4 (*during the night*); then 2 (*quickly*); then 6 (*opposite*).

<u>During the night</u>, <u>the old security guard spoke</u> <u>quickly</u> to the men <u>opposite</u> the supermarket.

                                                extra detail   extra detail

Remember:

- an adverb is a single word and an adverbial is a group of words
- adverbials and fronted adverbials can describe when, how or where something happens
- all the adverbs on this page end in 'ly', but not all words that end in 'ly' are adverbs!

ENGLISH
YEAR 6

HOMEWORK ACTIVITY: THE DISCOVERY	TIMING: 45 MINS

LEARNING OBJECTIVES
- To practise using adjectives and adverbs
- To improve a piece of text by adding detail to nouns and verbs

EQUIPMENT
- a dice

The start of the story below is not very interesting. The writer hasn't used adjectives, adverbs or adverbials.

A woman was walking. She saw something. She picked it up. The woman looked at it. She couldn't believe it. She was excited. She set off.

Rewrite the story adding detail to the nouns and verbs.

Example:

A woman was walking. ⟶ One rainy day last March, a grumpy old woman was walking slowly down an empty street.

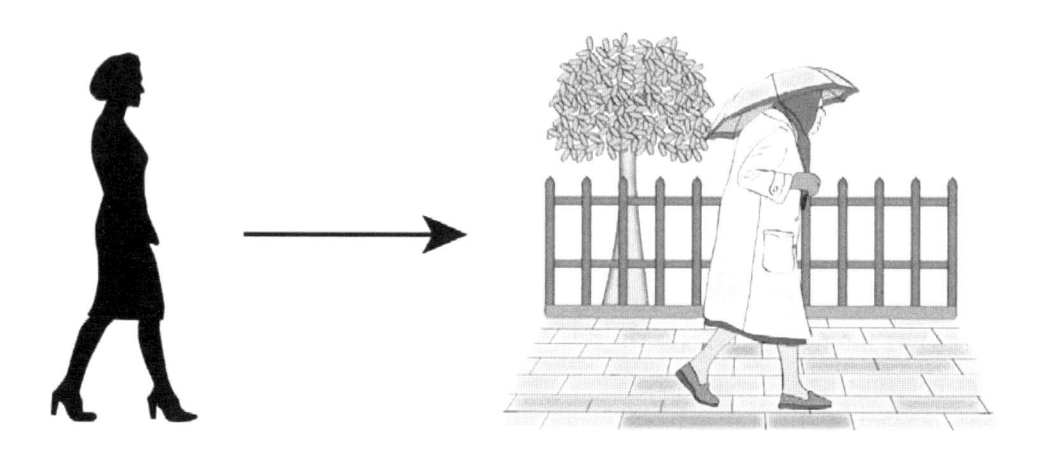

Remember:
Use adjectives to describe nouns: *a woman → a grumpy old woman*
Use adverbs to describe verbs: *was walking → was walking slowly*
Use adverbials to describe verbs: *down an empty street*
Use fronted adverbials to describe verbs: *One rainy day last March*

You don't need all of these for every sentence!

If you have time, continue the story. Remember to make your writing more interesting with adjectives, adverbs and adverbials.
What has the woman found? Where is she going? Does someone else appear?

ENGLISH — YEAR 6

20 Answers

Starter activity: Added detail

adjectives; adverbs

If you look closely, you will see lots of different insects in your local park. In the summer, you will find them scuttling quickly across the grass and hiding during the day under logs. They climb up long stems, shelter in cracks in walls, munch continuously on huge leaves and buzz around flowers. Some seem kind and very gentle: female earwigs lay their pearly eggs in spring. They lick their eggs carefully to stop them going mouldy. Others sound really ferocious: the devil's coach-horse beetle hunts tiny caterpillars by night. It squirts a nasty liquid from its arched tail to defend itself.

Main activity: Boastful Bella

1. Answers may vary. Examples might include:
   a) Your blue coat is older than mine.
   b) My new house is much larger than your old place.
   c) Your mobile is so slow and boring.
   d) We went on the most expensive holiday in the amazing Caribbean last week.
   e) Our friends have a beautiful yacht that has all the latest technology on board.
2. Answers may vary. Check the student has written three sentences for their adjective.

Main activity: Adverbs and adverbials

Answers may vary. Examples might include:
Soon afterwards, old Mrs Violet Bloom set off cheerfully under blue skies.
A week later, some scary-looking bikers rode noisily behind our house.

Homework activity: The discovery

Answers may vary. An example could be:
One rainy day last March, a grumpy old woman was walking slowly down an empty street. Suddenly, she saw something sparkly on the pavement in front of her. She picked it up in a flash. The old woman looked at it with her eyes wide open. She really couldn't believe it. She was so excited. She immediately set off back towards her house.

Glossary

Adjective
A word that describes a noun. It can come before or after the noun it describes.

Comparative adjective
A comparative adjective, such as *quicker* or *slowest*, is used to compare two or more nouns.

Adverb
A describing word that tells you more about a verb, an adjective, another adverb or a clause.

Adverbial phrase
A group of words that acts as an adverb. It can tell you how, where and when something is happening.

Fronted adverbial
A fronted adverbial phrase is placed at start of a sentence and separated from the main clause by a comma.

ENGLISH — YEAR 6

21 GRAMMAR: VERBS – PRESENT

LEARNING OBJECTIVES
- To use regular and irregular verb forms to express present time, including progressive and perfect forms

CONTENT DOMAINS
- G4.1a simple present
- G4.1b verbs in the perfect form
- G4.1d present progressive

STARTER ACTIVITY
- **Now or then?; 5 minutes; page 144**
  Assess the student's ability to correctly identify verbs in the simple present and present progressive tenses. Discuss the difference in form and meaning between simple present and present progressive verbs. Draw attention to the verb form *you read* as it could be either in simple present or simple past tense.

MAIN ACTIVITIES
- **Imagine the scene; 25 minutes; page 145**
  This is a discussion-based activity. Supplement the suggested questions with additional prompts to help the student verbalise lots of ideas before writing them down. Remind the student to describe and then record elements from the scene in the present tense.
- **Progressive or perfect?; 15 minutes; page 146**
  This activity focuses on recognising the difference between the progressive and perfect forms of the present tense. Some students will find it confusing that the perfect form describes an event in the past even though the verb form is classified as present. Avoid detailed discussion of this and elicit ways the student might tell the two forms apart.

PLENARY ACTIVITY
- **Verbs three ways; 5 minutes**
  On a whiteboard, write the infinitive of a verb such as *to walk*. Ask the student to write that verb in the three different present verb forms using a pronoun of their choice: *I walk*; *I am walking*; *I have walked*. Repeat for other verbs.

HOMEWORK ACTIVITY
- **Writing in the present; 45 minutes; page 147**
  This activity puts the student's learning into practice. Remind them to check their writing against the checklist and ask other people to listen to it. In the next session, ask the student to read their writing out loud, then discuss remaining areas of weakness and any misconceptions.

DIFFERENTIATION AND EXTENSION IDEAS
- **Now or then?** Extend by discussing the names of other verb forms encountered in the activity.
- **Imagine the scene** Support by modeling how to describe a scene in the present using a context your student will be familiar with. If appropriate, record their ideas on the table to allow them to think and express their ideas, or provide a picture or two from a magazine as stimulus.
- **Progressive or perfect?** Support the student in making the distinction by highlighting the different auxiliary verbs used in the progressive (to be) and perfect (to have) tenses.

PROGRESS AND OBSERVATIONS

ENGLISH
— YEAR 6 —

STARTER ACTIVITY: NOW OR THEN?

TIMING: 5 MINS

LEARNING OBJECTIVES
- To identify present tense verbs

EQUIPMENT
- highlighter

Verbs in the present tense describe something that happens regularly or is happening right now.

Highlight all the present tense verbs in the clauses below.

- he runs
- she is walking
- it is raining
- I have time
- Sachin was bored
- Jemma should listen
- I left
- she was worried
- Yasmina had forgotten
- Florence has a problem
- apostrophes are difficult
- his name is Joel
- they ate
- Harriet yawns

ENGLISH
— YEAR 6 —

MAIN ACTIVITY: IMAGINE THE SCENE	TIMING: 25 MINS

LEARNING OBJECTIVES	EQUIPMENT
• To use a range of present tense verbs • To practise using verbs in the simple present and present progressive tenses	none

You are going to plan a description in the present tense. Imagine standing or sitting somewhere interesting. It could be a park, a hill, a busy shopping centre or the middle of a desert.

Here are some questions to help you:

- Where am I?
- What can I feel?
- What can I smell?
- What can I see?
- What can I hear?

> I am by the sea. The sea is crashing on the rocks. The air smells salty. A seagull swoops over my head. I scrunch up my eyes against the bright sunshine.

Close your eyes for a minute and imagine yourself there. Discuss your ideas with your tutor. Try to speak in the present tense.

Now write your ideas below using the simple present or present progressive tense.

Example:
a seagull <u>swoops</u> (simple); the waves <u>are crashing</u> (progressive)

ENGLISH
— YEAR 6 —

MAIN ACTIVITY: PROGRESSIVE OR PERFECT?

TIMING: 15 MINS

LEARNING OBJECTIVES
- To recognise the present progressive and present perfect tenses

EQUIPMENT
- scissors

The present tense takes three forms.

```
          Present progressive
            I am running
                 |
Simple present      Present perfect
   I run  —  PRESENT  —  I have run
```

Cut out the sentences below, turn them face down and shuffle them.
Sort them into two piles: *present progressive* and *present perfect*.

Keeley is swimming in the river.	Have you seen the news?
Armando has been up to his old tricks.	I am driving on the motorway.
Angry dogs are barking behind the fence.	Farah has never visited the Eiffel Tower.
Nick is playing the electric guitar badly.	They have eaten all the biscuits!
My daughter has forgotten my birthday.	I am cycling to the seaside.
You are not staying here!	Have you remembered the address?
She has bought me some chocolates.	This film is really upsetting me.
Are we swimming for charity?	Hasn't it been a lovely day?

ENGLISH
— YEAR 6 —

HOMEWORK ACTIVITY: WRITING IN THE PRESENT   **TIMING: 45 MINS**

LEARNING OBJECTIVES
- To practise irregular spellings in the present tense
- To write a description in the present tense

EQUIPMENT
- highlighter

1. Highlight the correct spelling of each underlined present tense verb.

a) She kiss / kisses / kisss her mum goodnight every evening.

b) Maria go / gos / goes to the dentist for a check-up.

c) Vincent catchs / catch / catches the basketball just as the whistle blows / blowes / blow.

d) Dos / Does / Do your dog bite?

e) I have / has done my homework but my sister haven't / hasn't finished yet.

f) We are / am / is going to be late, isn't / aren't we?

2. On a separate piece of paper, write the description you planned in the *Imagine the scene* activity earlier, adding new ideas if you have any. Use the checklist to help you.

Tick

☐   I have used verbs in the present tense.

☐   I have spelled irregular verbs correctly.

☐   I have described things I can sense.

☐   I have used interesting and imaginative adjectives and verbs.

☐   I have created a powerful description of what is happening.

Read your writing to someone and ask them to give you a mark out of ten.

ENGLISH — YEAR 6

21 ANSWERS

STARTER ACTIVITY: NOW OR THEN?

he runs; she is walking; Florence has a problem; apostrophes are difficult; Harriet yawns; it is raining; his name is Joel; I have time

MAIN ACTIVITY: IMAGINE THE SCENE

Answers may vary. The student should use a mix of verbs formed in the simple present and the present progressive. Check for correct irregular spellings.

MAIN ACTIVITY: PROGRESSIVE OR PERFECT?

Present progressive	Present perfect
Keeley is swimming in the river.	Have you seen the news?
I am driving on the motorway.	Armando has been up to his old tricks.
Angry dogs are barking behind the fence.	Farah has never visited the Eiffel Tower.
Nick is playing the electric guitar badly.	They have eaten all the biscuits!
I am cycling to the seaside.	My daughter has forgotten my birthday.
You are not staying here!	Have you remembered the address?
This film is really upsetting me.	She has bought me some chocolates.
Are we swimming for charity?	Hasn't it been a lovely day?

HOMEWORK ACTIVITY: WRITING IN THE PRESENT

1. a) She kiss / **kisses** / kisss her mum goodnight every evening.
   b) Maria go / gos / **goes** to the dentist for a check-up.
   c) Vincent catchs / catch / **catches** the basketball just as the whistle **blows** / blowes / blow.
   d) Dos / **Does** / Do your dog bite?
   e) I **have** / has done my homework but my sister haven't / **hasn't** finished yet.
   f) We **are** / am / is going to be late, isn't / **aren't** we?
2. Discuss the checklist with the student. Check they have ticked all the boxes.

GLOSSARY

Simple present tense
This form of the verb describes something that regularly happens in the present. For example: *He plays chess.*

Irregular verb
A verb that does not follow the regular spelling patterns of the present or past tenses. For example: *He jumps* (present), *he jumped* (past) is regular; *she runs* (present), *she ran* (past) is irregular.

Present progressive tense
This form of the present tense describes something that is still going on at the moment of speaking. It is formed using the simple present tense of the verb *to be* and by adding the suffix *ing* to the verb. For example: *He is jumping*.

Present perfect tense
This form of the verb is used to show that something happened in past but not at a specific time. It is formed using *has* or *have* and the past participle of the verb. For example: *She has jumped*.

ENGLISH — YEAR 6

22 GRAMMAR: VERBS – PAST

LEARNING OBJECTIVES
- To use regular and irregular verb forms to express past tense, including progressive and perfect forms
- To select and use tenses consistently throughout writing

CONTENT DOMAINS
- G4.1a simple past
- G4.1b verbs in the perfect form
- G4.1d past progressive
- G4.2 tense consistency

STARTER ACTIVITY
- **In the past; 10 minutes; page 150**
  It would be useful for the student to be familiar with the simple and progressive forms of the present tense covered in lesson 21. Fold the activity sheet to hide the lower table before starting. Ensure the student recognises the general syntax of the three past tense verb forms (*-ed* endings, *was/were* and *had* constructions) and understands the term *irregular verbs*.

MAIN ACTIVITIES
- **Verb time machine; 20 minutes; page 151**
  This activity focuses on writing verbs in the simple past form. Reinforce regular spelling conventions (*-ed*) and guide the student to tackle a range of irregular verbs.
- **A tense situation; 15 minutes; page 152**
  This activity focuses on maintaining tense consistency. Help the student choose appropriate verbs and discuss how to form them consistently with the rest of the sentence. The top rung sentence is the only one that includes a shift in tense, due to a shift in time frame.

PLENARY ACTIVITY
- **I go, you went; 5 minutes**
  Say a verb in one of the present tense forms, such as *I go, I am going* or *I have gone*. Ask the student to say what you did in the equivalent past tense form, such as *you went, you were going* or *you had gone*. Repeat as time allows.

HOMEWORK ACTIVITY
- **The house; 45 minutes; page 153**
  This activity puts the student's learning into practice. Ask the student to use the simple or progressive past as they see fit. Review and discuss any remaining areas of weakness or misconceptions together in the next session.

DIFFERENTIATION AND EXTENSION IDEAS
- **Verb time machine** Support by preparing a list of appropriate verbs in advance, including a range of irregular verbs. Extend by asking the student to write a sentence for each of the past tense verbs they generate.
- **A tense situation** Extend by asking the student to write alternative endings for each sentence: *Yesterday I watched TV and then I went for a bike ride.*
- **The house** Support by underlining each verb that needs to be changed to the past tense.

PROGRESS AND OBSERVATIONS

ENGLISH
— YEAR 6 —

Starter activity: In the past

Timing: 10 mins

Learning objectives
- To recognise verbs in the past tense
- To sort verbs into the three past tense forms

Equipment
- highlighter

First, highlight all of the past tense verbs in each row.

we are jogging	we had jogged	we were jogging	we jog	we jogged
she falls	she was falling	she had fallen	she fell	she is falling
it is blowing	it blew	it blows	it was blowing	it had blown
he had run	he runs	he is running	he ran	he was running
they talked	they are talking	they were talking	they had talked	they talk

Now, sort them into the three different forms of the past tense.

simple past	past progressive	past perfect
I finished	I was finishing	I had finished

ENGLISH
YEAR 6

MAIN ACTIVITY: VERB TIME MACHINE **TIMING: 20 MINS**

LEARNING OBJECTIVES
- To turn a present tense verb into the simple past tense
- To recognise irregular past tense verbs

EQUIPMENT
- a dice

Roll a dice to generate a verb using the table below and write it down on a separate piece of paper. Repeat ten times.

roll	think of a verb beginning with ...	example	in the present tense
1	a, b, c or d	appear	I appear
2	e, f, g or h	go	I go
3	i, j, k or l	kick	I kick
4	m, n, o or p	move	I move
5	q, r, s or t	run	I run
6	u, v, w, x, y or z	walk	I walk

You have a clever verb time machine which normally changes a present tense verb into the past tense for you.

input
I appear

...going back in time
...going back in time
...back in time
...back

output
I appeared

However, today the verb time machine isn't working! An important message appeared on the screen just before it broke down. What do you think it means?

...system error...beware of irregular verbs...urgh..I'm not feeling well... beware of irregular verbs...went not goed...ran not runned...oh dear...%$@#!^&

On a separate piece of paper, change each of your present tense verbs you thought of into the past tense. Remember the verb time machine's advice!

ENGLISH
— YEAR 6 —

MAIN ACTIVITY: A TENSE SITUATION TIMING: 15 MINS

LEARNING OBJECTIVES
- To use the same tenses consistently in writing

EQUIPMENT
none

Uh oh, this is tense! This poor kitten is in a sticky situation. Can you help it escape by completing the rungs of the fireman's ladder?

Your answers should use the same tense as used in the first part of each sentence.

Sentence start	(verb)	ending
Lara ate the cake that you (bake)	_____	this afternoon.
Vicky has sent me a book but I (read)	_____	it already.
We will escape tonight and we (hide)	_____	in the woods.
Marc should say sorry and she (forgive)	_____	him for his mistake.
Glen has seen the whole series but I (watch)	_____	the first episode yet.
You can join our club if you (pay)	_____	the membership fees.
Normally I love ice cream but I really (hate)	_____	this weird new flavour.
Yesterday I watched TV and then I (play)	played	a football game on my console.

ENGLISH
YEAR 6

Homework activity: The House

Timing: 45 mins

Learning objectives
- To practise choosing the correct tense
- To use tenses consistently throughout a piece of writing

Equipment
- highlighter

The writer of the story below has confused the tenses. Can you rewrite it by putting all of the verbs in the past tense?

Start by highlighting the mistakes first. The first one is highlighted for you.

A Tense Moment

"I'm not sure about this," says Daniel.

"Come on, didn't be such a chicken," his friend Alexa was replying.

The dark, abandoned house has loomed over them. Daniel is looking at it with a frown. Alexa shakes her head and will walk up the steps confidently.

"Some sweet old granny probably lives here," she tells him.

A sudden gust of wind rattles the rotting shutters. Daniel had felt a lump in his throat.

"Wait a minute," he whispers, but it is too late. Alexa opens the front door just as the sun is disappearing behind a cloud.

The two children are standing in the chilly, gloomy silence, not sure whether to enter.

If you have time, continue the story. Here are some ideas to help you:

- Do the children go in or does something come out of the house?
- What might they say to each other? Use some direct speech.
- What do they find, see or hear?
- Is the house empty inside?

ENGLISH
— YEAR 6 —

22 ANSWERS

STARTER ACTIVITY: IN THE PAST
Simple past: we jogged, she fell, it blew, he ran, they talked
Past progressive: we were jogging, she was falling, it was blowing, he was running, they were talking
Past perfect: we had jogged, she had fallen, it had blown, he had run, they had talked

MAIN ACTIVITY: VERB TIME MACHINE
Answers may vary. Check for correct spelling of irregular past tense verb forms.

MAIN ACTIVITY: A TENSE SITUATION
Lara ate the cake that you <u>baked</u> this afternoon.
Vicky has sent me a book but I <u>have read</u> it already.
We will escape tonight and we <u>will hide</u> in the woods.
Marc should say sorry and she <u>should forgive</u> him for his mistake.
Glen has seen the whole series but I <u>haven't watched</u> the first episode yet.
You can join our club if you <u>can pay</u> the membership fees.
Normally I love ice cream but I really <u>hate</u> this weird new flavour.
Yesterday I watched TV and then I <u>played</u> a football game on my console.

HOMEWORK ACTIVITY: THE HOUSE
Answers may vary as the simple past and past progressive are interchangeable in some places. Examples might include:
"I'm not sure about this," said Daniel.
"Come on, don't be such a chicken," his friend Alexa replied.
The dark, abandoned house loomed over them. Daniel looked at it with a frown. Alexa shook her head and walked up the steps confidently.
"Some sweet old granny probably lived here," she told him.
A sudden gust of wind rattled the rotting shutters. Daniel felt a lump in his throat.
"Wait a minute," he whispered, but it was too late. Alexa opened the front door just as the sun disappeared behind a cloud.
The two children stood in the chilly, gloomy silence, not sure whether to enter.

GLOSSARY

Simple past tense
This verb form describes something that has already happened and has been completed in the past. For example: *he jumped*.

Irregular verb
A verb that does not follow the regular spelling patterns of the present or past tenses. For example: *he jumps* (present), *he jumped* (past); but *she runs* (present), *she ran* (past).

Past progressive tense
This form of the past tense is used to describe something that lasted some time in past. It is formed using the simple past tense of the verb *to be* and by adding the suffix *-ing* to the verb. For example: *he was jumping*.

Past perfect tense
This form of the verb is used to show that something happened in the past but not at a specific time. It is formed using *had* and the past participle of the verb. For example: *she had jumped*.

ENGLISH — YEAR 6

23 Grammar: Verbs – future and modal

Learning objectives
- To use modal verb forms to express degrees of possibility
- To use modal verb forms to express future time

Content domains
- G4.1c modal verbs

Starter activity
- **Might, will, must; 5 minutes; page 156**
  This activity introduces the student to a range of modal verbs. Classifying the words is of secondary importance: the activity serves more as a vehicle to familiarise the student with the words themselves and their role in modifying other verbs.

Main activities
- **Modal verbs; 20 minutes; page 157**
  This activity focuses on recognising and using modal verbs in context. Draw out possible alternative or irregular spellings for some negative modal verbs, such as *can't / cannot* or *will not / won't*.
- **In the future; 20 minutes; page 158**
  This activity focuses on the formation of the future tense. For simplicity, it does not include the use of the present tense for future time, e.g. *The train arrives at five*. Ensure the student varies the form of the future tense in their writing (*to be going to* and *will + verb*).

Plenary activity
- **The volcano; 5 minutes**
  Tell the student to imagine that they have discovered someone in danger trapped inside an active volcano. Ask them what they would or could do to help. What shouldn't they or mustn't they do? What might happen next? Ensure the student uses modal verbs in their responses.

Homework activity
- **Modal verbs crosswords; 45 minutes; page 159**
  This activity puts the student's learning into practice. Review and discuss any remaining areas of weakness or misconception in the next session.

Differentiation and extension ideas
- **Might, will, must** Extend by challenging the student to say or write a sentence using one or more of the modal verbs.
- **Modal verbs** Extend by asking the student to rewrite sentences 11–15 again, but to use different modal verbs. Discuss what difference this makes to their meaning.
- **Modal verbs crossword** Extend by removing the word bank of modal verbs to increase difficulty. Support by adding guiding letters in the crossword.

Progress and observations

ENGLISH
— YEAR 6 —

STARTER ACTIVITY: MIGHT, WILL, MUST **TIMING: 5 MINS**

LEARNING OBJECTIVES
- To understand the job of modal verbs

EQUIPMENT
- coloured pens or pencils

A modal verb comes before another verb to change its meaning.

Example:
It <u>will</u> rain any minute. We <u>should</u> find somewhere to shelter.

There are different kinds of modal verbs that show:

how possible something is	how certain something is	how necessary something is
It <u>might</u> rain.	We <u>will</u> escape.	They <u>must</u> leave.

Choose a colour for each category and colour in the key above. Then decide which category each of the words below belongs to, and colour it in to match your key.

will	could	can	would
may	might	shall	should
ought to	must	won't	mustn't

ENGLISH
YEAR 6

MAIN ACTIVITY: MODAL VERBS   **TIMING: 20 MINS**

LEARNING OBJECTIVES
- To identify modal verbs within some text
- To choose the correct modal verb in a sentence

EQUIPMENT
- highlighter

1. Highlight the modal verbs in these sentences.

a) William must miss his break time.
b) My family and I would really like to go to Barcelona.
c) One day, Jess might remember her sports kit.
d) You may never really understand.
e) Dad will have to record the football because his favourite programme is on.

2. You can make modal verbs negative by using *not* or the suffix *-n't*. Rewrite these sentences, making each of the modal verbs negative.

a) I could find my way around.

....

b) He should go immediately.

....

c) You can say that again.

....

d) Mum might win another time.

....

e) You ought to sit down.

....

3. Complete these sentences with a suitable modal verb.

a) Major Harris is going to space at last. He .... be very excited.

b) Jacob is really confused. He .... make his mind up.

c) It's starting to snow. We .... leave for home before it settles.

d) If you do that again, you .... be in big trouble.

e) Sorry, no more visitors today. Your friends .... come tomorrow instead.

ENGLISH
— YEAR 6 —

MAIN ACTIVITY: IN THE FUTURE **TIMING: 20 MINS**

LEARNING OBJECTIVES
- To write about events in the future
- To write the future tense in two different ways

EQUIPMENT
- a dice

Here's a prediction about what will happen in the future.

Highlight all of the verbs in the future tense. Can you find two different ways the writer uses the future tense?

In the future, ordinary humans are going to leave the Earth. The population will become too large for the Earth to support. We will need to find a way to get off the planet easily. Some scientists think that we will build a special 'space elevator'. It will be anchored at the equator and will rise up out of the Earth's atmosphere. It will be made of a super-strong and light material, such as carbon nanotubes. It won't be cheap to build, but it will provide a better way to escape Earth's gravity. Imagine one day when someone asks you where you are going on holiday, you might reply, "We are going to stay in a hotel on Mars."

Now, roll a dice to choose a topic and discuss what you think will happen in the future for that topic. On a separate sheet of paper, write a sentence about each topic using the future tense.

roll	topic
1	travel
2	medicine
3	food
4	entertainment
5	robots
6	clothes

Example:
If you rolled a 6, you could write the sentence:
In the future, people will wear clothes that will make them invisible.

HOMEWORK ACTIVITY: MODAL VERBS CROSSWORD

TIMING: 45 MINS

LEARNING OBJECTIVES
- To choose the correct modal verb to make sense in a sentence

EQUIPMENT
none

Use the modal verbs at the bottom of the page to complete the crossword. Work in pencil in case you make a mistake.

Across
1. She .... not want any visitors.
5. You .... to do your homework now.
6. You .... never believe me anyway.
8. I .... not be happy if you forget.

Down
1. They .... leave soon or they'll miss the bus.
2. Quick, we .... still get there on time.
3. Cheer up, it .... be good news.
4. You .... finish your tea first.
6. I .... not tell a lie for you!
7. My aunt .... speak four languages.

| may | might | can | will | should | shall | would | could | must | ought |

Next, on a separate sheet of paper, write 10 sentences of your own using the modal verbs that you have discovered in the crossword.

23 ANSWERS

STARTER ACTIVITY: MIGHT, WILL, MUST

How possible something is: might; may; could
How certain something is: will; would; shall; can; won't
How necessary something is: must; should; ought to; mustn't

MAIN ACTIVITY: MODAL VERBS

1. Answers may vary.
a) William must miss his break time.
b) My family and I would really like to go to Barcelona.
c) One day, Jess might remember her PE kit.

d) You may never really understand.
e) Dad will have to record the football because his favourite programme is on.

2. a) I couldn't find my way around.
b) He shouldn't go immediately.
c) You can't / cannot say that again.

d) Mum might not win another time.
e) You ought not to sit down.

3. a) Major Harris is going to space at last. He must be very excited.
b) Jacob is really confused. He can't make his mind up.
c) It's starting to snow. We should leave for home before it settles.

d) If you do that again, you will be in big trouble.
e) Sorry, no more visitors today. Your friends can come tomorrow instead.

MAIN ACTIVITY: IN THE FUTURE

In the future, ordinary humans are going to leave the Earth. The population will become too large for the Earth to support. We will need to find a way to get off the planet easily. Some scientists think that we will build a special 'space elevator'. It will be anchored at the equator and will rise up out of the Earth's atmosphere. It will be made of a super-strong and light material, such as carbon nanotubes. It won't be cheap to build, but it will provide a better way to escape Earth's gravity. Imagine one day when someone asks you where you are going on holiday, you might reply, "We are going to stay in a hotel on Mars."

Answers may vary. Examples include:
In the future, people will wear clothes that make them invisible.
By 2100, everyone is going to have a flying car.

HOMEWORK ACTIVITY: MODAL VERBS CROSSWORD

Across:
1. She may not want any visitors.
5. You ought to do your homework now.
6. You would never believe me anyway.
8. I shall not be happy if you forget.

Down:
1. They must leave soon or they'll miss the bus.
2. Quick, we might still get there on time.
3. Cheer up, it could be good news.
4. You should finish your tea first.
6. I will not tell a lie for you!
7. My aunt can speak four languages

Student's own answers.

GLOSSARY

Modal verb
A verb that comes before another verb to show how possible, certain or necessary something is. For example *may*, *should* or *must*.

Future tense
The tense used to describe something that will happen in the future. It can be written in a number of ways: using the modal verb *will*; using the modal verb *be going to*; and using the present tense.

ENGLISH — YEAR 6

24 GRAMMAR: CONJUNCTIONS AND PREPOSITIONS

LEARNING OBJECTIVES
- To use a range of conjunctions to link words, phrases and clauses
- To use a range of prepositions to express when, where or how
- To distinguish between co-ordinating and subordinating conjunctions

CONTENT DOMAINS
- G1.4 conjunctions
- G3.3 co-ordinating conjunctions
- G3.4 subordinating conjunctions
- G1.7 prepositions

STARTER ACTIVITY
- **Sorting diagram; 10 minutes; page 162**
  Assess the student's ability to correctly identify conjunctions and prepositions. Discuss how some words can be both, depending on what follows them (clause or a noun/pronoun). Remind the student that a clause must contain a verb and that a prepositional phrase does not.

MAIN ACTIVITIES
- **Making links; 20 minutes; page 163**
  This activity focuses on using co-ordinating and subordinating conjunctions to link clauses. Ensure the student understands that a subordinate clause – which includes the conjunction – does not make sense as a sentence on its own.
- **Preposition crossword; 15 minutes; page 164**
  This activity focuses on placing prepositions in context. If the student is unfamiliar with crosswords, remind them to count the letters and use known letters to guide them. When writing their own sentences, ensure the student uses each word as a preposition rather than a conjunction (e.g. *After my lunch*, but not: *After I have eaten lunch*).

PLENARY ACTIVITY
- **Quick write; 5 minutes**
  On a whiteboard, write a conjunction or preposition of your choice (e.g. *unless*). Challenge the student to say a sentence or phrase that includes the word. Repeat as time allows.

HOMEWORK ACTIVITY
- **Find some examples; 45 minutes; page 165**
  This activity assesses the student's ability to recognise conjunctions and prepositions and their roles in context. Remind the student to scan writing for conjunctions and prepositions. Review and discuss any remaining areas of weakness or misconception in the next session.

DIFFERENTIATION AND EXTENSION IDEAS
- **Making links** Extend by removing the conjunction word bank.
- **Preposition crossword** Extend by removing the preposition word bank underneath the clues. Challenge the student to write sentences with more than two prepositions.
- **Find some examples** Support by providing the student with a list of common conjunctions and prepositions.

PROGRESS AND OBSERVATIONS

ENGLISH
— YEAR 6 —

TUTORS GUILD

Starter activity: Sorting diagram

Timing: 10 mins

Learning objectives

- To understand the difference between conjunctions and prepositions

Equipment

none

Conjunctions join words, phrases and clauses together. Prepositions come before nouns or pronouns and tell you where something is or when something is happening.

Each of the phrases or sentences below contains an underlined conjunction or preposition. Copy each underlined word into the correct place on the Venn diagram. Can some of the words be both a conjunction and a preposition?

<u>under</u> the floorboards   <u>through</u> the front door   the person <u>next to</u> you

He was angry <u>but</u> didn't want to show it.   Have a sleep <u>while</u> you wait.

<u>after</u> the storm   the secret <u>behind</u> the curtain   a burger <u>and</u> chips

Conjunctions   **Prepositions**

(Venn diagram: "because" in left circle, "along" in right circle)

<u>for</u> a week's holiday   <u>until</u> two o'clock   You tripped <u>over</u> it?   <u>on</u> Tuesday

<u>Although</u> it was sunny, she played indoors.   Don't eat just <u>before</u> you swim.

The cat jumped <u>off</u> the chair.   <u>up</u> the ladder   Do you want tea <u>or</u> coffee?

ENGLISH
— YEAR 6 —

MAIN ACTIVITY: MAKING LINKS **TIMING: 20 MINS**

LEARNING OBJECTIVES
- To use conjunctions to link clauses
- To write sentences with co-ordinating and subordinating conjunctions

EQUIPMENT
none

You use conjunctions to link clauses in sentences.
This is a co-ordinating conjunction linking main clauses of equal importance:

Danny was thirsty *but* he didn't have any water.

This is a subordinating conjunction linking a main and subordinate clause:

Anna jumped in puddles *while* it was raining.

Complete the table below. Add the correct conjunction to each sentence. Write down whether they are co-ordinating or subordinating. The first one has been done for you.

clause	conjunction	clause	co-ordinating or subordinating?
Dad fell over	*and*	hurt himself.	co-ordinating
We can leave		you want.	
I can't sleep		it is dark.	
Izzy is silly		she's a good friend.	
You are really late		we've missed the film.	
I haven't got my homework		the dog ate it.	
He stayed awake		he was tired.	
The traffic was terrible		we passed Newcastle.	
I'm on a diet		I really want a pudding.	
We're going home		you like it or not.	
We've never visited Wales		have we been to Spain.	

Word bank				
nor	although	unless	so	whether
because	whenever	yet	until	but

Now, write some sentences using these or other conjunctions you know.

Example:
Someone took my pen <u>while</u> I wasn't looking.
My stepmum has lost the book <u>that</u> she bought today.

ENGLISH
— YEAR 6 —

MAIN ACTIVITY: PREPOSITION CROSSWORD

TIMING: 15 MINS

LEARNING OBJECTIVES
- To identify and write missing prepositions

EQUIPMENT
none

Use the prepositions at the bottom of the page to complete this crossword. Work in pencil in case you make a mistake. The first one has been done for you.

Across
3. My family loves travelling .... Ireland.
4. The boat sailed .... the river.
5. The couple strolled happily .... the bridge.
7. Let's keep this secret .... you and me.
8. We're going fishing .... Sunday.

Down
1. I've got a cricket match .... school. ✓
2. There's something moving .... that bag!
3. You hurt me but I won't hold it .... you.
4. There's a troll hiding .... the bridge.
6. The clumsy man fell .... the cliff!
8. Liverpool is a city .... Manchester.

| against | between | around | inside | up | next | under | across | off | ~~after~~ | near |

Now try to write some sentences that use two of these prepositions or others you know.

Example:
Let's meet <u>inside</u> the leisure centre <u>after</u> the game.

164

ENGLISH
— YEAR 6 —

HOMEWORK ACTIVITY: FIND SOME EXAMPLES **TIMING: 45 MINS**

LEARNING OBJECTIVES
- To find and copy examples of conjunctions and prepositions in action
- To decide what job they do in the writing

EQUIPMENT
none

Skim read some fiction or non-fiction books, magazine articles or websites and copy out examples of where the writer has used a conjunction or preposition. Remember, prepositions only come before nouns or pronouns.

For each, write down the job the word is doing in the writing.

These are the jobs that conjunctions do:
- link words or phrases
- link main clauses (co-ordinating)
- link main and subordinate clauses (subordinating)

These are the jobs prepositions do:
- show where something is
- show when or how something is happening

words from text	job
The poor farmer fell <u>down</u> the well.	preposition (where)
The thief escaped <u>once</u> the police had gone.	subordinating conjunction

ENGLISH
YEAR 6

24 Answers

Starter activity: Sorting diagram
Conjunctions: and; but; or; although; while
Prepositions: under; next to; through; behind; off; on; over; up; for
Both: after; before; until

Main activity: Making links
Dad fell over *and* hurt himself. (co-ordinating)
We can leave *whenever* you want. (subordinating)
I can't sleep *unless* it is dark. (subordinating)
Izzy is silly *but* she's a good friend. (co-ordinating)
You are really late *so* we've missed the film. (co-ordinating)
I haven't got my homework *because* the dog ate it. (subordinating)
He stayed awake *although* he was tired. (subordinating)
The traffic was terrible *until* we passed Newcastle. (subordinating)
I'm on a diet *yet* I really want a pudding. (co-ordinating)
We're going home *whether* you like it or not. (subordinating)
We've never visited Wales *nor* have we been to Spain. (co-ordinating)

Main activity: Preposition crossword

Across:
3. My family loves travelling <u>around</u> Ireland.
4. The boat sailed <u>up</u> the river.
5. The couple strolled happily <u>across</u> the bridge.
7. Let's keep this secret <u>between</u> you and me.
8. We're going fishing <u>next</u> Sunday.

Down:
1. I've got a cricket match <u>after</u> school.
2. There's something moving <u>inside</u> that bag!
3. You hurt me <u>but</u> I won't hold it against you.
4. There's a troll hiding <u>under</u> the bridge.
6. The clumsy man fell <u>off</u> the cliff!
8. Liverpool is a city <u>near</u> Manchester.

Homework activity: Find some examples
Answers may vary.

Glossary

Conjunction
A word that links words, phrases and clauses together to express the where, when and how.

Co-ordinating conjunction
A word that links words, phrases or clauses of equal importance.

Subordinating conjunction
A word that introduces a subordinate clause, which does not make sense as a sentence on its own.

Preposition
A word that shows where, when or how something is happening. It comes before a noun or pronoun.

ENGLISH — YEAR 6

25 Grammar: Sentence types

LEARNING OBJECTIVES
- To recognise the four sentence types by their grammatical patterns
- To punctuate the four sentence types accurately
- To write questions and commands in a number of forms

CONTENT DOMAINS
- G2.1 statements
- G2.2 questions
- G2.3 commands
- G2.4 exclamations

STARTER ACTIVITY
- **Four types; 5 minutes; page 168**
  Cut out the 10 sentences in advance. Assess the student's ability to identify each sentence type. Exclamations are currently defined as starting with *What* or *How* and may end in a full stop or exclamation mark. Explain that exclamation marks are not just used for exclamations but can be used to emphasise statements and commands.

MAIN ACTIVITIES
- **Question generator; 20 minutes; page 169**
  This activity focuses on writing questions in three different ways. Model further example(s) to start if appropriate. Continue the activity until the student has had the opportunity to write a range of questions in all three ways. Emphasise punctuation conventions (question marks, commas and apostrophes for contraction in question tags).
- **The story of a cup of tea; 20 minutes; page 170**
  This activity involves finding relevant material to write commands. Focus on the grammatical patterns involved, including imperative verbs, conjunctions and clauses. Address the misconception that commands always require exclamation marks because they can be emphasised orders (e.g. *Stop it!*).

PLENARY ACTIVITY
- **Quick talk; 5 minutes**
  Ask the student to explain the four sentence types and provide an example of their own for each.

HOMEWORK ACTIVITY
- **Sentence types; 45 minutes; page 171**
  This activity puts the student's learning into practice. Review and discuss any remaining areas of weakness or misconception in the next session.

DIFFERENTIATION AND EXTENSION IDEAS
- **Question generator** Support by preparing a list of question words and pronouns in advance. Extend by encouraging the student to add extra information.
- **The story of a cup tea** Support by providing a list of suitable conjunctions to help the student order their instructions. Support by reducing the amount of irrelevant text in the story.

PROGRESS AND OBSERVATIONS

ENGLISH
— YEAR 6 —

STARTER ACTIVITY: FOUR TYPES

TIMING: 5 MINS

LEARNING OBJECTIVES
- To recognise the four different sentence types

EQUIPMENT
none

There are four different sentence types in English: statements, questions, commands and exclamations.

Put a letter in the box next to each sentence below about the Ancient Greeks to show what type of sentence it is. What clues are there in the words or punctuation to guide you?

S = statement   Q = question   C = command   E = exclamation

☐ The Olympic Games took place every four years.

☐ Who ran the first marathon?

☐ Comb your hair before the battle.

☐ This play is very long, isn't it?

☐ The soldiers of Sparta were the fiercest army in Ancient Greece.

☐ Pray to Poseidon, the god of the sea, to protect us from this storm!

☐ What a magnificent temple!

☐ A trireme was the biggest Ancient Greek warship.

☐ Would you like some figs and cheese for breakfast?

☐ How beautiful your jewellery is!

ENGLISH
— YEAR 6 —

MAIN ACTIVITY: QUESTION GENERATOR   **TIMING: 20 MINS**

LEARNING OBJECTIVES
- To write a range of questions
- To form questions in three different ways

EQUIPMENT
- two dice

There are three ways of writing a question.
1. <u>What</u> is the time? (question word)
2. <u>Are you</u> going to the party? (subject and verb swap places: you ↔ are)
3. She is really upset, <u>isn't she?</u> (question tag)

Roll two dice three times to choose types of words from the table below that you can use to generate a question.

Example:
Your first roll is 12 (pronoun)   →   You choose the word 'he'
Your second roll is 5 (activity)   →   You choose the word 'skiing'
Your third roll is 4 (question word) →   You choose the word 'when'

first roll	subject	second roll	detail	third roll	which way?
2	pronoun	2	place	2	subject ↔ verb
3	noun	3	feeling	3	question tag
4	pronoun	4	time	4	question word
5	noun	5	activity	5	subject ↔ verb
6	pronoun	6	place	6	question tag
7	noun	7	feeling	7	question word
8	pronoun	8	time	8	subject ↔ verb
9	noun	9	activity	9	question tag
10	pronoun	10	place	10	question word
11	noun	11	feeling	11	subject ↔ verb
12	pronoun	12	time	12	question tag

Now write a question using the words you have chosen. Don't forget to use a question mark.

Example:
When did he go skiing in Switzerland?

Here are two more examples:

9 (noun) → elephant 8 (time) → yesterday 3 (question tag) → didn't it?	3 (pronoun) → they 11 (feeling) → excited 5 (subject ↔ verb) → are they
The elephant went missing yesterday, didn't it?	Are they excited about today's trip?

ENGLISH
— YEAR 6 —

MAIN ACTIVITY: THE STORY OF A CUP OF TEA　　　　**TIMING: 20 MINS**

LEARNING OBJECTIVES
- To write instructions (command type sentences)

EQUIPMENT
- highlighter

Here is a story about making a cup of tea.

It was a cold morning. "I'm so thirsty", thought Dad. He put on his dressing gown and went to the kitchen. Dad filled the kettle with fresh water from the tap. Next he plugged the kettle in. While the kettle was boiling, Dad put a teabag in a mug. The cat brushed around his ankles. "Alright, puss, I'll feed you in a minute," he said. As soon as the kettle had boiled, Dad put some boiling water into the mug. "I must remember to put the bins out", thought Dad. He left the teabag in the water for a minute and looked out of the window. There was frost on the car. He then removed the teabag with a teaspoon. Next, he added a little milk to the tea and stirred it with the teaspoon. Finally, he left the tea for a couple of minutes to cool before drinking it. "Ahh, that's better", he thought. The cat meowed loudly.

Your task is to write the instructions (command type sentences) for making a cup of tea.

First, highlight the words that are important for the instructions. Cross out any words that are not relevant.

Next, write a list of instructions. Remember to use an imperative (bossy) verb in each sentence.

Here are some examples of command sentences with the verbs underlined:

> First, <u>heat</u> a little oil in a frying pan.
>
> Once the packet is empty, <u>put</u> it in the recycling box.
>
> Finally, <u>brush</u> your teeth carefully.

ENGLISH
— YEAR 6 —

HOMEWORK ACTIVITY: SENTENCE TYPES **TIMING: 45 MINS**

LEARNING OBJECTIVES
- To write a range of sentence types
- To change one sentence type into another

EQUIPMENT
- highlighter

Write your answers to questions 1, 2, 4 and 5 on a separate piece of paper.

1. Change these statements to questions. The first one has been done for you.

a) The queen of the Greek gods was Hera. → Was Hera the queen of the Greek gods?

b) You are cross with me.

c) It is time to leave for the airport.

2. Change these questions to statements. The first one has been done for you.

a) Are you ready for your test? → You are ready for your test.

b) Is Callum still not feeling well?

c) She is going to be really late home, isn't she?

3. From the list below, mark which are commands (C) and which are exclamations (E). The first two have been done for you. Also highlight any that you think are neither commands nor exclamations.

Wait for me! **(C)**
If you see a snake, move away quietly.
Forget you ever saw me.
How amazing that movie was!
What a mess you are making!
When the alarm goes, make your way out.

What a beautiful day! **(E)**
How amazing was that movie?
Give it back or I'll tell Mum.
Do not touch my things!
What are you making?
Eat your vegetables please.

4. Write a question and then a statement in reply.
   For example: What time are you leaving? (question); I'm going at four o'clock. (statement)

5. Write a command and then a question in reply.
   For example: Tidy your room! (command); Why are you always bossing me around? (question)

ENGLISH — YEAR 6

25 Answers

Starter activity: Four types
Statements: The Olympic Games took place every four years; The soldiers of Sparta were the fiercest army in Ancient Greece; A trireme was the biggest Ancient Greek warship.
Questions: Who ran the first marathon?; This play is very long, isn't it?; Would you like some figs and cheese for breakfast?
Commands: Comb you hair before the battle; Pray to Poseidon, the god of the sea, to protect us from this storm!
Exclamations: What a magnificent temple!; How beautiful your jewellery is!

Main activity: Question generator
Answers may vary. Check for correct use of grammatical patterns and punctuation conventions.

Main activity: The story of a cup of tea
Answers may vary. An example might include:
First, fill the kettle with fresh water from the tap. Next, plug the kettle in. While the kettle is boiling, put a teabag in a mug. As soon as the kettle has boiled, put some boiling water into the mug. Leave the teabag in the water for a minute. Next, remove the teabag with a teaspoon. Add a little milk to the tea. Stir it with the teaspoon. Leave the tea for a couple of minutes to cool before drinking it.

Homework activity: Sentence types
1. b) Are you cross with me?, c) Is it time to leave for the airport?
2. b) Callum is still not feeling well. c) She is going to be really late home.
3. Commands: If you see a snake, move away quietly.; Forget you ever saw me.; Give it back or I'll tell Mum.; Don't touch my things!; When the alarm goes, make your way out; Eat your vegetables please.
Exclamations: How amazing that movie was!; What a mess you are making!
Other: How amazing was that movie?; What are you making?
4. Answers may vary.
5. Answers may vary.

Glossary

Sentence
A group of words that must contain a subject and a verb. It expresses a complete thought. It can have one or more clauses.

Statement
A sentence type in which a fact, opinion or idea is stated. It may end in a full stop or an exclamation mark for emphasis.

Question
A sentence type in which something is asked and grammatical patterns, such as question words, inversion or question tags, are present. It always ends with a question mark.

Command
A sentence type in which an instruction or order is given and an imperative verb is present. A command may end in a full stop or an exclamation mark for emphasis.

Exclamation
A sentence with a particular syntax. An exclamation begins with *What* or *How* and usually ends with an exclamation mark, e.g. *How relaxing our holiday has been!*

ENGLISH — YEAR 6

26 Grammar: Subject and Object

Learning Objectives
- To recognise the difference between the subject and object
- To recognise the difference between the active and passive verb forms
- To change a sentence from active to passive and vice versa

Content Domains
- G1.9 subject and object
- G4.4 passive and active

Starter Activity
- **Subject, verb, object ; 10 minutes; page 174**
  Ensure the student can correctly identify the subject, verb and object in each sentence. All sentences are in the active voice. Reinforce the concept that an object may or may not be present.

Main Activities
- **Active and passive; 15 minutes; page 175**
  This activity focuses on recognising active and passive sentences. Discuss with the student how the passive voice is constructed (*to be* and *by* are key words). Emphasise how the word order remains subject, verb and object whether the sentence is active or passive: it's the voice of the verb that changes.
- **Active to passive; 20 minutes; page 176**
  This activity focuses on changing active voice sentences to the passive. Discuss with the student how the object swaps place with and becomes the subject. Ensure the student identifies and writes the correct auxiliary verb and participle for the passive (e.g. *It was broken*, not *It were broke*).

Plenary Activity
- **I am an alien; 5 minutes**
  Tell the student you are an alien and you've just heard of subjects, verbs and objects but don't understand anything about them. Challenge the student to write an example sentence and explain. Repeat for active and passive as time allows.

Homework Activity
- **Changing voice; 45 minutes; page 177**
  This activity puts the student's learning into practice. Review and discuss any remaining areas of weakness or misconception in the next session.

Differentiation and Extension Ideas
- **Subject, verb, object** Support by reducing the number of sentences.
- **Active and passive voice** Extend by removing the example answers. Challenge the student to think of active or passive sentences that follow directly on, e.g. *A gust of wind blew the door wide open.* → *The rain soaked the doormat. (active).*
- **Changing voice** Support by removing the amount of text or simplifying it. Highlight each sentence in two different colours (active and passive) to guide the student. Alternatively, copy and print out the text separated into lines with room to write the converted sentences in between.

Progress and Observations

ENGLISH
YEAR 6

STARTER ACTIVITY: SUBJECT, VERB, OBJECT

TIMING: 10 MINS

LEARNING OBJECTIVES
- To identify the subject, verb and object in a sentence

EQUIPMENT
- three highlighters

Look at this example:

The tennis player	hits	the ball.
the subject is 'doing' the verb to the object	verb	object

Identify the subject, verb and object in each of these sentences using three different highlighters. Some sentences don't have objects.

1. I like ice-cream.
2. Our dog bit the postman!
3. The tired doctor forgot her car keys.
4. My least favourite memory is my first day at school.
5. His sister won five hundred pounds.
6. My naughty cousin ran away.
7. Some people hate dogs. Uncle Jim doesn't like them for sure.
8. You might become a famous singer.
9. Nobody could put Humpty Dumpty back together again.
10. My annoying cat is meowing.

ENGLISH
YEAR 6

MAIN ACTIVITY: ACTIVE AND PASSIVE VOICE **TIMING: 15 MINS**

LEARNING OBJECTIVES
- To understand the difference between the active and passive voices
- To write sentences in the active and passive voices

EQUIPMENT
- highlighter

A verb is in the active voice when the subject is performing the action.

The school hired the new head teacher.
subject   active verb   object

A verb is in the passive voice when the verb is being done to the subject by someone or something.

The new head teacher was hired by the school.
subject   passive verb   object

1. Identify whether each of these sentences is in the active or passive voice. Write each sentence on a separate piece of paper and annotate it like the examples above to help you.

   a) Bargain hunters crowded the shops. ....Active........
   b) The tree was uprooted by the violent storm. ....
   c) My aunt won a long distance race at the age of 70. ....
   d) The movie was ruined by people talking. ....
   e) Crops in Africa are destroyed by plagues of locusts. ....
   f) The supermarket has run out of sausages. ....

2. Link the subjects, verbs and objects correctly in the sentence below. Write them correctly on a separate piece of paper and label each one *active* or *passive*.

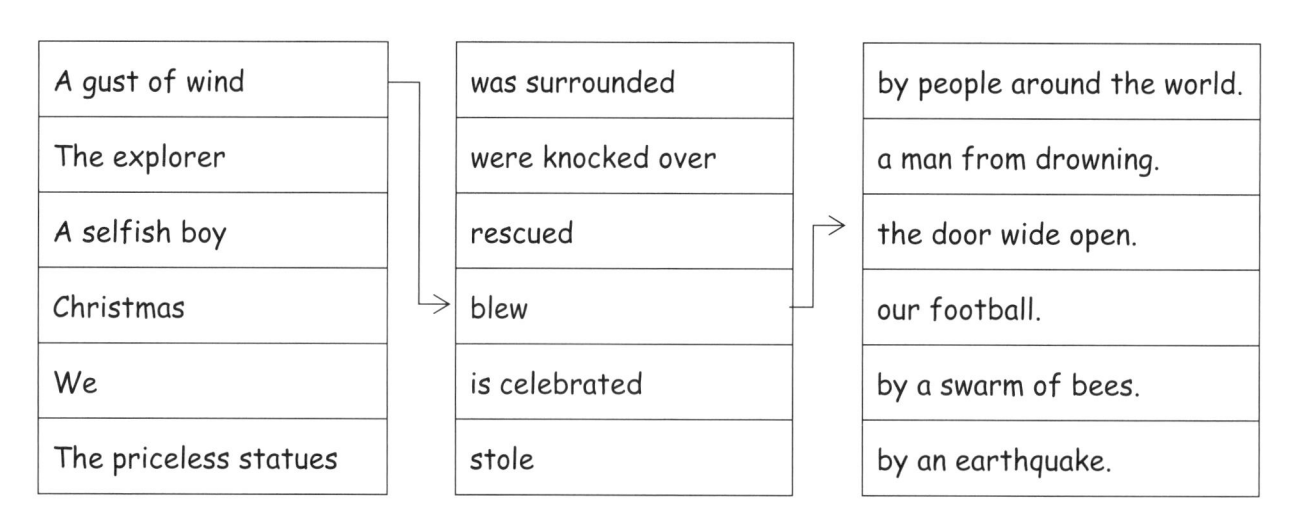

A gust of wind	was surrounded	by people around the world.
The explorer	were knocked over	a man from drowning.
A selfish boy	rescued	the door wide open.
Christmas	blew	our football.
We	is celebrated	by a swarm of bees.
The priceless statues	stole	by an earthquake.

Now write one active and one passive sentence of your own for each of the subjects in the first column.

ENGLISH
— YEAR 6 —

MAIN ACTIVITY: ACTIVE TO PASSIVE

TIMING: 20 MINS

LEARNING OBJECTIVES
- To change active voice sentences to the passive voice

EQUIPMENT
- scissors

You can change an active sentence into a passive sentence.

In the table below, write a suitable simple present or past tense verb in the middle column. Then, cut out each row and reorder the words to make a passive sentence. Add any of the words from the word bank.

Example:
The cat chased the mice. → The mice were chased by the cat.

You may need to change the verb form.

Example:
I ate the meal. → The meal was eaten by me.

the cat	chased	the mice
you		a package
the actor		a new car
Lucy		the computers
lots of people		Italian food
squirrels		nuts
her sisters		a special cake
an explorer		some lost ruins

Word bank

is	are	was	were	by

HOMEWORK ACTIVITY: CHANGING VOICE

TIMING: 45 MINS

LEARNING OBJECTIVES
- To practise changing active voice sentences to the passive voice
- To practise changing passive voice sentences to the active voice

EQUIPMENT
none

Sometimes the active voice or passive voice sound clumsy.

Example:
The child ate his lunch quickly (active)
sounds much clearer and less clumsy than
His lunch was eaten quickly by the child (passive).

Rewrite this news report on a separate piece of paper, changing the active voice to the passive and the passive voice to the active.

A Night at the Zoo

Last Friday, a gorilla was almost stolen from the zoo by a masked man. CCTV caught the whole thing on camera. The zoo was entered by the man after dark. The gorilla enclosure was approached by him. A special gorilla mask was put on by him. Then his chest was beaten loudly by him. The masked man fascinated the gorilla. The enclosure gate was opened by the man. The gorilla was offered a banana by him. The man was followed by the gorilla towards the park entrance. On the way, the gorilla was taken by the man to visit the other animals. The meerkats were scared away by the gorilla. Luckily, the zoo keepers stopped both the man and gorilla. The gorilla was taken back to his enclosure by the zoo keepers. It was given another banana by them. The police arrested the masked man. They were told by the man that he was sorry.

Here's a reminder:

A verb is in the active voice when the subject is performing the action.

<u>The school</u> hired the new head teacher.
subject   active verb   object

A verb is in the passive voice when the action of the verb is being done to the subject by someone or something.

<u>The new head teacher</u> was hired by the school.
subject   passive verb   object

26 Answers

Starter activity: Subject verb object

subject	verb	object
1. I	like	ice-cream.
2. Our dog	bit	the postman!
3. The tired doctor	forgot	her car keys.
4. My least favourite memory	is	my first day at school.
5. His sister	won	five hundred pounds.
6. My naughty cousin	ran away.	
7. Some people, Uncle Jim	hate, doesn't like	dogs, them.
8. You	might become	a famous singer.
9. Nobody	could put	Humpty Dumpty
10. My annoying cat	is meowing.	

Main activity: Active and passive voice

1. a) active
   b) passive
   c) active
   d) passive
   e) passive
   f) active

2. A gust of wind blew the door wide open. (active)
   The explorer was surrounded by a swarm of bees. (passive)
   A selfish boy stole our football. (active)
   Christmas is celebrated by people around the world. (passive)
   I rescued a man from drowning. (active)
   The priceless statues were knocked over by an earthquake. (passive)

Main activity: Active to passive

Answers may vary. Answers might include:
The cat chased the mice. → The mice were chased by the cat.
You sent the package. → The package was sent by you.
The actor drove a new car. → A new car was driven by the actor.
Lucy fixes the computers. → The computers are fixed by Lucy.
Lots of people enjoy Italian food. → Italian food is enjoyed by lots of people.
Squirrels eat nuts. → Nuts are eaten by squirrels.
Her sisters baked a special cake. → A special cake was baked by her sisters.
An explorer discovered some lost ruins. → Some lost ruins were discovered by an explorer.

Homework activity: Changing voice

Last Friday, a masked man almost stole a gorilla from the zoo. The whole thing was caught on camera by CCTV. The man entered the zoo after dark. He approached the gorilla enclosure. He put on a special gorilla mask. Then he beat his chest loudly. The gorilla was fascinated by the masked man. The man opened the enclosure gate. He offered the gorilla a banana. The gorilla followed the man towards the park entrance. On the way, the man took the gorilla to visit the other animals. The gorilla scared the meerkats away. Luckily, the man and gorilla were both stopped by the zoo keepers. The zoo keepers took the gorilla back to his enclosure. They gave it another banana. The masked man was arrested by the police. The man told them that he was sorry.

Glossary

Subject
The main focus of a clause or sentence. It is who or what the clause or sentence is about. It can be a noun, pronoun or noun phrase.

ENGLISH — YEAR 6

27 GRAMMAR: CLAUSES

LEARNING OBJECTIVES	CONTENT DOMAINS
• To identify main clauses, relative clauses and other subordinate clauses • To link clauses using co-ordinating and subordinating conjunctions • To use commas to mark clauses	• G3.1 sentences and clauses • G3.1a relative clauses • G3.4 subordinate clauses

STARTER ACTIVITY

- **The laws of the clause; 10 minutes; page 180**
  This activity contains detailed information about clauses that will be useful for reference in all of the activities. Try not to overburden the student with explanation at this point. The focus of this activity should be on the student recognising that a clause must contain a subject and verb.

MAIN ACTIVITIES

- **Main or subordinate clause; 20 minutes; page 181**
  This activity focuses on recognising and manipulating main and subordinate clauses. If necessary, refer the student back to the starter activity and their prior work on conjunctions (see page 161). Ensure the student uses a separating comma when placing a subordinate clause before a main clause.
- **Santa and his relative Clauses; 15 minutes; page 182**
  This activity focuses on inserting relative clauses into the middle of main clauses. For simplicity, the relative pronouns *that* and *whom* have been omitted in this activity.

PLENARY ACTIVITY

- **Applause for the clause; 5 minutes**
  Ask the student to name some terms and rules for using clauses (these could be based on closed questions about the information in the starter activity). Award three claps for each one and tally them up. Finally, clap the full number together as applause for their responses.

HOMEWORK ACTIVITY

- **Link and add; 45 minutes; page 183**
  This activity puts the student's learning into practice. Read the story out loud to the student, without the insertion instructions so they hear it clearly. Model an example of adding a relative clause or conjunction if necessary. Review and discuss any remaining areas of weakness or misconception in the next session.

DIFFERENTIATION AND EXTENSION IDEAS

- **Main or subordinate clause** Support by providing a list of suitable subordinating conjunctions (see answers).
- **Santa and his relative Clauses** Support by widening the topic to include the student's own family, friends or things they are more familiar with for their own examples. Extend by asking the student to write sentences using *that* and *whom*.
- **Link and add** Support by removing the requirement to add either the relative clauses or the conjunctions to focus the student on one of these tasks only.

PROGRESS AND OBSERVATIONS

ENGLISH
YEAR 6

Starter activity: The laws of the clause

Timing: 10 mins

Learning Objectives
- To recognise main and subordinate clauses in context

Equipment
- highlighter

What are clauses? Here are some rules about clauses to help you understand.

> **The laws of a clause**
> 1. A clause is a group of words.
> 2. A clause contains a subject and a verb.
> 3. You can join clauses together using conjunctions.
> 4. There are two types of clause.

> **Type 1: the main clause**
> A main clause makes sense on its own as a sentence.
> **Example:**
> *The dog barked.*
>
> You can join main clauses using a co-ordinating conjunction.
> **Example:**
> *The dog barked and my sister slept.*

> **Type 2: the subordinate clause**
> A subordinate clause is introduced by a subordinating conjunction. It does not make sense on its own as a sentence.
> **Example:**
> *while my sister was sleeping*
>
> You need a main clause to go with it.
> **Example:**
> *The dog barked while my sister was sleeping.*

1. **Highlight the main clause in this sentence.**

After she cooks dinner, Mum will help me with my homework.

2. **Highlight the subordinate clause in this sentence.**

My sister can't get to sleep if the dog is barking.

> There is also a special type of subordinate clause. It is called a relative clause. It adds detail to a noun.
>
> *The astronaut, <u>who was from Glasgow</u>, spent a year on the space station.*

ENGLISH
YEAR 6

MAIN ACTIVITY: MAIN OR SUBORDINATE CLAUSE   **TIMING: 20 MINS**

LEARNING OBJECTIVES
- To identify main and subordinate clauses
- To use conjunctions to link clauses
- To use subordinate clauses in different positions

EQUIPMENT
- two highlighters

1. Highlight the main clauses in the sentences below in one colour and the subordinate clauses in another:

a) The football match was cancelled because the referee was ill.
b) While the car is broken, I am walking everywhere.
c) You need to pack your things before we leave tomorrow.
d) Even though my friend is annoying, I still like her.

2. Add a suitable subordinating conjunction to link the clauses in the table below. The first one has been done for you.

A bird flew in the window	when	I was talking on the phone.
You are not playing games		you have tidied your room.
I managed to find the way		I don't speak much Chinese.
Please come and stay		you need a break.
We should go that way		you have a better idea.
The rain has not stopped		we left home.
There was a loud bang		the car pulled into the garage.

Now cut out each row and swap the positions of the main and subordinate clauses. Write each new sentence in your book. Don't forget the correct punctuation.

Example:
A bird flew in the window when I was talking on the phone. → When I was talking on the phone, a bird flew in the window.

ENGLISH
— YEAR 6 —

MAIN ACTIVITY: SANTA AND HIS RELATIVE CLAUSES   **TIMING: 15 MINS**

LEARNING OBJECTIVES

- To write relative clauses to add detail to nouns

EQUIPMENT

none

You are going to write some sentences about Santa, his relatives and his things.

A relative clause contains extra detail about the noun that comes before it.

Example:
Santa Claus, who lives at the North Pole, delivers presents at Christmas.
[proper noun]   [relative clause]   [main clause]
                  [relative pronoun *who*]

Now it's your turn to write about Santa's relatives. Use the relative pronouns *who* or *whose* to add a relative clause between the commas. On a separate piece of paper, write two more sentences featuring two new relatives.

person	, insert a relative clause,	main clause
Mrs Claus	, who … ,	cooks gingerbread biscuits.
The elves	, who … ,	help Santa in the toy factory.
Rudolph the Reindeer	, whose … ,	pulls the sleigh through the sky.
Santa's cat Sharp Claus	, whose … ,	sleeps by the fire.

Now write about Santa's things. Use the relative pronoun *which* to add a relative clause between the commas. On a separate piece of paper, write two more sentences featuring two new things.

thing	, insert a relative clause,	main clause
Santa's sleigh	, which … ,	flies all around the world.
The presents	, which … ,	are delivered on Christmas Eve.

ENGLISH
YEAR 6

HOMEWORK ACTIVITY: LINK AND ADD

TIMING: 45 MINS

LEARNING OBJECTIVES
- To practise linking clauses
- To practise adding relative clauses

EQUIPMENT
none

This story only uses simple sentences. Rewrite and improve the story by linking the clauses and adding relative clauses where shown.

After the storm, Shanice and Angela [insert a relative clause] went to the park. [link with a conjunction] They wanted to play on the swings. They were pleased. [link with a conjunction] They discovered no-one else was there.

Now continue the story on a separate piece of paper.

Why not try the following ideas?

- Link your clauses with co-ordinating or subordinating conjunctions.
- Add extra detail to nouns using relative clauses.
- Start a sentence with a subordinate clause.

ENGLISH
YEAR 6

27 Answers

Starter activity: The laws of the clause
1. After she cooks dinner, Mum will help me with my homework.
2. My sister can't get to sleep if the dog is barking.

Main activity: Main or subordinate clause
1. Answers may vary. Check for correct placement of commas, capital letters and full stops.
a) The football match was cancelled (main clause) because the referee was ill (subordinate clause).
b) While the car is broken (subordinate clause), I am walking everywhere (main clause).
c) You need to pack your things (main clause) before we leave tomorrow (subordinate clause).
d) Even though my friend is annoying (subordinate clause), I still like her (main clause).

2. <u>Until</u> you have tidied your room, you are not playing games.
<u>Although</u> I don't speak much Chinese, I managed to find the way.
<u>Whenever</u> you need a break, please come and stay.
<u>Unless</u> you have a better idea, we should go that way.
<u>Since</u> we left home, the rain has not stopped.
<u>As</u> the car pulled into the garage, there was a loud bang.

Main activity: Santa and his relative clauses
Answers may vary. Examples might include:
Mrs Claus, who has white hair and round glasses, cooks gingerbread biscuits.
The elves, who love wrapping up presents, help Santa in the toy factory.
Rudolph the Reindeer, whose nose is bright red, pulls the sleigh through the sky.
Santa's cat Sharp Claus, whose fur is black as coal, sleeps by the fire.
Santa's sleigh, which is red and gold, flies all around the world.
The presents, which are only for good children, are delivered on Christmas Eve.

Homework activity: Link and add
Answers may vary. An example might include:
After the storm, Shanice and Angela, <u>who were best friends</u>, went to the park <u>because</u> they wanted to play on the swings. They were pleased <u>when</u> they discovered no-one else was there. The swings, <u>which were old and rotten</u>, were empty. Shanice jumped on one <u>although</u> it was still dripping wet. She knew she would get soaked <u>but</u> she didn't care.

Glossary

Clause
A group of words that contains a subject (noun, pronoun or noun phrase) and a verb. It can be in the active or passive voice and may also contain an object. It is not the same as a sentence, as clauses can be subordinated whereas sentences cannot.

Main clause
A clause that contains subject and a verb and makes sense on its own as a sentence.

Subordinate clause
A clause that is introduced by a subordinating conjunction and contains a subject and a verb. It does not make sense as a sentence on its own. A subordinate clause can be placed before or after a main clause with appropriate punctuation.

Relative clause
A type of subordinate clause that adds detail to a noun. It always comes after the noun it is describing and begins with a relative pronoun (*who, whose, that* or *which*).

ENGLISH — YEAR 6

28 Grammar: Standard English

LEARNING OBJECTIVES

- To recognise standard and Non-Standard forms of English, including dialect and slang
- To recognise formal and informal language and structures
- To use the correct subject-verb agreement

CONTENT DOMAINS

- G7.1 Standard English
- G7.2 formal and informal vocabulary
- G7.3 formal and informal structures

STARTER ACTIVITY

- **Slang and dialect; 10 minutes; page 186**
  This activity familiarises the student with the concept of Non-Standard English. Ensure that you can locate the places on the map before starting.

MAIN ACTIVITIES

- **Standard English; 10 minutes; page 187**
  This activity focuses on changing Non-Standard English to Standard English. Check the student understand subject-verb agreement (*we was / were*), modal verbs (*could of / have*), adverbs (*good / well*), subject and object pronouns (*Theo and me / I*) and double negatives (*didn't do nothing / anything*).
- **Formal and informal language; 25 minutes; page 188**
  This longer activity focuses on recognising the vocabulary and structures of formal and informal language, and then planning a formal letter. Give prompts when discussing the questions and support as appropriate with completing the plan (see Formal letter plan on page 189).

PLENARY ACTIVITY

- **Fill in the blanks; 5 minutes**
  On a whiteboard, write a word or phrase used in formal language with one or more letters missing (e.g. *Yo_rs s_ncer_ly,*). Challenge the student to fill in the missing letter(s). Repeat with different formal words or phrases as time allows.

HOMEWORK ACTIVITY

- **Formal letter plan; 45 minutes; page 190**
  The student uses their completed plan to write a formal letter on a separate sheet of paper. Remind the student to lay the letter out as discussed and pay particular care with the syntax, punctuation and spelling of the formal language. Review together at the next session, addressing any misconceptions and correcting mistakes.

DIFFERENTIATION AND EXTENSION IDEAS

- **Formal and informal language** Extend by asking the student to translate the text speak orally or in writing into Standard English to reinforce how Standard English can still be informal.
- **Formal letter writing** Support by adding more scaffolding to the text boxes, such as filling in a fictitious name and address for the addressee. Extend by removing the existing text.

PROGRESS AND OBSERVATIONS

ENGLISH
— YEAR 6 —

TUTORS' GUILD

STARTER ACTIVITY: SLANG AND DIALECT

TIMING: 10 MINS

LEARNING OBJECTIVES
- To recognise slang and dialect from around the UK and Ireland
- To recognise that slang and dialects are not Standard English

EQUIPMENT
none

The word 'slang' means informal language. A dialect is a way of speaking in a particular area. Slang and dialects are not Standard English.

Draw lines to match each of these slang words and dialect expressions with their meaning.
Can you find the places on the map where you might hear them?

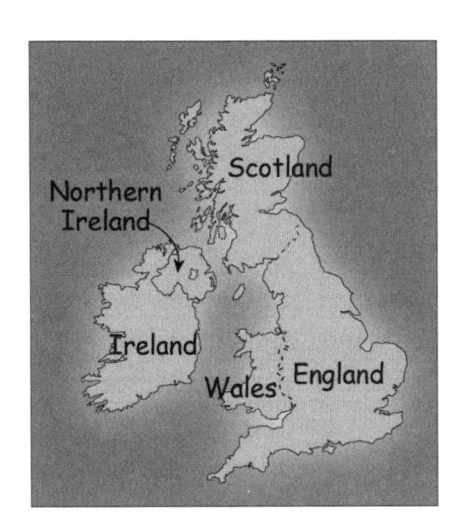

Emmet	Crisps (Ireland)
Popty ping	Stop being foolish! (Kent)
Apples and pears	Police (Liverpool)
The bizzies	Tomorrow morning (Scotland)
Mardy	Tourist (Cornwall)
The morn's morn	Stairs (London)
A bag of taytos	You big, soft baby (Birmingham)
Geet walla	Bad-tempered (Yorkshire)
Having a buzz	Microwave (Wales)
Yow big saft babbie	Very large (Newcastle)
He dint ortera dun it	Having a good time (Manchester)
Stop acting the giddy goat!	He shouldn't have done it (Norfolk)

Do you know any more slang? Are there any words that are just used in your area? How would you write these words in Standard English?

ENGLISH
— YEAR 6 —

MAIN ACTIVITY: STANDARD ENGLISH **TIMING: 10 MINS**

LEARNING OBJECTIVES
- To recognise Standard and Non-Standard English
- To change Non-Standard English to Standard English

EQUIPMENT
none

1. Draw lines to match the pairs of sentences.

Non-Standard English
Mo and Jayden was in the park.
The goalie done good.
Jack ain't coming.
You wanna come round mine?
These biscuits is well nice.
I didn't do nothing.
United should of won the league.

Standard English
Jack isn't coming.
Do you want to come to my place?
United should have won the league.
I didn't do anything.
Mo and Jayden were in the park.
These biscuits are really nice.
The goalkeeper did well.

2. Now rewrite the sentences below as Standard English. Use the examples above to help you.

a) We're gonna play at Ellie's.

....

b) I never get no answers right.

....

c) You could of told me, couldn't ya?

....

d) Ain't it well funny me and Tasha look the same?

....

e) She don't know nothing about it.

....

ENGLISH
— YEAR 6 —

MAIN ACTIVITY: FORMAL AND INFORMAL LANGUAGE   **TIMING: 25 MINS**

LEARNING OBJECTIVES
- To recognise formal and informal language
- To plan a formal letter

EQUIPMENT
- highlighter

Read the letter and text message below. They are about the same thing but use very different language.

Dear Sir,

I am writing to complain about the noise pollution at the local pool today. In my opinion, it is not acceptable that young children are ruining the peaceful atmosphere with loud music from their mobile telephones. They even bring speakers with them.
I would be grateful if your staff would please remind the children to turn off their music and respect the enjoyment of other pool users.

Yours faithfully,
I Hedaicke
Mr Ivor Hedaicke

Hi m8 ☺, i M weL Grr bout wot hapnd @ d pool 2day. IMO yung kidz shdnt b allowd 2 plA rubbish music on der fones. dey evN brng speakers w dem. it's rly anoyN 4 othR people k ☹? tel yor staff 2 git d kidz 2 shut ^ & shO sum rSpect. c U l8er

Which one is formal language? Which one is informal?

It is important that you use language suited to a situation. Which one do you think is most suitable for the man's complaint? Use a highlighter to identify any formal language.

You are going to write a letter about a problem in your local park or street. To create your letter plan, discuss the following questions with your tutor and write what you discuss on the homework sheet.

- What do you need to put at the top right of your letter?
- What do you need to put top left?
- Who are you writing to? How do you address them?
- Why are you writing?
- What is the problem? Who is to blame? How does it affect you or others?
- What do you want to be done about it? How do you end your letter?

ENGLISH
— YEAR 6 —

HOMEWORK ACTIVITY: FORMAL LETTER PLAN

TIMING: 45 MINS

LEARNING OBJECTIVES
- To write a formal letter from a plan
- To use formal language

EQUIPMENT
none

Your address

Date

Name, title and address of person you are writing to

Dear

I am writing to

I would be grateful if

Yours

Signature

Title and name

28 Answers

Starter activity: Slang and dialect

1. Emmet; Tourist (Cornwall)
2. Popty ping; Microwave (Wales)
3. Apples and pears; Stairs (London)
4. The bizzies; Police (Liverpool)
5. Mardy; Bad-tempered (Yorkshire)
6. The morn's morn; Tomorrow morning (Scotland)
7. A bag of taytos; Crisps (Ireland)
8. Geet walla; Very large (Newcastle)
9. Having a buzz; Having a good time (Manchester)
10. Yow big, saft babbie; You big, soft baby (Birmingham)
11. He dint ortera dun it; He shouldn't have done it (Norfolk)

Main activity: Standard English

1. Mo and Jayden was in the park. → Mo and Jayden were in the park.
   The goalie done good. → The goalkeeper did well.
   Jack ain't coming. → Jack isn't coming.
   You wanna come round mine? → Do you want to come to my place?

   These biscuits is well nice. → These biscuits are really nice.
   I didn't do nothing. → I didn't do anything.
   United should of won the league. → United should have won the league.

2. a) We're going to play at Ellie's.
   b) I never get any answers right.
   c) You could have told me, couldn't you?
   d) Isn't it really funny that Tasha and I look the same?
   e) She doesn't know anything about it.

Main activity: Formal and informal language

Answers may vary: Dear Sir, I am writing to; In my opinion, it is not acceptable; I would be grateful; respect the enjoyment of other pool users. Yours faithfully, I Hedaicke Mr Ivor Hedaicke

Homework activity: Formal letter plan

Answers may vary. Check for correct layout conventions and use of formal language.

Glossary

Standard English
Grammatically correct language that uses standard nouns, verb forms, pronouns and adverbs, and avoids dialect and slang. It may be formal or informal and may contain contractions.

Dialect
A way of speaking in a particular area.

Slang
Casual language that is Non-Standard English.

Formal language and structures
Formal language and structures are more common in writing. They are often used in more serious contexts and with people whom you don't know well. Formal vocabulary often involves longer words with Greek and Latin roots.

Informal language and structures
Informal language and structures are more common in speech. They are often used in relaxed contexts and with people whom you know well. Informal vocabulary often involves shorter words with Anglo-Saxon roots.

Subject-verb agreement
The Standard English convention of making the verb form used agree correctly with the subject that precedes it.

ENGLISH — YEAR 6

29 PUNCTUATION: BASIC SENTENCE PUNCTUATION

LEARNING OBJECTIVES
- To use capital letters to mark the start of a sentence
- To use a full stop, question mark or exclamation mark to mark the end of a sentence

CONTENT DOMAINS
- G5.1 capital letters
- G5.2 full stops
- G5.3 question marks
- G5.4 exclamation marks
- G5.7 inverted commas

STARTER ACTIVITIES
- **Start and finish; 5 minutes; page 186**
  Assess the student's ability to demarcate the start and end of sentences correctly. The activity increases in difficulty with the use of direct speech. Discuss where a choice of punctuation is possible.

MAIN ACTIVITIES
- **What is a sentence?; 20 minutes; page 187**
  This activity focuses on differentiating between clauses and phrases. No subordinate clauses are included, as students may confuse subordinate clauses with sentences because a verb is present.
- **Write and respond; 20 minutes; page 188**
  Encourage the student to use their imagination whilst focussing on using the correct punctuation. For the KS2 tests, students are expected to use exclamation marks in a sentence that begins with *What* or *How*. However, students should be taught that exclamation marks can also be used with sentence fragments to express strong emotions.

PLENARY ACTIVITIES
- **Write the rules; 5 minutes**
  Ask the student to write down the basic rules for punctuating the start and end of a sentence. For example: *Every sentence must start with ... and end with ...*

HOMEWORK ACTIVITIES
- **One long sentence; 45 minutes; page 189**
  This activity puts the student's learning into practice. When setting the homework, ask the student to read the article out loud to make sure they understand what is required. Review and discuss any remaining areas of weakness or misconception in the next session.

DIFFERENTIATION AND EXTENSION IDEAS
- **Start and finish** Support by removing the direct speech to decrease the difficulty.
- **What is a sentence?** Extend by adding a subordinating conjunction to the start of one of the sentences. Discuss how this affects its status as a sentence, demonstrating how not all clauses are sentences.
- **Write and respond** Support by trying the activity out orally before writing down the sentences. Alternatively, roll the dice to determine the student's choices.

PROGRESS AND OBSERVATIONS

ENGLISH
— YEAR 6 —

STARTER ACTIVITY: START AND FINISH **TIMING: 5 MINS**

LEARNING OBJECTIVES

- To show how a sentence starts and finishes

EQUIPMENT

none

The punctuation is missing at the start and finish of each of the sentences below.

Add the correct punctuation and capital letters.

1. next year I want to win the lottery and go to Spain

2. isn't that your brother over there

3. what a beautiful day

4. if I were you, I'd take an umbrella with you

5. "we never knew the King was a karate expert," they said

6. "why don't we play basketball later" I asked

7. "stop" shouted the guard

8. the excited scientist looked at his creation and said, "how amazing"

9. "oh, Brian," I replied with a shake of my head, "you are always late "

ENGLISH
— YEAR 6 —

MAIN ACTIVITY: WHAT IS A SENTENCE? **TIMING: 20 MINS**

LEARNING OBJECTIVES
- To identify a sentence

EQUIPMENT
- two highlighters

Before you can punctuate a sentence properly, you need to be able to recognise one. A sentence can be very short, very long or anywhere in between, but it must contain a subject and a verb and make sense on its own.

The smoke rises. → This is a sentence. It contains a subject (*the smoke*) and a verb (*rises*).

The rising smoke → This is a phrase, not a sentence. It contains a subject (*the smoke*) and an adjective (*rising*), but no verb.

Highlight the sentences and phrases in the table below in different colours. All the punctuation has been removed.

you are brilliant	an incredible invention	the cat hunts a mouse
Danny's new time machine	my auntie smells of lavender	my worst nightmare
the treasure was lost forever	camping in France	I might be famous one day
the long jump is my favourite	the tall, thin, menacing stranger	are you joking
get out of my house now	Jill's nasty accident last week	far, far away from home
superman flies fast	the astronaut was singing	just wait a minute
pigeons are a nuisance	the ringing of the church bells	would we ever escape

On a separate piece of paper, rewrite the sentences using the correct punctuation at the start and end of each one.

Finally, try to join up some of the phrases to make sentences. You will need to add verbs.

Example:
my worst nightmare + camping in France → My worst nightmare is camping in France.

ENGLISH
YEAR 6

MAIN ACTIVITY: WRITE AND RESPOND **TIMING: 20 MINS**

LEARNING OBJECTIVES

- To end a sentence with a full stop, question mark or exclamation mark

EQUIPMENT

- a dice

This is an activity to play with your tutor. You are going to make up some sentences that must end in a full stop, question mark or exclamation mark. Roll a dice and use the table below to guide you.

Roll 1 or 4 for . (full stop), then roll to pick a subject.
Roll 2 or 5 for ? (question mark), then roll to pick a question word.
Roll 3 or 6 for ! (exclamation mark), then roll to pick a mood.

first roll	1 or 4 – choose a . (full stop)	2 or 5 – choose a ? (question mark)	3 or 6 – choose a ! (exclamation mark)
	+	+	+
second roll	subject	question word	mood
1	a place	who	angry
2	a person	what	upset
3	an animal	when	surprised
4	an activity	where	excited
5	an emergency	which	bossy
6	a problem	how	amazed

Here's how it works:

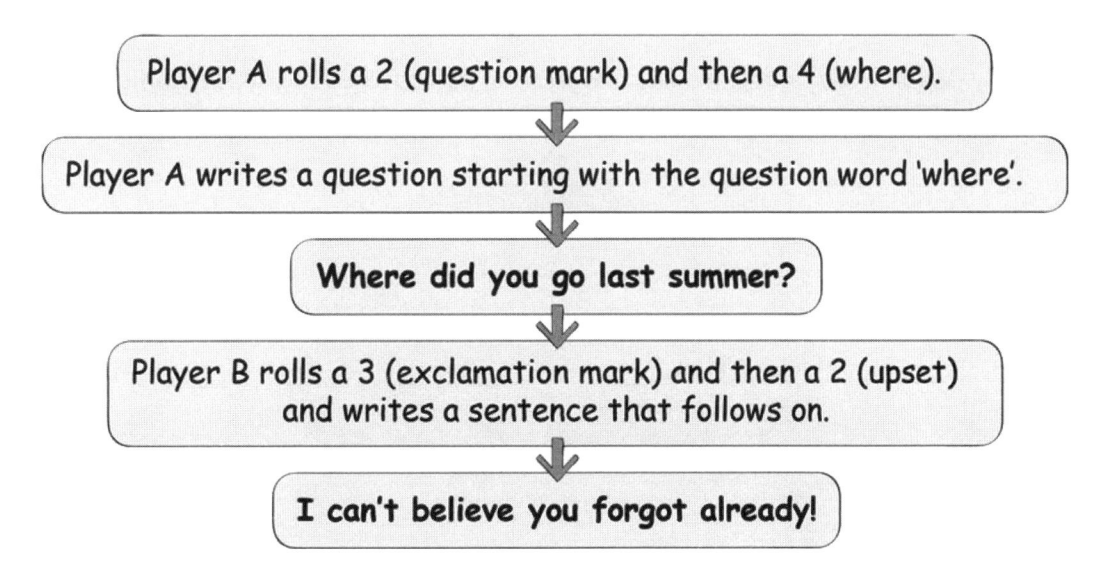

- Player A rolls a 2 (question mark) and then a 4 (where).
- Player A writes a question starting with the question word 'where'.
- Where did you go last summer?
- Player B rolls a 3 (exclamation mark) and then a 2 (upset) and writes a sentence that follows on.
- I can't believe you forgot already!

Homework activity: One long sentence

Timing: 45 mins

Learning objectives
- To punctuate each sentence accurately

Equipment
none

This writer has written an article about food in Holland, but has forgotten to include the punctuation to show where and how each sentence starts and ends.

Put in the capital letters, full stops, question marks and exclamation marks. All other punctuation is correct.

did you know peanut butter is actually a Dutch speciality our word for peanut butter is pindaklass, which means peanut cheese it's very popular, especially for breakfast we even put peanut butter sauce on our chips does that sound weird we also put tomato sauce, mayonnaise, onions and curry on them is this making you feel hungry how about some poffertjes poffertjes are small, fluffy pancakes they are cooked in a special pan and topped with butter and powdered sugar they taste amazing do you like donuts then you would probably like olienbollen, which are deep-fried dough balls people serve them on New Year's Eve and you can buy them at winter markets sometimes they have raisins inside another winter dish is called stamppot it's mashed potatoes with vegetables like carrots and cabbage usually served with a smoked sausage what else do we eat well, we eat strawberries on toast and put chocolate sprinkles on buttered bread we also love deep-fried cheese and syrup waffles pea soup is popular salty and sweet liquorice are really popular too finally, we eat raw herring fish covered in chopped onions what a smell

stamppot

poffertjes

29 Answers

Starter activity: Start and finish

1. Next year I want to win the lottery and go to Spain.
2. Isn't that your brother over there?
3. What a beautiful day!
4. If I were you, I'd take an umbrella with you.
5. "We never knew the King was a karate expert," they said.
6. "Why don't we play basketball later?" I asked.
7. "Stop!" shouted the guard.
8. The excited scientist looked at his creation and said, "How amazing!"
9. "Oh, Brian," I replied with a shake of my head, "You are always late."

Main activity: What is a sentence?

Sentences: You are brilliant.; The cat hunts a mouse.; My auntie smells of lavender.; The treasure was lost forever.; I might be famous one day.; The long jump is my favourite.; Are you joking?; Get out of my house now!; Superman flies fast.; The astronaut was singing.; Just wait a minute!; Pigeons are a nuisance.; Would we ever escape?

Phrases: an incredible invention; Danny's new time machine; my worst nightmare; camping in France; the tall, thin, menacing stranger; Jill's nasty accident last week; far, far away from home; the ringing of the church bells

Main activity: Write and respond

Answers may vary.

Homework activity: One long sentence

Did you know peanut butter is actually a Dutch speciality? Our word for peanut butter is pindaklass, which means peanut cheese. It's very popular, especially for breakfast. We even put peanut butter sauce on our chips! Does that sound weird? We also put tomato sauce, mayonnaise, onions and curry on them. Is this making you feel hungry? How about some poffertjes? Poffertjes are small, fluffy pancakes. They are cooked in a special pan and topped with butter and powdered sugar. They taste amazing! Do you like donuts? Then you would probably like olienbollen, which are deep-fried dough balls. People serve them on New Year's Eve and you can buy them at winter markets. Sometimes they have raisins inside. Another winter dish is called stamppot. It's mashed potatoes with vegetables like carrots and cabbage usually served with a smoked sausage. What else do we eat? Well, we eat strawberries on toast and put chocolate sprinkles on buttered bread. We also love deep-fried cheese and syrup waffles. Pea soup is popular. Salty and sweet liquorice are really popular too. Finally, we eat raw herring fish covered in chopped onions. What a smell!

Glossary

Phrase
A group of words that means something on its own without a verb.

Sentence
A set of words that contains a subject (the focus of the sentence) and a predicate (what is said about the subject). The predicate always contains a verb and often an object.

Clause
A part of a sentence that contains a verb. A main clause can be used as a complete sentence on its own.

Subordinate clause
A clause that only makes sense along with a main clause. It does not make sense as a sentence on its own. It is introduced by a subordinating conjunction.

ENGLISH
YEAR 6

30 PUNCTUATION: COMMAS

LEARNING OBJECTIVES
- To use commas to separate items in lists
- To use commas for clear meaning
- To avoid splicing main clauses together with commas

CONTENT DOMAINS
- G5.5 commas in lists
- G5.6a commas to clarify meaning or avoid ambiguity in writing

STARTER ACTIVITIES
- **What are commas for?; 5 minutes; page 198**
  Assess the student's knowledge of the functions of commas. Encourage the student to explain as clearly as possible using grammatical terms, such as *subordinate clauses* and *fronted adverbials*.

MAIN ACTIVITIES
- **Separate the shopping; 20 minutes; page 199**
  Encourage the use of adjectives, plurals and quantities in the memory game (for example: *some juicy tomatoes, two kilos of rice*). Ask the student to read each list out loud for meaning before inserting or changing the commas. The use of the serial comma is not covered in this activity.
- **Master and servant; 20 minutes; page 200**
  Ask the student to try placing a subordinate clause at the front of a sentence and using a comma to separate the clauses. Then ask them to join two main clauses. Correct any misconception that a comma can be used to do this (comma splicing) and establish that a co-ordinating conjunction is always required. Discuss how two subordinate clauses cannot be joined and still make sense.

PLENARY ACTIVITIES
- **Subordinate conjunctions; 5 minutes**
  Ask the student to draw a spider diagram of subordinate conjunctions.

HOMEWORK ACTIVITIES
- **Missing commas; 45 minutes; page 201**
  This activity puts the student's learning into practice. Encourage the student to read the whole story for sense first. Review and discuss any remaining areas of weakness or misconception in the next session.

DIFFERENTIATION AND EXTENSION IDEAS
- **Separate the shopping** Extend or support by editing the sentences and commas to increase or decrease difficulty.
- **Master and servant** Support by reordering the clauses so that they are pre-matched or asking the student to write their own. Extend by removing the subordinating conjunctions and asking student to add their own before writing any sentences.
- **Homework** Extend by removing all commas for the story text to assess the student's ability to use commas in other circumstances, such as direct speech.

PROGRESS AND OBSERVATIONS

ENGLISH
— YEAR 6 —

TUTORS' GUILD

STARTER ACTIVITY: WHAT ARE COMMAS FOR? **TIMING: 5 MINS**

LEARNING OBJECTIVES
- To discuss what commas are for

EQUIPMENT
none

Commas are really useful.

Discuss with your tutor what you know about commas and the different jobs they do. Write your thoughts in the bubbles below.

Here are some questions to get you started.

- When should you use a comma?
- Can you use a comma in anything other than a sentence?

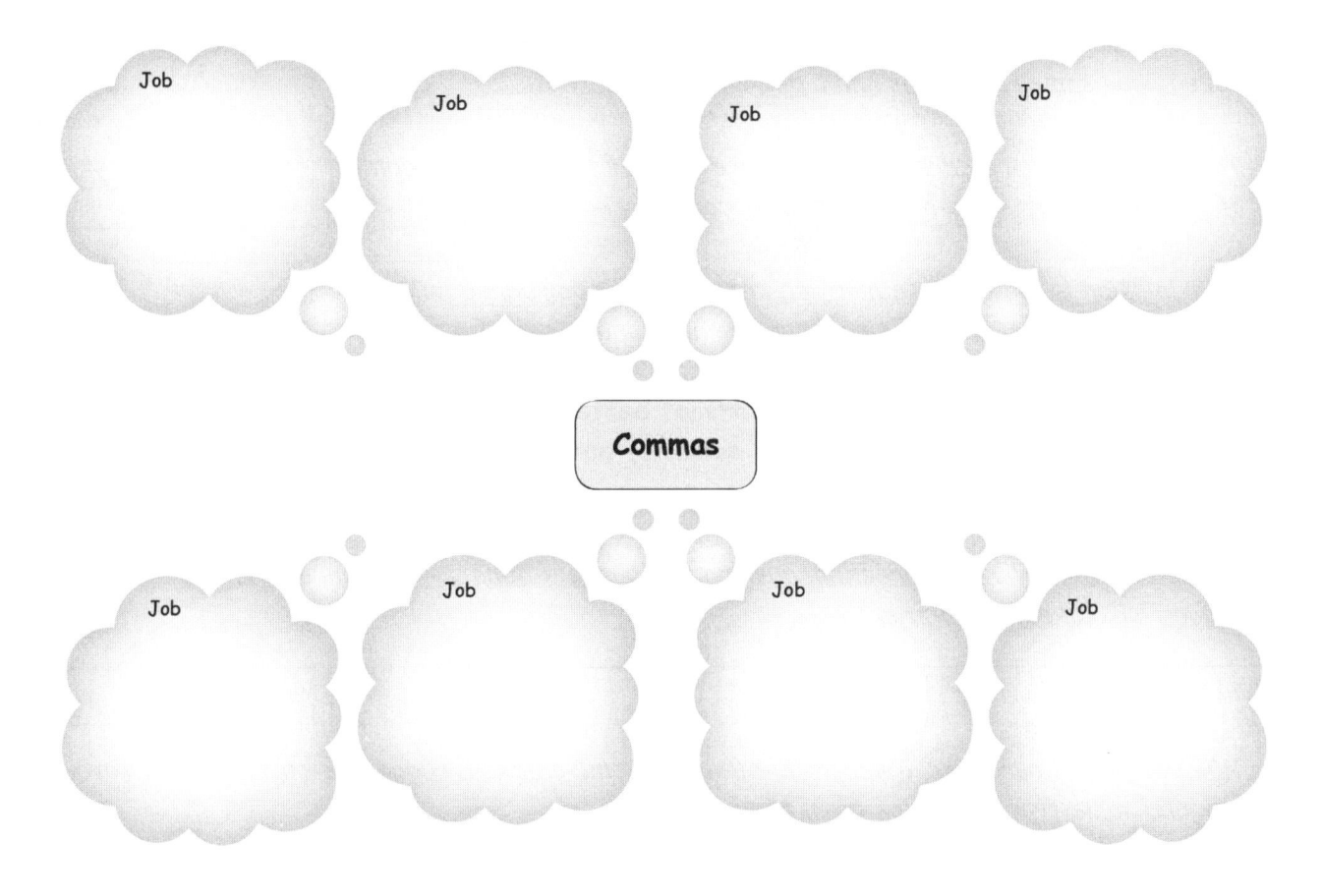

Job Job Job Job

Commas

Job Job Job Job

ENGLISH
— YEAR 6 —

MAIN ACTIVITY: SEPARATE THE SHOPPING

TIMING: 20 MINS

LEARNING OBJECTIVES
- To separate items in a list using commas
- To spot where commas have been used by mistake

EQUIPMENT
none

First, play the *Yesterday I went to the shop and I bought ...* memory game with your tutor for 5 minutes. Who can remember the list the best?

Now answer the questions below.

1. Once a week your dad sends you to the shop with a note about what to buy. Unfortunately, he always forgets to put any commas in his notes. Insert the commas in the correct places to make each shopping list clearer in meaning.

   a) *Please pick up some potatoes a bunch of grapes three bananas a dozen eggs some red onions and a pint of milk.*

   b) *Today we need some cereal a pasta sauce a tin of tomatoes a couple of yellow peppers some honey but no bacon and eggs.*

   c) *Your mission is to buy some mint ice cream coffee powdered milk chocolate biscuits a tub of single cream cakes and slices of mango.*

2. Your sister thinks she can place the commas better than you. She can't! She's covered these lists in commas, but they are all wrong! Rewrite each list correctly.

   a) *Please buy the following: green, beans frozen, burgers buns sliced, ham a bottle, of tomato, sauce fish, cakes, and pizzas.*

   ----

   b) *Will you please purchase, a kilogram, of sugar, some chicken, nuggets a, cucumber my favourite, jam and some fish and, chips from the takeaway?*

ENGLISH
— YEAR 6 —

MAIN ACTIVITY: MASTER AND SERVANT   **TIMING: 20 MINS**

LEARNING OBJECTIVES
- To separate subordinate clauses and main clauses using a comma
- To avoid joining two main clauses with a comma

EQUIPMENT
none

Look at the clauses below. Some are masters (main clauses) and some are servants (subordinate clauses). Choose two clauses and join them together to make a sentence.

Example:

The man walked slowly although his dog was trying to pull him along faster.
[*master* or main clause]   [*servant* or subordinate clause, this clause doesn't make sense on its own]

Write out each of your sentences on a separate piece of paper. For some, try putting the subordinate clause first and adding a comma. Make sure you start and end each sentence with the correct punctuation.

Masters (main clauses)
William ate his tea
the cat meows loudly
I enjoyed dancing
she goes for a run every day
I don't like it
we hid under a tree
Sophie eats apples
the old man clapped
the gorilla beats its chest
I went skiing

Servants (subordinate clauses)
although it was snowing heavily
whenever it's feeling happy
before he went to bed
because it's good for her health
when the play ended
every time I stroke it
except on Thursdays
until I hurt my knee
when the dog barks
while it was raining

We know masters and servants go together. What about other combinations? How would you join two masters (main clauses) together? What about two servants (subordinate clauses)? Is that possible? Discuss and practise this with your tutor.

Listen here, Subordinatus Clausus, you are meaningless without me.

Remember: a clause always contains a verb.

ENGLISH
YEAR 6

HOMEWORK ACTIVITY: MISSING COMMAS	TIMING: 45 MINS

LEARNING OBJECTIVES
- To find and correct the comma mistakes
- To use your knowledge of commas in lists
- To use your knowledge of commas and clauses

EQUIPMENT
- highlighter

Can you tell what's wrong with the story below? It is missing a lot of commas.

Copy out the story, putting in commas where you think they are needed. Highlight the mistakes in the text before you start writing. If you have time, continue the story.

Forgetful Jarrod

Even though it was cold Jarrod left for school without his coat. By the time he got there he was shivering. When he sat down in the classroom he realised he had forgotten his pencil case his reading book his packed lunch and the reply slip about the end-of-year party. Oh no, he thought. Unless I return it today I won't be able to go. Urgently, Jarrod put up his hand. "Mr Gibbs, can I go home again please?" he asked. "I've forgotten something important." "Not again, Jarrod," sighed his teacher. "Yesterday you forgot your glasses your trainers your history homework and that atlas you borrowed. Every time you come through that door you've forgotten something. When it's raining you forget your coat. Whenever it's hot you come without a cap your water and any sun-cream! What is it you've forgotten this time?"

ENGLISH
YEAR 6

30 ANSWERS

STARTER ACTIVITY: WHAT ARE COMMAS FOR?

The functions of commas are: to separate items in lists of nouns, verbs or adjectives; to separate main and subordinate clauses; to separate relative clauses; to separate extra information; to separate fronted adverbs or adverbials; to mark the end of parenthesis; in direct speech; in salutations in letters; to separate groups of three-digit numbers.

MAIN ACTIVITY: SEPARATE THE SHOPPING

1. a) Please pick up some potatoes, a bunch of grapes, three bananas, a dozen eggs, some red onions and a pint of milk.
   b) Today we need some cereal, a pasta sauce, a tin of tomatoes, a couple of yellow peppers, some honey but no bacon and eggs.
   c) Your mission is to buy some mint ice cream, coffee, powdered milk, chocolate biscuits, a tub of single cream, cakes and slices of mango.
2. a) Please buy the following: green beans, frozen burgers, buns, sliced ham, a bottle of tomato sauce, fish cakes and pizzas.
   b) Will you please purchase a kilogram of sugar, some chicken nuggets, a cucumber, my favourite jam and some fish and chips from the takeaway?

MAIN ACTIVITY: MASTER AND SERVANT

Answers may vary but examples might include:
The old man clapped when the play ended. (master + servant; no comma required)
Until I hurt my knee, I enjoyed dancing. (servant + master; comma required)
The gorilla beats its chest whenever it's feeling happy. (master + master; coordinating conjunction required)
Although it was raining when the dog barks. (servant + servant; still does not make sense without a main clause)

HOMEWORK ACTIVITY: MISSING COMMAS

Even though it was cold, Jarrod left for school without his coat. By the time he got there, he was shivering. When he sat down in the classroom, he realised he had forgotten his pencil case, his reading book, his packed lunch and the reply slip about the end-of-year party. Oh no, he thought. Unless I return it today, I won't be able to go. Urgently, Jarrod put up his hand. "Mr Gibbs, can I go home again please?" he asked. "I've forgotten something important."
"Not again, Jarrod," sighed his teacher. "Yesterday you forgot your glasses, your trainers, your history homework and that atlas you borrowed. Every time you come through that door, you've forgotten something. When it's raining, you forget your coat. Whenever it's hot, you come without a cap, your water and any sun-cream! What is it you've forgotten this time?"

GLOSSARY

Comma
A punctuation mark mostly used to separate different parts of a sentence to make the meaning clear.

Main clause
A clause that makes sense on its own as a sentence. It must contain a subject and a verb.

Subordinate clause
A clause that does not make sense on its own as a sentence. It is introduced by a subordinating conjunction and can come before or after a main clause. It must contain a subject and a verb.

Conjunctions
Words that link words, phrases or clauses together. Co-ordinating conjunctions link things of equal importance. Subordinating conjunctions introduce subordinate clauses.

ENGLISH
YEAR 6

31 Punctuation: Parenthesis

Learning Objectives
- To identify and use pairs of brackets, dashes or commas to indicate parenthesis

Content Domains
- G5.9 punctuation for parenthesis

Starter Activity
- **Place the pairs; 5 minutes; page 204**
  Assess the student's knowledge of how to use punctuation to indicate a parenthesis.

Main Activities
- **My fantasy family tree; 20 minutes; page 205**
  Encourage the student to experiment with the formation of the relative clause, as shown in the example. Emphasise that relative pronouns can sometimes be dropped in a parenthesis.
- **Extra information; 20 minutes; page 206**
  Encourage the student to use contextual clues to match each sentence with its parenthesis. Check the student understands that a pair of brackets can be used at the end of a sentence, but a pair of dashes or commas must come in the middle. Discuss how a parenthesis can be a word, phrase, clause or even a sentence.

Plenary Activity
- **Now you teach me; 5 minutes**
  Ask the student to describe how they would add some extra information to a sentence. Encourage the student to explain as clearly as possible using grammatical terms, such as *parenthesis, a pair of dashes,* etc.

Homework Activity
- **Adding parenthesis; 20 minutes; page 207**
  This activity puts the student's learning into practice. Review and discuss any remaining areas of weakness or misconception in the next session.

Differentiation and Extension Ideas
- **Place the pairs** Support by discussing grammatical terms, such as relative clauses and relative pronouns, with the student.
- **Extra information** Support by matching the sentences to their parentheses for the student. Instruct them whether to use brackets or dashes, and where in each sentence to place each parenthesis.
- **Adding parenthesis** Support by including the start of a parenthesis in the questions, e.g. *My friend Poppy, who ... , thinks that time travel is possible.*

Progress and Observations

ENGLISH
— YEAR 6 —

STARTER ACTIVITY: PLACE THE PAIRS   **TIMING: 5 MINS**

LEARNING OBJECTIVES
- To put a pair of commas, brackets or dashes around extra information

EQUIPMENT
none

You can add extra information (a parenthesis) to a sentence using a pair of commas, brackets or dashes. If you took the parenthesis away, the sentence would still make sense.

1. Where would the pair of commas go in these sentences?

a) His friend who works in the clothes shop loves to dress smartly.

b) The banana which was covered in black spots tasted horrible.

c) Emily aged 14 from Leeds won a magic competition.

2. Where would the pair of brackets go in these sentences?

a) My school trip to the sewage farm was great it was a bit smelly though.

b) The wedding singer a tiny man with thick glasses kept dropping his microphone.

3. Where would the pair of dashes go in these sentences?

a) Creeping out from behind the door I had been hiding there for ages I shouted, "Boo!"

b) I believe you lots of other people wouldn't when you say you are telling the truth.

ENGLISH
— YEAR 6 —

MAIN ACTIVITY: MY FANTASY FAMILY TREE **TIMING: 20 MINS**

LEARNING OBJECTIVES
- To add extra information to a sentence
- To use commas to separate a relative clause

EQUIPMENT
- a dice

You are going to create a fantasy family tree. Imagine it is the year 1523. First, choose to be either a brave Knight or a powerful Queen. Now roll the dice and use the family generator below to create the rest of your family tree, writing a description in each box. One of your grandfathers has been done for you.

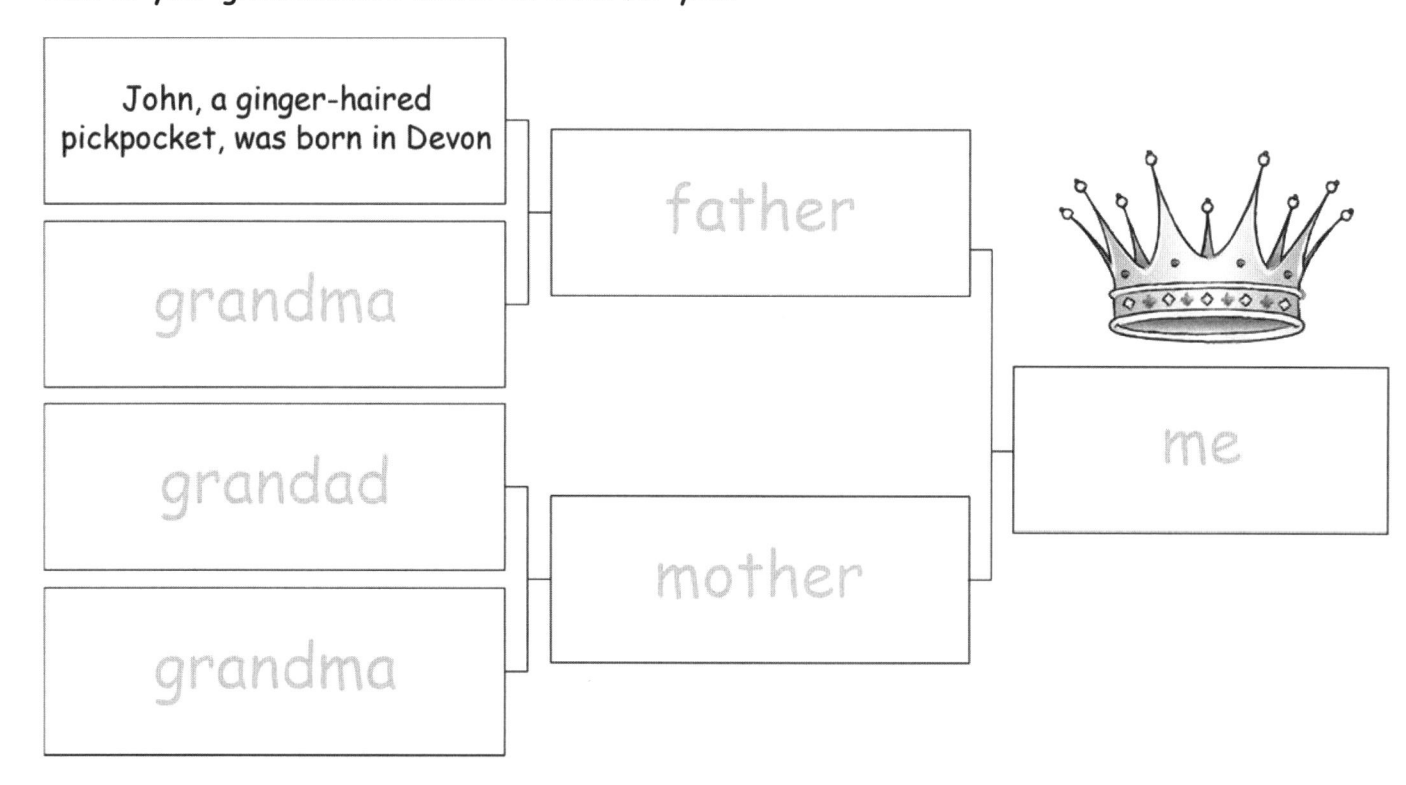

[Family tree diagram: John, a ginger-haired pickpocket, was born in Devon → father; grandma → father; grandad → mother; grandma → mother; father and mother → me (with crown)]

To generate each family member, roll the dice 5 times and write a description that includes a parenthesis (here a relative clause) between a pair of commas.

The example above was generated by rolling 3, 2, 1, 4, and 6 and writing:

John, a ginger-haired pickpocket, was born in Devon.

This could also have been written as: Ginger-haired John, who was born in Devon, was a pickpocket.

number rolled	first roll: name begins with	second roll: appearance	third roll: profession	fourth roll: event	fifth roll: place
1	A-D	blue-eyed	pickpocket	lived	Scotland
2	E-H	ginger-haired	dragon slayer	died	prison
3	I-L	stick-thin	alchemist	attacked	Wales
4	M-P	big-bellied	grave robber	born	castle
5	Q-U	long-legged	mole catcher	escaped	river
6	V-Z	double-chinned	hermit	married	Devon

ENGLISH
— YEAR 6 —

MAIN ACTIVITY: EXTRA INFORMATION **TIMING: 20 MINS**

LEARNING OBJECTIVES
- To use a pair of brackets to add extra information
- To use a pair of dashes to add extra information

EQUIPMENT
none

You can use a pair of brackets or dashes to add extra information to a sentence.

Draw lines to match each sentence to the extra information you could add to it. The first one has been done for you.

sentence	extra information (parenthesis)
The grey wolf lives in remote areas of North America.	that boy I go to karate with
My sister is moving to Spain.	the first man in space
I went paintballing for my birthday.	we never usually win anything
Jenny hates jogging.	the one who lives in Bristol
Amazingly, my school won the cup.	yes, that really was her name
Felix can be really annoying.	it was really fun
Yuri Gagarin orbited the Earth for one hour.	also named Canis lupus
Mrs Shufflebottom was always late for the bus.	she prefers a good walk

Now write each sentence out, adding the extra information in a suitable place and separating it with a pair of brackets or dashes.

ENGLISH
YEAR 6

HOMEWORK ACTIVITY: ADDING PARENTHESIS

TIMING: 20 MINS

LEARNING OBJECTIVES
- To add extra information to a sentence
- To use commas, brackets and dashes to add extra information

EQUIPMENT
none

1. Rewrite these sentences on a separate piece of paper and add some extra information (a parenthesis) between the commas, brackets or dashes. Here's an example:

    My brother – ... – never eats any breakfast. →
    My brother – the one who sleeps all day – never eats any breakfast.

    a) My friend Poppy, ... , thinks time travel is possible.
    b) We watched a long play at the theatre (...).
    c) The cup, ... , was knocked over by the cat.
    d) His auntie – ... – got married in a cave.
    e) The traffic started moving at last (...).
    f) My pet – ... – is 10 years old now.

2. Now add a parenthesis containing some extra information to these sentences.

    a) Dad's cousin flies all over the world.
    b) The painting was sold at auction.
    c) My mum always wanted to be a singer.
    d) Liam and Jamie went to see the head teacher again.

If you have time, write some sentences of your own using commas, brackets or dashes to add a parenthesis.

31 ANSWERS

STARTER ACTIVITY: PLACE THE PAIRS

1. a) His friend, who works in the clothes shop, loves to dress smartly.
   b) The banana, which was covered in black spots, tasted horrible.
   c) Emily, aged 14 from Leeds, won a magic competition.
2. a) My school trip to the sewage farm was great (it was a bit smelly though).
   b) The wedding singer (a tiny man with thick glasses) kept dropping his microphone.
3. a) Creeping out from behind the door – I had been hiding there for ages – I shouted, "Boo!"
   b) I believe you – lots of other people wouldn't – when you say you are telling the truth.

MAIN ACTIVITY: MY FANTASY FAMILY TREE

Answers may vary.

MAIN ACTIVITY: EXTRA INFORMATION

The grey wolf (also named Canis lupus) lives in remote areas of North America.
My sister – the one who lives in Bristol – is moving to Spain. (Brackets also acceptable).
I went paintballing for my birthday (it was really fun).
Jenny hates jogging (she prefers a good walk).
Amazingly, my school won the cup (we never usually win anything).
Felix – that boy I go to karate with – can be really annoying. (Brackets also acceptable).
Yuri Gagarin – the first man in space – orbited the Earth for one hour. (Brackets also acceptable).
Mrs Shufflebottom – yes, that really was her name – was always late for the bus. (Brackets also acceptable).

HOMEWORK ACTIVITY: ADDING PARENTHESIS

1. Answers may vary. Examples might include:
a) My friend Poppy, who lives in Brighton, thinks time travel is possible. b) We watched a long play at the theatre (it was really boring). c) The cup, which was full of coffee, was knocked over by the cat. d) His auntie – the adventurous one – got married in a cave. e) The traffic started moving at last (we were now three hours late). f) My pet – a brown rabbit – is 10 years old now.
2. Answers may vary. Examples might include:
a) Dad's cousin, who works for a charity, flies all over the world. b) The painting, which was worth £10,000, was sold at auction. c) My mum always wanted to be a singer (even though she couldn't sing in tune). d) Liam and Jamie – definitely the two naughtiest boys in Year 6 – went to see the head teacher again.

GLOSSARY

Parenthesis
Extra information inserted into a sentence. It is separated by a pair of commas, brackets or dashes. If you take the parenthesis away, the sentence will still make sense.

Commas
A punctuation mark used to separate different parts of a sentence, such as clauses or extra information, to make the meaning clear.

Brackets
A punctuation mark used in pairs with the opening bracket at the beginning of the extra information and a closing bracket at the end.

Dashes
A punctuation mark used in the same way as a pair of brackets. A dash is longer than a hyphen and always has a space either side of it.

Relative clause
A clause that adds detail to a noun. It always comes after the noun it is describing. It is a type of subordinate clause separated from the main clause by commas. It often starts with a relative pronoun.

ENGLISH
YEAR 6

32 Punctuation: Colons and semi-colons

Learning objectives
- To use colons to introduce lists
- To use semi-colons within lists
- To use colons or semi-colons between clauses

Content domains
- G5.10 colons
- G5.11 semi-colons

Starter activity
- **Punctuation Pete; 10 minutes; page 210**
  Ensure the student can correctly identify each type of punctuation mark. Discuss which punctuation marks always come in pairs. Ask the student what they know about colons and semi-colons. Remind the student that it is a punctuation convention to start a sentence with a capital letter.

Main activities
- **Shopping lists; 20 minutes; page 211**
  This activity focuses on using colons and semi-colons in lists of nouns and noun phrases. Consolidate the student's understanding by repeating the first two parts of the activity before moving onto the final part.
- **Colon or semi-colon?; 15 minutes; page 212**
  This activity focuses on using colons and semi-colons between clauses. This usage is less common than in lists and is more difficult to grasp. Encourage the student to use the terms *explanation* and *same theme* to inform their choice.

Plenary activity
- **Change my mark; 5 minutes**
  On a whiteboard, draw a punctuation mark of your choice (e.g. a full stop). Challenge the student to alter it to make and name a different punctuation mark (e.g. comma). Swap roles.

Homework activity
- **The VIP party; 45 minutes; page 213**
  This activity puts the student's learning into practice. Remind the student that their sentences should contain the same punctuation as the examples. Review and discuss any remaining areas of weakness or misconception in the next session.

Differentiation and extension ideas
- **Shopping lists** Extend or support by adding or removing words from the table. If appropriate, discuss how semi-colons are used to avoid ambiguity when listing expanded noun phrases that include commas.
- **The VIP party** Support by removing the requirement for the student to write their own sentences for questions 3 and 4 to decrease difficulty.

Progress and observations

ENGLISH
YEAR 6

STARTER ACTIVITY: PUNCTUATION PETE

TIMING: 10 MINS

LEARNING OBJECTIVES
- To find and name a range of punctuation marks

EQUIPMENT
- highlighter

Punctuation Pete loves to steal punctuation marks. Highlight all the different types of punctuation mark in the text below and copy them into his bag.

The policeman shouted, "Stop! You'll never get away with it."

Punctuation Pete, the crafty thief, replied, "Do you really think you can catch me?" With that, the light-fingered robber sprinted away.

The policeman (who was called Old Bill) set off after him. He was soon out of breath: he was over sixty and a bit overweight.

Punctuation Pete slowed down. He thought he had escaped – or had he? Old Bill had called for help; Punctuation Pete was soon captured.

Punctuation Pete needs help naming a few of the punctuation marks he's never seen before. Write the names of the missing ones in the table below. Some have been done for you.

punctuation mark	name	punctuation mark	name
.	full stop	:	
,	comma	-	
!	exclamation mark	;	
?		" "	
'		( )	
–		A	capital letter

ENGLISH
— YEAR 6 —

MAIN ACTIVITY: SHOPPING LISTS **TIMING: 20 MINS**

LEARNING OBJECTIVES
- To use a colon to introduce a list
- To use semi-colons to separate items in a list

EQUIPMENT
- a dice

Complete the table below with some ideas of your own. You are going to use it to generate some shopping lists.

number rolled	first roll: item of clothing	second roll: colour	third roll: amount	fourth roll: detail
1	shirt	black	one	quick drying
2	coat		two / pair	with deep pockets
3		blue		
4	bow tie			small and itchy
5		crimson	five	
6	skirt		six / half a dozen	

First, roll the dice four times to choose four items of clothing. Write a shopping list introduced by a colon (:) and separate each item with a comma. Here is an example:

Your first roll is 4 (bow tie), then 6 (skirt), then 2 (coat) and your fourth roll is 1 (shirt).
You could write:
I am going to buy the following items: a bow tie, a skirt, a coat and a shirt.

Look at the second roll column, and roll four more times, this time to choose some colours. Rewrite your sentence to include these adjectives to describe your items of clothing.

Next, roll the dice four more times to choose an amount of each item and four final times to choose the details (you'll find these in the third and fourth roll columns).

So far, it's been correct to use commas to separate your items but when you add the extra information from the third and fourth rolls, you will have to use semi-colons to separate them.

Write your shopping list, introducing the items by a colon (:) and separating them by semi-colons (;) like this:

Today I am shopping for: five grey shirts with deep pockets; six small, itchy, gold bow ties; a quick-drying lime shirt; and three blue skirts with red stripes.

ENGLISH
— YEAR 6 —

MAIN ACTIVITY: COLON OR SEMI-COLON? **TIMING: 15 MINS**

LEARNING OBJECTIVES
- To use a colon before a clause that explains
- To use a semi-colon before a clause with the same theme

EQUIPMENT
- scissors

A colon can be used to introduce another clause that gives more detail.

Example:
I'm feeling really full: I ate too many sweets at the cinema.

A semi-colon can be used to join clauses that have the same theme.

Example:
Boris joined the hockey team; his friend Adam joined a cricket club.

Cut out the clauses and punctuation marks below. Match the clauses and place either a colon or a semi-colon between each pair.

Ben is very silly	dig a tunnel under the wall.	:
I am so tired	it broke down on the way home.	;
My dad bought a new car	he sometimes plays tricks on his friends.	:
Zara couldn't stop worrying	I will send you the package.	;
There is only one way to escape	she gets on well with mine.	:
Text me your address tomorrow	her cat had been missing for days.	;
I am terrible at learning languages	we stayed up really late last night.	:
Maryam doesn't like her sisters	my cousin can speak four.	;

ENGLISH
YEAR 6

HOMEWORK ACTIVITY: THE VIP PARTY

TIMING: 45 MINS

LEARNING OBJECTIVES
- To practise using colons and semi-colons
- To practise using a range of punctuation

EQUIPMENT
none

1. Read the sentences below and write the names of the punctuation marks used below each sentence.

a) The Princess wore the following to the ball: a beautiful gown, a tiara, white gloves and a pair of glass slippers.

----

b) The guest list for the party included: the actress with purple hair, Suzie Sparrow; Doug Power, the Kingdom's Strongest Man; Zizi Belle, the daughter of a famous lady-in-waiting; and an undercover reporter from Neverland called Sir Sebastian Gossip.

----

c) The Prince said, "There is only one reason for leaving her slipper: she must want me to find her."

----

d) The horses turned back into the mice; the carriage transformed back into a pumpkin.

----

2. Write one more sentence to add to those in question 1 on a separate piece of paper using the same punctuation marks that you found in the sentences.

3. Now write a short paragraph about what happens at the party. Try to use as many of the following punctuation marks as you can:
. , ! ? ' — : - ; "" () A

Here are some ideas to get you started:
- Who is talking to each other? Use direct speech.
- Add extra information using commas, dashes or brackets.
- Someone could explain something. Use a colon.
- List all the things the guests could eat.

32 ANSWERS

STARTER ACTIVITY: PUNCTUATION PETE

Punctuation in Pete's bag: , " . " ? ( ) : ! - ;

punctuation mark	name	punctuation mark	name
.	full stop	:	colon
,	comma	-	hyphen
!	exclamation mark	;	semi-colon
?	question mark	" "	inverted commas
'	apostrophe	( )	brackets
–	dash	A	capital letter

MAIN ACTIVITY: SHOPPING LISTS

Answers may vary. Check for correct placement of colons, semi-colons and commas within the lists of nouns and noun phrases.

MAIN ACTIVITY: COLON OR SEMI-COLON?

Colons (explain):
Ben is very silly: he sometimes plays tricks on his friends.
I am so tired: we stayed up so late last night.
Zara couldn't stop worrying: her cat had been missing for days.
There is only one way to escape: dig a tunnel under the wall.
Semi-colons (same theme):
My dad bought a new car; it broke down on the way home.
Text me your address tomorrow; I will send you the package.
Maryam doesn't like her sisters; she gets on well with mine.
I am terrible at learning languages; my cousin can speak four.

HOMEWORK ACTIVITY: THE VIP PARTY

1. a) capital letter, colon, comma, full stop
   b) capital letter, colon, commas, semi-colons, hyphens, full stop
   c) capital letter, comma, inverted commas (speech marks), colon, full stop
   d) capital letter, semi-colon, full stop
2. Student's own answers.
3. Student's own answers.

GLOSSARY

Colon
A punctuation mark used to introduce a list, a quotation or an example. It can also introduce an explanation in a separate independent clause. A colon should always be followed by a lower-case letter, except for the personal pronoun *I*.

Semi-colon
A punctuation mark used to separate items in a list of phrases. It is also used to separate two main clauses with the same theme (that are linked in meaning and are equally important).

33 Punctuation: Apostrophes

Learning Objectives

- To use apostrophes to show possession
- To understand the difference between plural and possessive –s
- To use apostrophes to indicate a contraction

Content Domains

- G5.8 apostrophes to mark singular and plural possession in nouns
- G5.8 the grammatical difference between plural and possessive –s
- G5.8 apostrophes to mark contracted forms

Starter Activity

- **Hunting for apostrophes; 5 minutes; page 216**
  Assess the student's knowledge of the apostrophe, both for possession and for contraction. Encourage the student to explain their reasons. Address the misconception that *its* (possessive pronoun) needs an apostrophe.

Main Activities

- **Who does it belong to?; 20 minutes; page 217**
  Make sure the student asks themselves whether the owner is a singular or plural noun each time and knows how to place the apostrophe accordingly. Singular nouns ending in –s, such as *Angus* or *octopus*, should be followed by 's. Discuss and model how to use apostrophes with irregular plurals, such as *women* and *children*. Reiterate that possessions are not just objects you own, but can also be abstract nouns, such as *mistakes* or *beliefs*.
- **Make it shorter; 20 minutes; page 218**
  This activity invites the student to remove letters and place an apostrophe to make a contracted word. Demonstrate how *should've* is the contraction of *should have* and discuss why it is often confused with *should of* (which is incorrect) because of its sound.

Plenary Activity

- **Correct my mistakes; 5 minutes**
  Write a phrase with a deliberate contraction or possession mistake, such as: *The childs' toy* or *They do'nt like sweet's*. Ask the student correct the use of apostrophes in the phrases provided.

Homework Activity

- **Sorting apostrophes; 45 minutes; page 219**
  This activity puts the student's learning into practice. Encourage the student to read the whole story for sense first. Review and discuss any remaining areas of weakness or misconception in the next session.

Differentiation and Extension Ideas

- **Who does it belong to?** Support by removing irregular plurals from the list of owners.
- **Make it shorter** Support by replacing trickier pairs such as *shall not/shan't* with more common contractions.
- **Homework** Support by providing a particular book or text aimed at the reading ability of the student.

Progress and Observations

ENGLISH
YEAR 6

STARTER ACTIVITY: HUNTING FOR APOSTROPHES

TIMING: 5 MINS

LEARNING OBJECTIVES
- To spot where the writer has forgotten to use apostrophes

EQUIPMENT
none

It's hard to make sense of apostrophes sometimes. This writer doesn't understand how to use them, so they didn't bother to use any at all! Can you help by adding apostrophes where they are needed?

People often confuse *its* and *it's*. Remember, *it's* always means *it is*.

Sharks senses

A sharks senses help it to survive in its habitat. Its eyesight is generally good and sharks eyes often have special eyelids to protect them. A sharks sense of smell is well-developed. There are also tiny pores on a sharks snout that detect electrical signals. Its hearing is excellent and theyre often attracted to low-pitched sounds. Sharks taste buds help them identify their food. Without all these senses, sharks couldnt hunt, avoid their enemies attacks or find their way. Sharks are amazing, arent they?

ENGLISH
— YEAR 6 —

MAIN ACTIVITY: WHO DOES IT BELONG TO?	TIMING: 20 MINS

LEARNING OBJECTIVES

- To use apostrophes to show that something belongs to someone or something
- To understand how to use apostrophes with singular and plural nouns

EQUIPMENT

- small coin or token

Flip a small coin or token to land on a space in each of the tables below. On a separate piece of paper, write the words from the squares your token lands on. Use these words to write a phrase by joining the owner to its possession using an apostrophe. Flip the coin eight times for each table, so you end up with eight sentences.

Don't worry if they don't make sense!

Example:
the dog + weapon = the dog's weapon

In this case, the apostrophe means: the weapon of (belonging to) the dog

owners

the dog	the cat
a vicar	those doctors
the knight	some pupils
that actress	his neighbours
the whale	my cousins
Angus	some women
Lily	their children
an octopus	the foxes
the boss	the ladies
this witness	your workmen

possessions

food	growling
clothes	mistakes
weapon	beliefs
smiles	discussions
story	illness
decision	chairs
conversation	interests
escape	attack
orders	package
evidence	tools

ENGLISH
— YEAR 6 —

MAIN ACTIVITY: MAKE IT SHORTER **TIMING: 20 MINS**

LEARNING OBJECTIVES
- To use apostrophes to show where letters have been removed
- To write shortened (contracted) words using apostrophes

EQUIPMENT
- scissors
- glue stick

Sometimes we shorten or join words together by removing letters and putting an apostrophe in their place. These are called contractions.

Cut out each pair of words and the apostrophes. Now cut away any unwanted letters to shorten each pair of words into a single word. Stick them together, putting the apostrophe in the correct place. Here's an example:

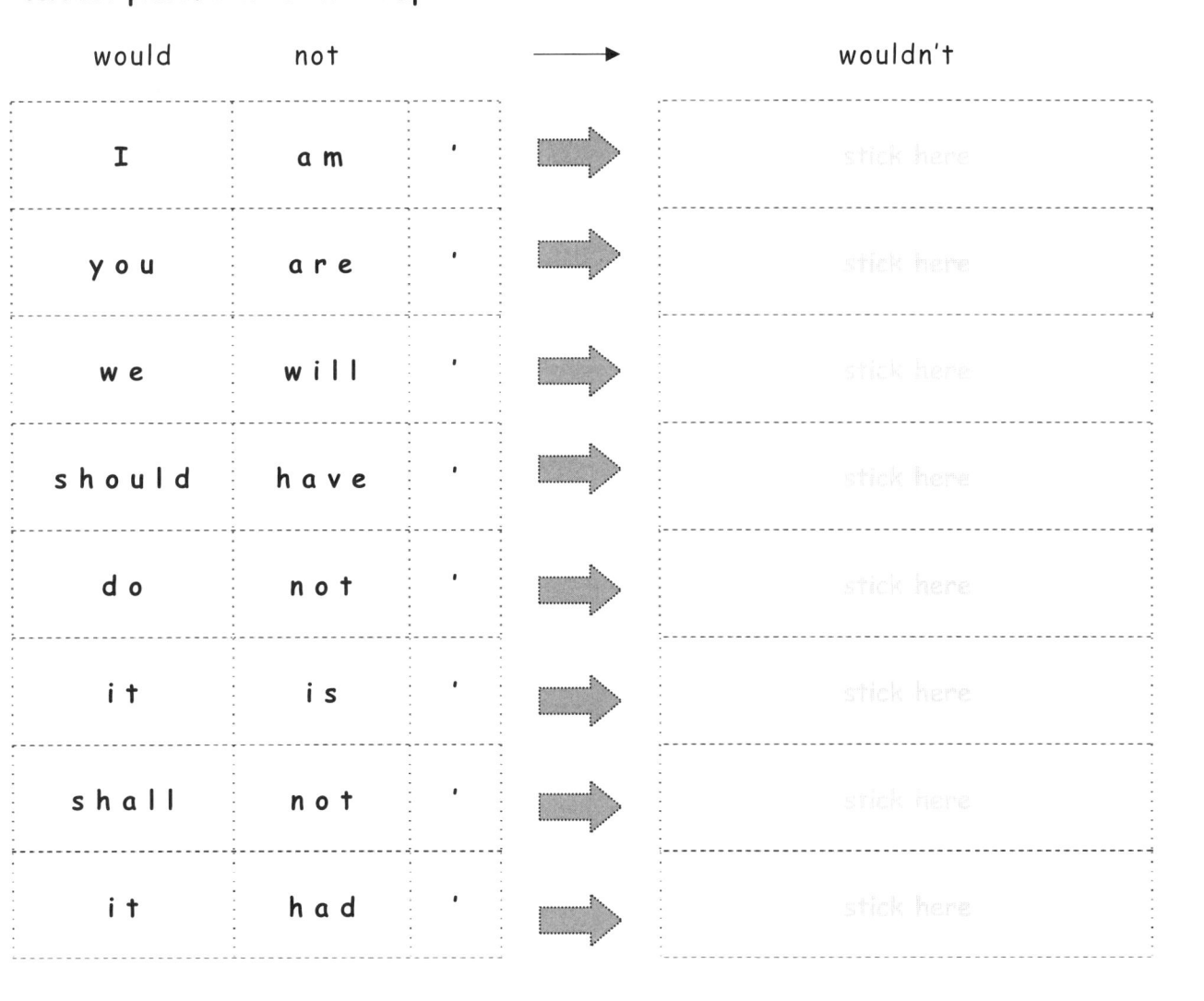

would	not	→	wouldn't
I	am	' →	stick here
you	are	' →	stick here
we	will	' →	stick here
should	have	' →	stick here
do	not	' →	stick here
it	is	' →	stick here
shall	not	' →	stick here
it	had	' →	stick here

If you have time, write a short sentence to include each of the contractions you have made.

ENGLISH
— YEAR 6 —

TUTORS' GUILD

HOMEWORK ACTIVITY: SORTING APOSTROPHES

TIMING: 45 MINS

LEARNING OBJECTIVES
- To find examples of where writers have used apostrophes
- To show you know why an apostrophe has been used

EQUIPMENT
- fiction and non-fiction books, magazines and newspapers

Read extracts from a selection of books, magazines or newspapers to find where the writers have used apostrophes.

Using the different sections in the books below, write down the examples you find – this will help you understand why the apostrophes have been used. Try to find lots of examples for each section. Can you find any mistakes?

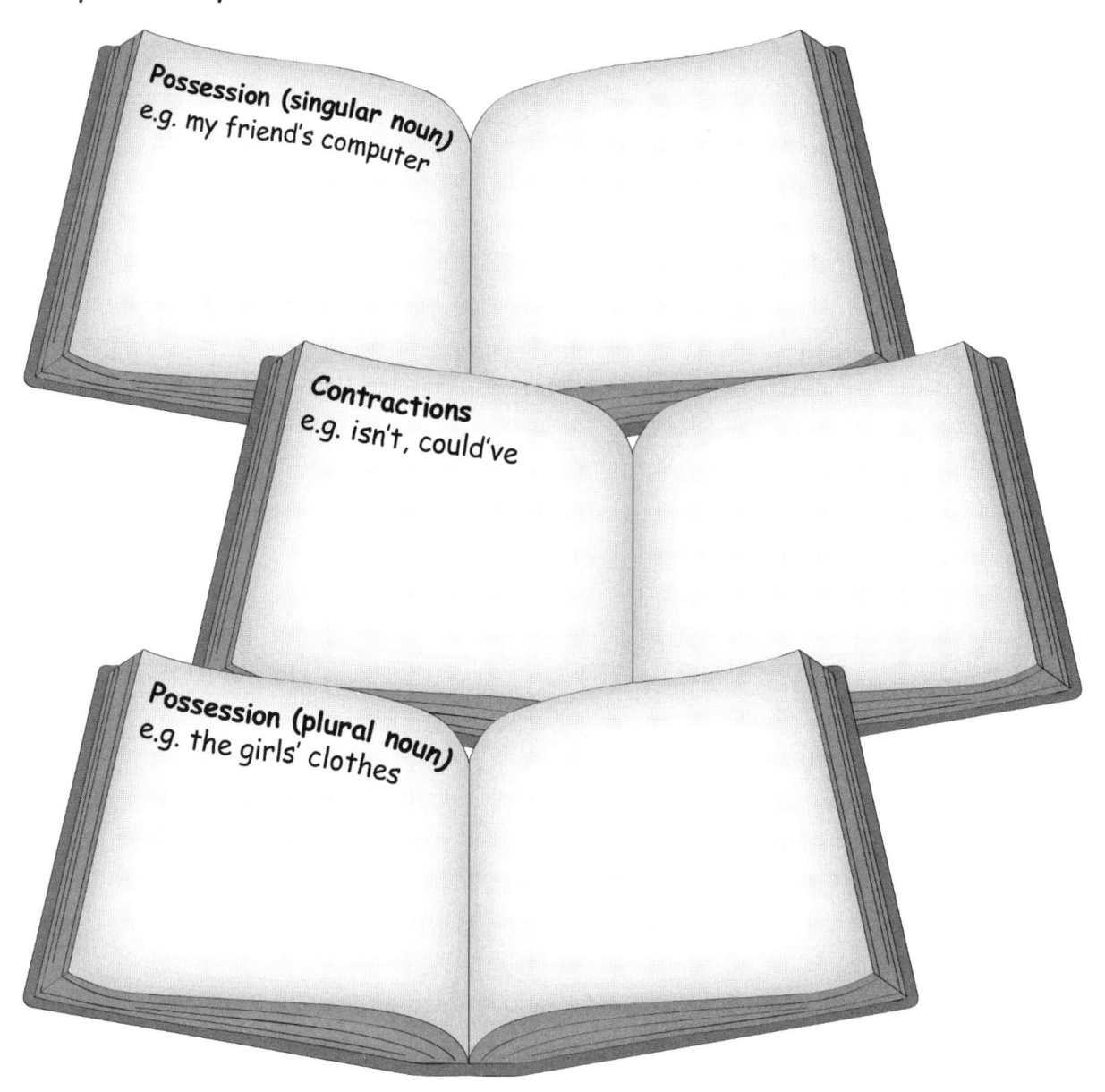

Possession (singular noun)
e.g. my friend's computer

Contractions
e.g. isn't, could've

Possession (plural noun)
e.g. the girls' clothes

33 Answers

Starter activity: Hunting for apostrophes

Sharks' senses

A shark's senses help it to survive in its habitat. Its eyesight is generally good and sharks' eyes often have special eyelids to protect them. A shark's sense of smell is well-developed. There are also tiny pores on a shark's snout that detect electrical signals. Its hearing is excellent and they're often attracted to low-pitched sounds. Sharks' taste buds help them identify their food. Without all these senses, sharks couldn't hunt, avoid their enemies' attacks or find their way. Sharks are amazing, aren't they?

Main activity: Who does it belong to?

Answers may vary. Examples might include:
the dog's food (singular noun)
Angus's escape (singular noun ending in *s*)
some pupils' discussions (regular plural noun)
your workmen's mistakes (irregular plural noun)

Main activity: Make it shorter

I'm; you're; we'll; should've; don't; it's; it'd
Answers may vary. Examples might include:
I'm hungry and it's time for a snack.
We would've got here quicker if we'd known about the traffic.

Homework activity: Sorting apostrophes

Answers may vary. Check that the student has classified their examples correctly and address any remaining mistakes / misconceptions. Reiterate the difference between the possessive pronoun *its* and the contraction *it's*.

Glossary

Apostrophe
A punctuation mark used to show possession and where letters are missing in a contraction.

Possession
Describes when something belongs to (is possessed by) someone or something. It is marked by an apostrophe.

Contraction
Words that are shortened and joined are called contractions. They are common in informal speech and writing. Contractions are allowed in Standard English, but not in formal writing.

Noun
A naming word for a person, place, thing or idea. A noun can be singular (one) or plural (more than one).

ENGLISH
YEAR 6

34 PUNCTUATION: PUNCTUATING SPEECH

LEARNING OBJECTIVES

- To use inverted commas to indicate direct speech
- To understand how to order punctuation in direct speech
- To change reported speech to direct speech and vice versa

CONTENT DOMAINS

- G5.7 inverted commas

STARTER ACTIVITIES

- **What did they say? 5 minutes; page 222**
  All punctuation except full stops and apostrophes has been removed to make it more difficult for the student to identify the spoken words. Discuss how punctuation, such as inverted commas, commas, question marks would make it easier to distinguish different elements. At this stage, ask the student to simply place a pair of inverted commas either side of their highlighted text ("...").

MAIN ACTIVITIES

- **Punctuating direct speech; 20 minutes; page 223**
  This activity focuses on placing the reporting clause before or after the direct speech, but not in the middle. Ensure the student understands how to place commas inside or outside the inverted commas depending on the position of the reporting clause.
- **Direct speech ↔ reported speech; 20 minutes; page 224**
  Make sure that the student is including / excluding words, punctuation and changing pronouns as appropriate when converting from one to the other.

PLENARY ACTIVITIES

- **My tutor said … ; 5 minutes**
  Say a sentence or phrase, such as *I'm really hungry*. Ask the student to write it down then add speech marks and the reporting clause, e.g. *"I'm really hungry," my tutor said.* Repeat with different phrases as time allows.

HOMEWORK ACTIVITIES

- **The conversation; 45 minutes; page 225**
  This activity puts the student's learning into practice. When setting this homework, read the story together and ask the student for some initial ideas. Explain that only the inverted commas are missing; all the other punctuation is correct. Review and discuss any remaining areas of weakness or misconception in the next session.

DIFFERENTIATION AND EXTENSION IDEAS

- **What did they say?** Support by including some missing punctuation (except speech marks).
- **Punctuating direct speech** Extend by asking the student to rewrite the sentences, swapping the position of the reporting clause and making the subsequent punctuation changes.
- **Direct ↔ reported speech** Support by preparing direct speech bubbles with the inverted commas and punctuation in place. Extend by challenging the student to place the reporting clause before as well as after any direct speech.

PROGRESS AND OBSERVATIONS

ENGLISH
— YEAR 6 —

STARTER ACTIVITY: WHAT DID THEY SAY?   **TIMING: 5 MINS**

LEARNING OBJECTIVES
- To identify spoken words in writing

EQUIPMENT
- highlighter

Inverted commas are used to show what someone is saying. Before you can put them in the right place, you need to be sure you can spot the exact words that are being spoken.

Highlight the words that should be between a pair of inverted commas in the sentences below.

1. Billy's cat jumped off the sofa and onto my foot I explained.

2. She said we really must hide or the aliens will capture us.

3. Why don't we all take a trip to the beach they asked.

4. Oh dear Mum moaned I'm really not enjoying this meal.

5. The old man bellowed get down from there.

6. I've got to tell you he said sighing that's the worst joke I've ever heard.

7. You promised to tell me I cried.

8. Frankie said that I make the best cakes Mum said with a smile.

ENGLISH
YEAR 6

MAIN ACTIVITY: PUNCTUATING DIRECT SPEECH　　　　**TIMING: 20 MINS**

LEARNING OBJECTIVES
- To use the correct punctuation in the correct order with direct speech

EQUIPMENT
- scissors

First, cut out the punctuation cards below.

| " | " | , | . | ? | ! |

Next, cut out each row of sentences, separating them into two sections as shown. Now arrange each sentence in the right order, adding the correct punctuation cards each time and write them down on a separate piece of paper. Here's an example:

" What time is it ? " asked the farmer .

I've lost my favourite game	Roman said sadly.
My football coach told me	Great effort out there today.
Please can we get a puppy	begged my sister.
Stay right where you are	warned the soldier.
The teacher said warmly	You deserve a certificate.
Weren't you a cute baby	my girlfriend remarked.
I think I'm in danger	whispered the spy.

ENGLISH
— YEAR 6 —

MAIN ACTIVITY: DIRECT ↔ REPORTED SPEECH   **TIMING: 20 MINS**

LEARNING OBJECTIVES
- To change reported speech to direct speech
- To change direct speech to reported speech

EQUIPMENT
- a dice

Look at the sentences below. Draw lines to match the direct speech to its equivalent reported speech.

Mum asked impatiently whether it was time to catch the train yet.	"I've never been on holiday to Wales before," Amy said.
The woman announced that our flight was delayed.	"That was the most incredible film ever!" exclaimed Sam.
Amy said that she had never been on holiday to Wales before.	"Is it time to catch the train yet?" asked Mum impatiently.
Sam exclaimed that it was the most incredible film ever.	"Your flight is delayed," announced the woman.

Now you are going to make up your own direct or reported speech. Roll a dice four times and use the table below to guide you.

number rolled	first roll: direct or reported speech?	second roll: who's speaking?	third roll: how they are speaking?	fourth roll: subject?
1	direct speech	a boy	said	a pet
2	reported speech	a girl	shouted	a journey
3	direct speech	a man	asked	a plan
4	reported speech	a woman	wondered	a hobby
5	direct speech	a superhero	explained	a place
6	reported speech	a villain	replied	a friend

Here's an example. Your first roll is 1 (direct speech); your second roll is 5 (superhero); your third is 3 (asked); your third is 1 (a pet). You first write some direct speech based on those rolls. Then you change it into reported speech.

"Has anyone see my cat, Cuddles?" asked HeroBoy.   ⟶   HeroBoy asked whether anyone had seen his cat, Cuddles

ENGLISH
— YEAR 6 —

HOMEWORK ACTIVITY: THE CONVERSATION **TIMING: 45 MINS**

LEARNING OBJECTIVES
- To punctuate direct speech accurately
- To continue the conversation

EQUIPMENT
none

On a separate piece of paper rewrite the sentences in the conversation below, putting in the missing inverted commas.

Then write the next part of the conversation using lines of direct speech. Don't forget to start a new line every time someone new speaks.

Why can't I come with you? asked my brother. I promise to be quiet.

No way, I said firmly. It's far too dangerous for you.

Please, Connor, he begged. I could be your lookout.

I pretended to think about it and then replied, Nah, you're too scared of the dark. You would be rubbish at it.

Right, if you won't let me, I'm telling Mum and Dad, Joe said crossly.

Oh, really? I said. Tell, would you? Joe clenched his jaw and nodded. Well, you know what I'd do in that case, don't you? I added menacingly.

Ideas to get you started:

- What does Joe say next? What is Connor threatening to do? Who else might join the conversation?

- Introduce another character, such as a parent, friend or sister.

- Think from Joe's point of view? How would you persuade someone in this situation?

Tick

☐ I have checked that I've put speech marks around direct speech.

☐ I have tried to put other punctuation in the correct place.

☐ I have used a new line for a new speaker.

34 Answers

Starter activity: What did they say?

1. Billy's cat jumped off the sofa and onto my foot I explained.
2. She said we really must hide or the aliens will capture us.
3. Why don't we all take a trip to the beach they asked.
4. Oh dear mum moaned I'm really not enjoying this meal.
5. The old man bellowed get down from there.
6. I've got to tell you he said sighing that's the worst joke I've ever heard.
7. You promised to tell me I cried.
8. Frankie said that I make the best cakes Mum said with a smile.

Main activity: Punctuating direct speech

"I've lost my favourite game," Roman said sadly.
My football coach told me, "Great effort out there today."
"Please can we get a puppy?" begged my sister.
"Stay right where you are!" warned the soldier.
The teacher said warmly, "You deserve a certificate."
"Weren't you a cute baby?" my girlfriend remarked.
"I think I'm in danger," whispered the spy.

Main activity: Direct speech ↔ reported speech

"I've never been on holiday to Wales before," Amy said. → Amy said that she had never been on holiday to Wales before.
"That was the most incredible film ever!" exclaimed Sam. → Sam exclaimed that it was the most incredible film ever.
"Is it time to catch the train yet?" asked Mum impatiently. → Mum impatiently asked whether it was time to catch the train yet.
"Your flight is delayed," announced the woman. → The woman announced that our flight was delayed.

Homework activity: The conversation

"Why can't I come with you?" asked my brother. "I promise to be quiet."
"No way," I said firmly. "It's far too dangerous for you."
"Please, Connor," he pleaded. "I could be your lookout."
I pretended to think about it and then replied, "Nah, you're too scared of the dark. You would be rubbish at it."
"Right, if you won't let me, I'm telling Mum and Dad," Joe said crossly.
"Oh, really?" I said. "Tell, would you?" Joe clenched his jaw and nodded. "Well, you know what I'd do in that case, don't you?" I added menacingly.
Extending the conversation: answers will vary.

Glossary

Inverted commas
A type of punctuation mark that goes around direct speech. Either single inverted commas or double quotation marks are acceptable in British English.

Direct speech
What a person actually says. It always goes inside a pair of speech marks. For example: *She said, "I like cabbage."*

Reported speech
Where the writer reports what a person says. For example: *She said that she liked cabbage.* (Sometimes called indirect speech)

ENGLISH — YEAR 6

35 Punctuation: Hyphens and single dashes

Learning objectives
- To use hyphens to make meaning clear
- To use hyphens to make compound words and add prefixes
- To use a single dash between clauses to show an interruption in speech or thought, or a shift of direction

Content domains
- G5.12 single dashes
- G5.13 hyphens

Starter activities
- **Do you really mean that?; 5 minutes; page 228**
  Discuss how the missing hyphens affect the meaning of each sentence and how adding the hyphen makes the meaning clearer. Emphasise that such ambiguities are not common in English and that the student should only hyphenate when they know why they are doing it.

Main activities
- **Hyphenated personalities; 20 minutes; page 229**
  When matching the words, emphasise that the compound adjectives should describe personality traits and not physical looks (discourage *pig-faced* or *narrow-headed*). Use the crossword element to focus any discussion about meanings.
- **Hyphen or dash?; 20 minutes; page 230**
  Discuss the objectives to guide the student's understanding of the different functions of hyphens and dashes. Encourage the student to read each sentence out loud to help them locate the missing single dashes.

Plenary activities
- **Tell me when; 5 minutes**
  Ask the student to explain when a hyphen is needed and ask them to write an example. Then ask the student to explain when to use a single dash and write an example.

Homework activities
- **Skim and classify; 30 minutes; page 231**
  This activity puts the student's learning into practice. Remind the student to skim for single dashes only and to ignore pairs of dashes used to add extra information in the middle of a sentence. Review and discuss any remaining areas of weakness or misconception in the next session.

Differentiation and extension ideas
- **Hyphenated characteristics** Support by adding letters or parts of words into the crossword squares.
- **Hyphen or dash?** Support by indicating whether a hyphen or single dash is required in the middle column. Extend by discussing compound nouns, such as *mother-in-law*, and hyphenating numbers.

Progress and observations

ENGLISH
— YEAR 6 —

STARTER ACTIVITY: DO YOU REALLY MEAN THAT?

TIMING: 5 MINS

LEARNING OBJECTIVES
- To use hyphens to make the meaning more clear

EQUIPMENT
- highlighter

Missing out a punctuation mark like a hyphen (-) can change the meaning of a sentence.

Highlight the words in each of the sentences below that need to be joined or split by a hyphen. Write the correctly hyphenated words on the line underneath.

1. We saw a man eating tiger in the jungle.

   ----

2. The football player loved his club and wanted to resign.

   ----

3. I'm trying hard to eat fat free meals.

   ----

4. I am going to a run down town tomorrow.

   ----

5. Nearly new clothes: a little used suit for sale.

   ----

6. Beware of the ball chasing dogs in the park.

ENGLISH
YEAR 6

MAIN ACTIVITY: HYPHENATED PERSONALITIES   **TIMING: 20 MINS**

LEARNING OBJECTIVES
- To make compound adjectives with hyphens
- To match the adjectives to their definitions

EQUIPMENT
none

Compound adjectives are a great way of describing someone's personality.
Draw lines to match the words in the two columns. Then write their compound adjectives with hyphens in the third column.

Example:
cold → blooded = a cold-blooded criminal (a cruel and hardened criminal)

pig	hearted	
even	headed	
cold	fisted	
green	witted	
tight	tempered	
thin	eyed	
narrow	faced	
quick	skinned	
two	behaved	
well	minded	

Now complete this crossword with the words you've made. Use the clues below and don't forget the hyphens. Work in pencil in case you make a mistake.

Across
3. gets jealous
5. keeps their money to themselves
6. stays calm and relaxed
7. won't change their mind
8. is unloving and unsympathetic
9. is crafty or dishonest

Down
1. thinks fast and cleverly
2. doesn't listen to other people's views
4. is polite and respectful
5. can't take a joke or criticism

ENGLISH
YEAR 6

MAIN ACTIVITY: HYPHEN OR DASH? **TIMING: 20 MINS**

LEARNING OBJECTIVES
- To use a hyphen to make a compound word
- To use a single dash to show an interruption or change of direction

EQUIPMENT
- none

Decide whether each sentence below needs a hyphen, a dash or both. Then rewrite each sentence with the correct punctuation.

1. My uncle is forty three in a week's time.

   ....

2. It looks like winter is over until the next storm of course.

   ....

3. Sachin's favourite time of year was mid August.

   ....

4. A strange noise from downstairs woke Teddy. It's only the wind, he thought or was it?

   ....

5. I can't find my glasses oh, there they are.

   ....

6. My mum gets on really well with her mother in law.

   ....

7. This seventeenth century painting is priceless.

   ....

8. My brother is a very self confident person I'm not.

   ....

ENGLISH
— YEAR 6 —

HOMEWORK ACTIVITY: SKIM AND CLASSIFY   **TIMING: 30 MINS**

LEARNING OBJECTIVES
- To find examples of hyphens and single dashes
- To decide what job they do in the writing

EQUIPMENT
- fiction and non-fiction books, magazines and newspapers

Your task is to skim a selection of fiction or non-fiction books, magazine articles or websites and copy out examples of where a writer has used hyphens or single dashes.

For each example you find, use the numbers below to indicate the job the punctuation is doing in the writing. The first one has been done for you.

The jobs that hyphens do:
1. make compound words
2. add a prefix
3. mark a line break

The jobs single dashes do:
4. mark an interruption
5. mark a change of direction
6. introduce an explanation

examples of hyphens and single dashes	punctuation job
the foul-breathed, slime-covered troll	1

35 Answers

Starter activity: Do you really mean that?
1. We saw a man eating tiger in the jungle; man-eating
2. The football player loved his club and wanted to resign; re-sign
3. I'm trying hard to eat fat free meals; fat-free
4. I am going to a run down town tomorrow; run-down
5. Nearly new clothes: a little used suit for sale; little-used
6. Beware of the ball chasing dogs in the park; ball-chasing

Main activity: Hyphenated personalities

pig-headed	→	7. Across
even-tempered	→	6. Across
cold-hearted	→	8. Across
green-eyed	→	3. Across
tight-fisted	→	5. Down
thin-skinned	→	5. Across
narrow-minded	→	2. Down
quick-witted	→	1. Down
two-faced	→	9. Across
well-behaved	→	4. Down

Main activity: Hyphen or dash?
1. My uncle is forty-three in a week's time.
2. It looks like winter is over – until the next storm of course.
3. Sachin's favourite time of year was mid-August.
4. A strange noise from downstairs woke Teddy. It's only the wind, he thought – or was it?
5. I can't find my glasses – oh, there they are.
6. My mum gets on really well with her mother-in-law.
7. This seventeenth-century painting is priceless.
8. My brother is a very self-confident person – I'm not.

Homework activity: Skim and classify
Answers may vary. Check that each example has been classified correctly.

Glossary

Hyphen
A punctuation mark used to make compound words and add prefixes to root words. It is also used to avoid ambiguity (e.g. *a little worn dress / a little-worn dress*), or to show a word break over a line. A hyphen is shorter than a dash.

Single dash
A punctuation mark used to show an interruption in speech or thought, or a shift of direction. A dash is longer than a hyphen.

ENGLISH — YEAR 6

36 SPELLING: WORD FAMILIES

LEARNING OBJECTIVES

- To classify words according to common root words
- To add a variety of common suffixes and prefixes to root words
- To recognise and write different plural noun forms accurately

CONTENT DOMAINS

- G6.2, S41 prefixes
- G6.3, S38, S42, S43, S46 suffixes
- G6.4 word families

STARTER ACTIVITIES

- **Root them up; 7 minutes; page 234**
  Use the activity to assess the student's ability to find words with common roots and group them. Tell the student that some of the groups will have more words than others. Ensure the student understands that a root word can occur at the beginning, middle or end of a word.

MAIN ACTIVITIES

- **Word builder; 20 minutes; page 235**
  This activity challenges the student to write words using some of the most common prefixes, root words or suffixes. One point is scored for each correct word recorded. A bonus point can be scored for expanding the opponent's word. Use this activity as a fun way of discussing which prefixes and suffixes can be added to words.
- **Plurals; 20 minutes; page 236**
  Discuss how most (but not all) plural nouns follow the rules on the sheet, and how the ending of the singular noun dictates the pluralisation rule. Ensure that the student avoids the common misconception that an apostrophe is needed when forming a plural noun, e.g. *my friends* not *my friend's*. For the second activity, follow the rules on the sheet. There are no irregular plurals in the card choices. Encourage the student to aim for accuracy over speed at first.

PLENARY ACTIVITIES

- **A-Z plurals; 3 minutes**
  Start by saying aloud a plural noun beginning with *a* such as *ants*. Ask the student to follow on with a plural noun beginning with *b* such as *buses*. Take it in turns to work as quickly as possible to the end of the alphabet.

HOMEWORK ACTIVITIES

- **Thou crusty botch of nature!; 45 minutes; page 237**
  This activity encourages the student to write 'insulting' noun phrases by adding negating prefixes to adjectives and creating compound nouns. Encourage the student to use their imagination to come up with funny ideas.

DIFFERENTIATION AND EXTENSION IDEAS

- **Root them up** Support by filling in more words or root words on the tables.
- **Word builder** Extend by first rolling one dice to choose a column, then rolling two dice to select one of the options from that column.
- **Against the clock** Extend by replacing or supplementing the words on the card to include irregular plurals such as roofs, chefs or potatoes.
- **A-Z plurals** Extend by narrowing this activity to a particular topic, such as animal names.

PROGRESS AND OBSERVATIONS

ENGLISH
— YEAR 6 —

TUTORS' GUILD

STARTER ACTIVITY: ROOT THEM UP

TIMING: 7 MINS

LEARNING OBJECTIVES
- To put words with common roots into groups
- To identify root words within longer words

EQUIPMENT
none

A farmer has planted lots of different root words in a field. These words have all grown into longer words. Now they are ready for you to root them up and sort them.

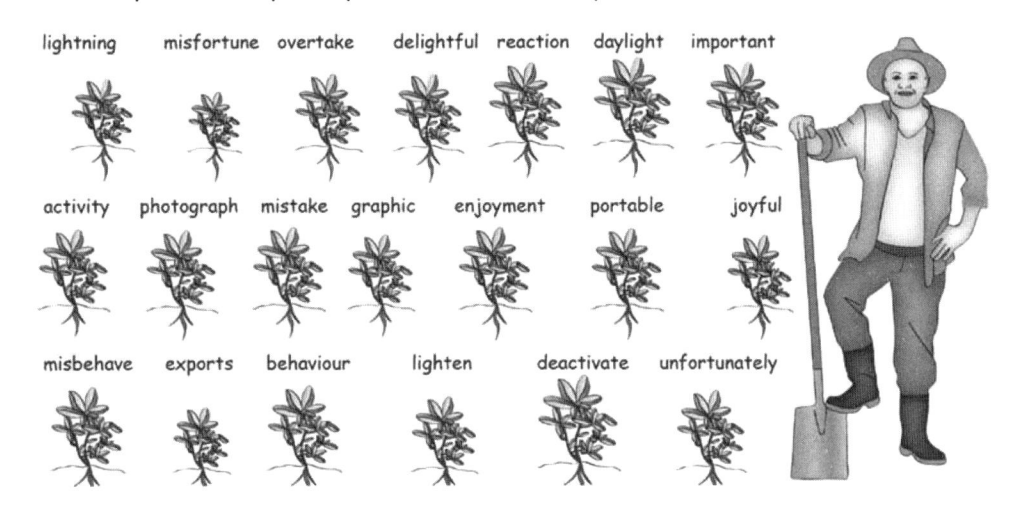

lightning   misfortune   overtake   delightful   reaction   daylight   important

activity   photograph   mistake   graphic   enjoyment   portable   joyful

misbehave   exports   behaviour   lighten   deactivate   unfortunately

In the tables below, write down any of the words you think share the same root. Can you identify the root words themselves from the longer words?

One group has been started for you.

lightning
delightful
word
word
root?

word
word
word
word
root?

word
word
word
word
root?

word
word
word
word
root?

word
word
word
word
root?

word
word
word
word
root?

word
word
word
word
root?

word
word
word
word
root?

ENGLISH
YEAR 6

MAIN ACTIVITY: WORD BUILDER **TIMING: 20 MINS**

LEARNING OBJECTIVES
- To write words using prefixes, root words and suffixes

EQUIPMENT
- two dice

Play this word game with your tutor. Start by rolling one of the dice.

> If you roll 1 or 2 choose a prefix from the list of 12 below.
> If you roll 3 or 4 choose a root word from the list of 12 below.
> If you roll 5 or 6 choose a suffix from the list of 12 below.

Say out loud and then write on a separate piece of paper a word that uses that prefix, root word or suffix. You can use any word you know.

Example:
You roll a 5. You choose the suffix '*-ness*' from the table. You say and write the word '*happiness*'.

You get one point for each correct word you write down. You can also claim a bonus point if you can make your tutor's word even longer. If you can, say "I can do better!" In the example above, you would write down '*unhappiness*'.

prefixes	root words	suffixes
im-	ject	-s or -es
re-	act	-ed
un-	vent	-ly
tri-	phone	-er or -or
auto-	tele	-ing
mis-	port	-tion
ir-	photo	-able or -ible
inter-	press	-al or -ial
super-	cap	-ness
dis-	micro	-ty or -ity
il-	octo	-ment
sub-	bio	-ic

ENGLISH
— YEAR 6 —

TUTORS GUILD

MAIN ACTIVITY: PLURALS　　　　　　　　　　TIMING: 20 MINS

LEARNING OBJECTIVES
- To know how to write most plural nouns

EQUIPMENT
- stopwatch or timer
- scissors

Plural nouns describe more than one of the same thing. There are a few rules about how you spell them.

1. Discuss these rules with your tutor and write the plural nouns in the last column. One has been done for you.

singular		rule		plural
dog		s		dogs
lunch		es		
day	+	s	=	
puppy		ies (-y)		
knife		ves (-fe)		
piano		s		

2. Your tutor will read ten singular nouns from the list below. On a separate piece of paper, write the plural of each word. Your tutor will time you, so try to write all ten plurals as quickly as you can! Play again and see if you can beat your score and your time.

watch	house	city	half
school	army	kangaroo	fish
boy	box	leaf	meal
church	worry	zoo	inch
balloon	valley	baby	banana
mountain	party	monkey	tray

ENGLISH
YEAR 6

HOMEWORK ACTIVITY: THOU CRUSTY BOTCH OF NATURE!   **TIMING: 45 MINS**

LEARNING OBJECTIVES
- To write some funny insults
- To add prefixes to adjectives
- To create compound nouns

EQUIPMENT
- none

The characters in William Shakespeare's plays could be really rude to each other! Here are some examples of the insults Shakespeare wrote:

"Thou mountain of mad flesh!"
"Come, you are a tedious fool!"
"Thou art as loathsome as a toad"

On a separate piece of paper, write a short play scene in which two characters throw insults at each other. There are two easy ways to create your insults.

Make adjectives negative by adding prefixes.
Example:
add *im-* to the adjective *polite* to make *impolite*.

Create compound nouns. For example, someone who spoils someone else's fun might be described as:

a fun-spoiler or an *enjoyment-vacuum*.

Use the prefix and adjective bank below to help you create your insults. You could start your play like this:

Character A: You really are an impolite enjoyment-vacuum!
Character B: Me? It is you who is the ungrateful fun-spoiler!

Prefix bank
un-   in-   im-
dis-   il-

Adjective bank

believable	considerate	kind	mature	patient	responsible
literate	bearable	sane	clean	perfect	friendly
grateful	helpful	competent	important	respectful	pleasant

Tick

☐ I have used words with prefixes.

☐ I have created some compound nouns.

36 Answers

Starter activity: Root them up

activity; deactivate; reaction (root word: act)
lightning; delightful; lighten, daylight (root word: light)
joyful; enjoyment (root word: joy)
portable; important, exports (root word: port)
mistake; overtake (root word: take)
graphic; photograph (root word: graph)
misbehave; behaviour (root word: behave)
unfortunately; misfortune (root word: fortune)

Main activity: Word builder

Answers may vary.

Main activity: Plurals

1. dogs; lunches; days; puppies; knives; pianos
2. watches; houses; cities; halves; schools; armies; kangaroos; fish(es); boys; boxes; leaves; meals; churches; worries; zoos; inches; balloons; valleys; babies; bananas; mountains; parties; monkeys; trays

Homework activity: Thou crusty botch of nature!

Check the student's work for correct choice and spelling of prefixes and adjectives. Check that their compound nouns make sense. There are no specific rules on forming compound nouns (e.g. *paperclip, paper-clip* and *paper clip* are all acceptable), unless a hyphen is required to eliminate ambiguity.

Glossary

Root word
The simplest form of a word before any prefix or suffix is added to it. For example: *friend* is the root word of *unfriendly*. Words in word families look similar and mean similar things because they share the same root.

Prefix
A letter or group of letters that are fixed (added) to the beginning of a word. When you add a prefix, you change the meaning of the word, often giving it an opposite / negative meaning or a new meaning.

Suffix
A letter or a group of letters that are fixed (added) at the end of a word. When you add a suffix, you change the meaning of the word. For example: *-ed* is added to the end of *walk* to make *walked*.

Plural
Nouns that describe more than one of the same thing. For example: *one cat* but *two cats*. They are usually formed by adding the suffix *-s*, although there are a number of other pluralisation rules and irregular plurals too.

Compound noun
A noun made from two or more words. For example: *playgroup, ice-breaker* or *cat food*. A compound noun can be written as a single word, as a word with a hyphen or as two words. There are no clear rules about this.

ENGLISH — YEAR 6

37 SPELLING: SYNONYMS, ANTONYMS AND HOMOPHONES

LEARNING OBJECTIVES

- To understand how words are related by meaning as synonyms and antonyms
- To recognise homophones
- To use the correct homophones depending on context

CONTENT DOMAINS

- G6.1 synonyms and antonyms
- S61 homophones, near homophones and other words that are often confused

STARTER ACTIVITY

- **Opposites snap!; 6 minutes; page 240**
  Cut out the cards before the lesson. Assess the student's ability to spot antonyms. Ensure they can read and understand the meaning of each word before you start.

MAIN ACTIVITIES

- **Synonym sorter; 15 minutes; page 241**
  This activity challenges the student to sort words into groups of synonyms. Reinforce the concept that synonyms can be words that are similar (but not exactly the same) in meaning.
- **Synonym/antonym sentences; 10 minutes; page 241**
  Ask the student to think of a synonym and an antonym for the given word (in brackets). It is usually easier to start with the antonym. Remind the student to check that their words will make sense in context.
- **Be the tutor; 15 minutes; page 242**
  This activity challenges the student to correct a piece of text by identifying the incorrect homophones and then writing the correct ones.

PLENARY ACTIVITY

- **Homophone quick-write; 4 minutes**
  Say some common homophones in context. For example: *My pen is over there. The word I want you to write is 'there'.* Ask the student to write the homophone and correct any misconceptions / mistakes.

HOMEWORK ACTIVITY

- **Word search; 45 minutes; page 243**
  This activity consolidates the student's ability to find and classify synonyms, antonyms and homophones.

DIFFERENTIATION AND EXTENSION IDEAS

- **Opposites snap!** Support by reducing the number of cards you use in the game to increase the chances of a pair of antonyms being placed.
- **Synonym sorter** Extend by challenging the student to think of more synonyms that would fit into the sorted groups.

PROGRESS AND OBSERVATIONS

ENGLISH
YEAR 6

Starter activity: Opposites snap!

Timing: 6 mins

Learning objectives
- To recognise words with the opposite meaning (antonyms)

Equipment
- scissors

An antonym is a word that is opposite in meaning to another word.

Cut out the cards below. All the words have opposite meanings. Play a game of matching pairs with your tutor.

Shout 'snap!' and claim the cards when you find a pair of antonyms.

after	before	never	always
old	young	question	answer
interesting	boring	lost	found
near	far	open	close
many	few	rise	set
heavy	light	save	spend

ENGLISH
— YEAR 6 —

MAIN ACTIVITY: SYNONYMS AND ANTONYMS **TIMING: 25 MINS**

LEARNING OBJECTIVES
- To recognise words with the same meaning (synonyms)
- To write synonyms and antonyms

EQUIPMENT
- coloured pens / pencils

A synonym is a word that has the same meaning as another word.

1. Have a go at being a synonym sorter! Colour in each pair of synonyms you find in the table below. Use a different colour for each set to make six sets of synonyms.

massive	pretty	merry	huge
happy	cheerful	friendly	shout
immense	roar	big	affectionate
yell	beautiful	stroll	step
stunning	pleased	kind	walk
hike	loving	fabulous	bellow

2. Now try some synonym / antonym sentences. Look at the word in brackets after each of the sentences below. Complete each sentence by writing a synonym of the word in the first gap and an antonym in the second gap. The first one has been done for you.

a) My <u>filthy</u> dog needed a long bath to get <u>clean</u>. (dirty)

b) The sand was _____ but the sea was _____. (hot)

c) The food was too _____, except for my boiled egg which was _____ (hard).

d) I sometimes _____ so much it almost makes me _____ (laugh)

e) "You must all be _____," warned our teacher. "You are all too _____." (quiet)

f) We must be _____ the finish line now. It can't be _____. (close)

ENGLISH
— YEAR 6 —

MAIN ACTIVITY: BE THE TUTOR **TIMING: 15 MINS**

LEARNING OBJECTIVES
- To find the incorrect homophones
- To write the correct homophones

EQUIPMENT
- highlighter

Homophones are words that are spelled the same but have different meanings.

Example:
piece (meaning a part of something) and *peace* (meaning quiet).

Imagine you are the tutor. One of your students has given you their work to mark. Highlight the incorrect homophones in their text below.

"What's the whether like now?" asked Tamwar.
"The son is out at last! Let's go two the park!" his brother Haroon replied.
"Thank goodness for that," muttered there dad. "Now I can get some piece and quite."
"Sea you later, Dad!" they shouted.
"Bee back by won o'clock," he reminded them.
"Can't we be aloud out later?" complained Haroon.
"No, the hole family is coming for lunch."
The too boys ran to the park.
"Over there," said Tamwar happily. "It's are friends. Their playing football."

Number each mistake from 1-14. Write the correct homophone in each case in the table below.

	correct homophone		correct homophone
1		8	
2		9	
3		10	
4		11	
5		12	
6		13	
7		14	

ENGLISH
YEAR 6

HOMEWORK ACTIVITY: WORD SEARCH

TIMING: 45 MINS

LEARNING OBJECTIVES
- To find all the synonyms, antonyms and homophones, and group them

EQUIPMENT
none

Complete this word search by circling the words in the list when you find them in the grid. Once you have found all 18 words, put them into pairs of synonyms, antonyms or homophones, and write each pair in the correct column in the table below.

Words can go in the following directions: → ↓

P	L	A	I	N	F	H	E	A	R	F	Q
S	Z	E	M	O	A	N	X	N	U	N	H
V	N	F	C	U	K	O	V	E	R	F	R
Y	P	L	A	N	E	B	R	E	A	K	V
M	G	R	U	M	B	L	E	M	O	O	H
I	U	V	J	J	W	E	X	C	D	K	X
N	O	U	J	S	R	X	N	B	D	H	C
U	N	P	T	I	N	Y	E	R	E	E	E
T	F	J	C	K	L	W	A	A	V	R	N
E	M	E	S	S	Y	U	T	K	E	E	T
R	O	T	M	A	I	U	U	E	N	D	D
D	U	N	D	E	R	O	D	O	U	R	A

PLAIN
MOAN
TINY
UNDER
HEAR
BREAK
HERE
MESSY
ODD
ODOUR
BRAKE
GRUMBLE
PLANE
EVEN
OVER
SCENT
MINUTE
NEAT

synonyms	antonyms	homophones

ENGLISH
YEAR 6

37 ANSWERS

STARTER ACTIVITY: OPPOSITES SNAP!
after / before; never / always; old / young; question / answer; interesting / boring; lost / found; near / far; open / closed; many / few; rise / set; heavy / light; save / spend

MAIN ACTIVITY: SYNONYMS AND ANTONYMS

Synonym sorter
1. happy = cheerful = merry = pleased
   walk = step = hike = stroll
   friendly = kind = affectionate = loving
   shout = roar = bellow = yell
   big = massive = immense = huge
   beautiful = stunning = pretty = fabulous

Synonym/antonym sentences
2. b) The sand was scorching but the sea was cold. (hot)
   c) The food was too tough, except for my boiled egg which was soft. (hard)
   d) I sometimes giggle so much it almost makes me cry. (laugh)
   e) "You must all be silent," warned our teacher. "You are all too noisy." (quiet)
   f) We must be near the finish line now. It can't be far. (close)

MAIN ACTIVITY: BE THE TEACHER

"What's the whether like now?" asked Tamwar.
"The son is out at last! Let's go two the park!" his brother Haroon replied.
"Thank goodness for that," muttered there dad. "Now I can get some piece and quite."
"Sea you later, Dad!" they shouted.
"Bee back by won o'clock," he reminded them.
"Can't we be aloud out later?" complained Haroon.
"No, the hole family is coming for lunch."
The too boys ran to the park.
"Over there," said Tamwar happily. "It's are friends. Their playing football.

1. weather
2. sun; 3. to
4. their; 5. peace; 6. quiet
7. see
8. be; 9. one
10. allowed
11. whole
12. two
13. our; 14. they're

HOMEWORK ACTIVITY: WORD SEARCH

```
P L A I N + H E A R + +
+ + + M O A N + + + + +
+ + + + + O V E R + + +
+ P L A N E B R E A K +
M G R U M B L E + O + +
I + + + + + + + D + S +
N + + + + + N B D H C +
U + + T I N Y E R E E E
T + + + + + A A V R N +
E M E S S Y + T K E E T
+ + + + + + + E N + + +
+ U N D E R O D O U R +
```

synonyms	antonyms	homophones
grumble / moan	under / over	plain / plane
minute / tiny	odd / even	break / brake
scent / odour	neat / messy	here / hear

GLOSSARY

Synonym
Words that have the same or a very similar meaning, such as *happy* and *cheerful.*

Antonym
Words that have opposite meanings, such as *beautiful* and *ugly*.

Homophone
Words that sound the same but are spelled differently and have different meanings, such as *peace* and *piece*. Words that sound almost the same, such as *quite* and *quiet* are called near homophones.

ENGLISH — YEAR 6

38 SPELLING: TRICKY SPELLINGS

LEARNING OBJECTIVES

- To spell frequently occurring words with unstressed vowels or silent letters
- To understand and apply the *i* before *e*, except after *c* spelling rule
- To spell frequently occurring words that include the letter string *-ough*

CONTENT DOMAINS

- S58 words with the /i:/ sound spelt *ei* after *c*
- S59 words containing the letter string *-ough*
- S60 words with silent letters

STARTER ACTIVITIES

- **What's missing? 5 minutes; page 246**
  Cut out and assemble the letter fans prior to the lesson. Assess the student's ability to identify the missing vowel in each word (see list on answer sheet).

MAIN ACTIVITIES

- **Silent submarines; 15 minutes; page 247**
  Encourage the student to say each word out loud using the available letters before identifying the missing silent letter.
- **Are you tough enough?; 15 minutes; page 248**
  Make sure the student can differentiate between the seven different *–ough* sounds. Give contextual clues to guide them. For example: *This word means when there's no water.* (drought).
- ***i* before *e*?; 10 minutes; page 248**
  Make sure the student understands and applies the rule correctly, and is not fooled by *ancient* (no *ee* sound). There are no exceptions included.

PLENARY ACTIVITIES

- **Quick write; 5 minutes**
  Say some of the target words in context or without. For example: *receipt* or *Would you like the receipt?* Ask the student to write the target word and correct any misconceptions or mistakes.

HOMEWORK ACTIVITIES

- **Spelling mistakes; 45 minutes; page 249**
  This activity puts the student's learning into practice. Encourage them to read the whole story for sense first. Review and discuss any remaining areas of weakness or misconception in the next session.

DIFFERENTIATION AND EXTENSION IDEAS

- **What's missing?** Support by writing each word (e.g. g e n _ r a l) or giving an example of the word in context.
- **Silent subs** Extend by removing the list of missing letters.
- ***i* before *e*?** Extend by supplementing the words with exception words, such as *seize*, *either* and *weird*.

PROGRESS AND OBSERVATIONS

ENGLISH
— YEAR 6 —

TUTORS' GUILD

STARTER ACTIVITY: WHAT'S MISSING?

TIMING: 5 MINS

LEARNING OBJECTIVES
- To identify the missing (unstressed) vowel in each word

EQUIPMENT
- scissors
- mini whiteboard

When your tutor reads out a word to you, hold up the fan showing the letter you think is missing. On a separate piece of paper, try writing the word with the missing letter in the right place.

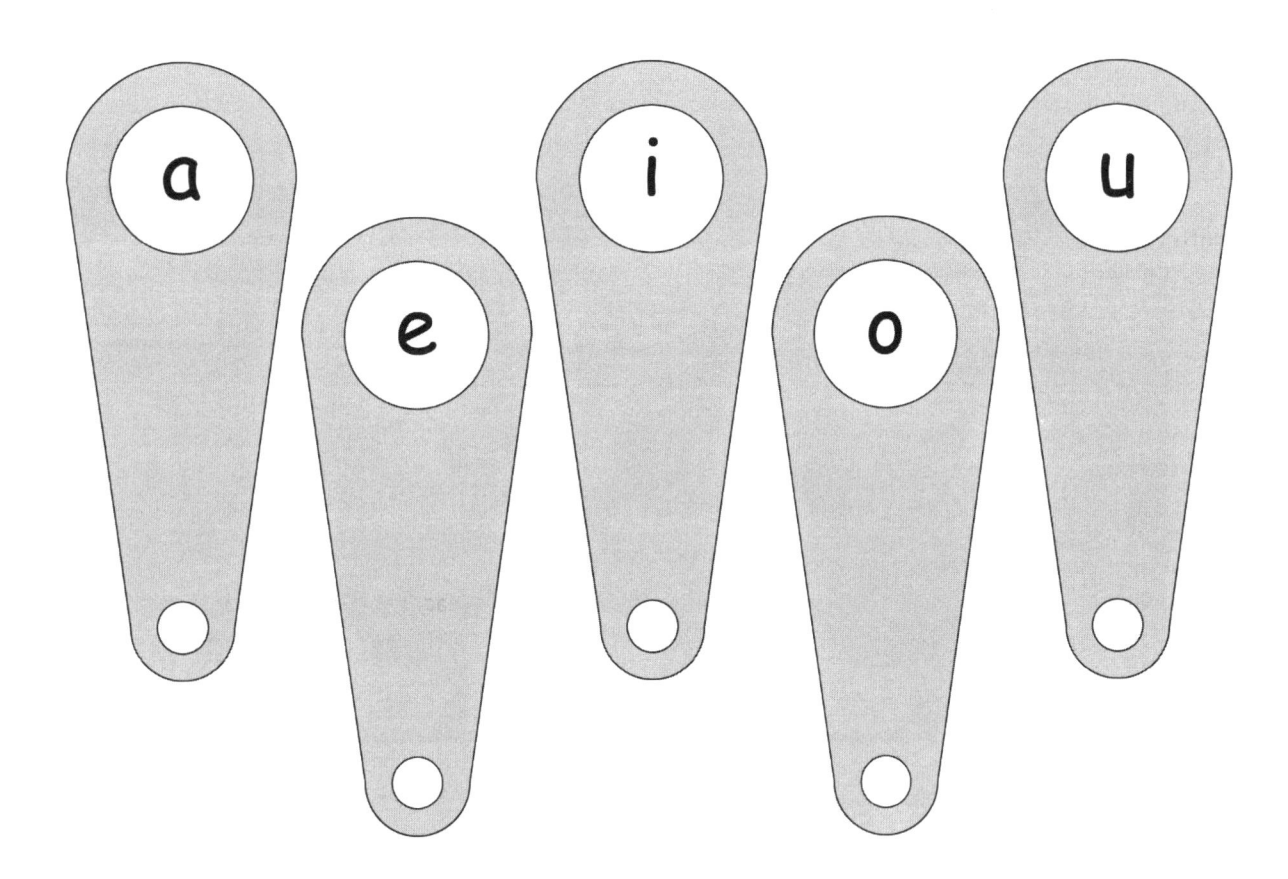

ENGLISH
— YEAR 6 —

MAIN ACTIVITY: SILENT SUBMARINES

TIMING: 15 MINS

LEARNING OBJECTIVES
- To identify silent letters in words
- To write the words in sentences

EQUIPMENT
none

Imagine you are the captain of a ship trying to find a fleet of submarines. The map below shows their location, but only parts of their names.

Find all fourteen submarines by filling in the silent letters in each of their names.

Your radio operator has just intercepted a vital clue from the submarines. He thinks the clue reveals the missing letters, but they are all jumbled up:

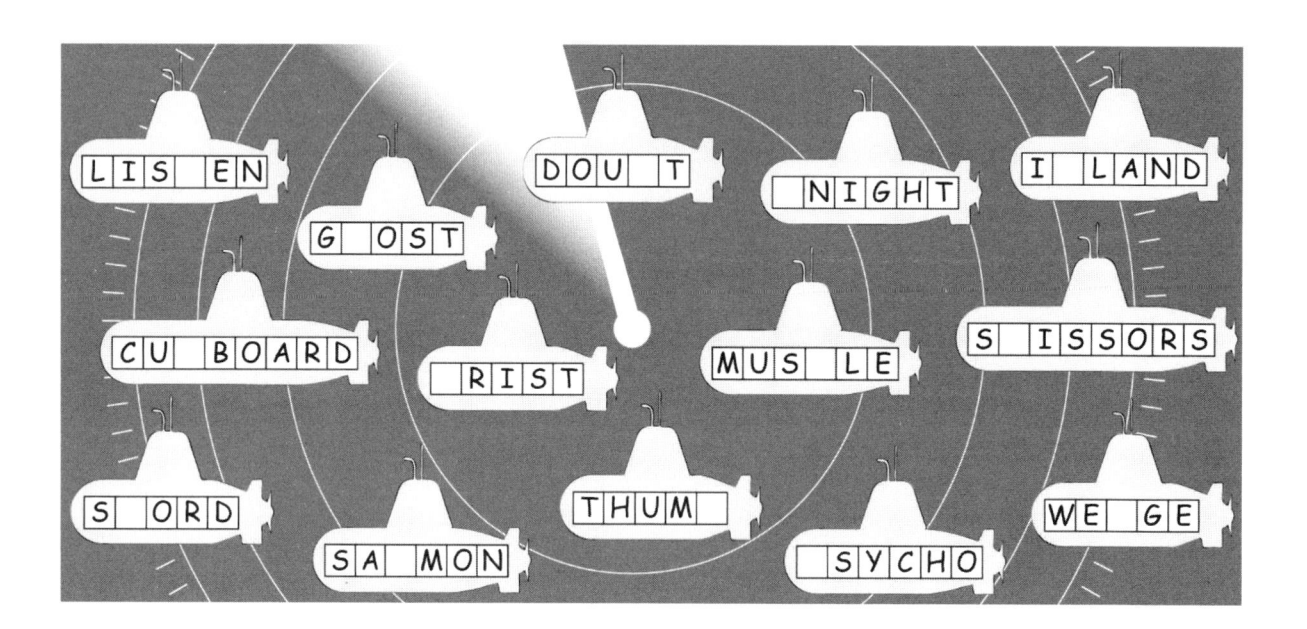

| c | s | b | k | p | l | b | w | d | h | w | c | t | p |

Submarine names shown:
- LIS_EN
- DOU_T
- _NIGHT
- I_LAND
- G_OST
- CU_BOARD
- _RIST
- MUS_LE
- S_ISSORS
- S_ORD
- THUM_
- SA_MON
- _SYCHO
- WE_GE

Once you have found all of the submarine names, try writing some sentences on a separate piece of paper using the words you have revealed.

ENGLISH
— YEAR 6 —

MAIN ACTIVITY: TRICKY LETTER STRINGS **TIMING: 15 MINS**

LEARNING OBJECTIVES
- To sort words with the –ough letter string
- To understand when to use ie or ei

EQUIPMENT
- highlighter

1. Are you tough enough to solve this puzzle? All of these words contain the letter string *-ough*.

   Read the words below out loud and sort them according to their sound. Write each one in the correct box in the table below. One has been done for you.

   ~~tough~~   plough   rough   though   fought   borough   ought   through
   dough   enough   cough   drought   thought   although   bought   thorough
   trough   nought   bough   brought

'uff'	'oh'	'oo'	'awt'
tough			

'uh'	'off'	'ow'

2. Remember the rule: *i* before *e*, except after *c* when the sound is *ee*. This rule works most of the time. Complete the missing letters in the words below using the *i* before *e* rule to help you.

   a) f ___ ___ r c e

   b) c ___ ___ l i n g

   c) c a l o r ___ ___ s

   d) a c h ___ ___ v e m e n t

   e) r e c ___ ___ v e

   f) b e l ___ ___ f

   g) a n c ___ ___ n t

   h) p ___ ___ c e

248

ENGLISH
YEAR 6

Homework activity: Spelling mistakes

Timing: 45 mins

Learning objectives
- To find and correct all the spelling mistakes
- To use your knowledge of silent letters, -ough words and the i before e rule

Equipment
- highlighter

Your friend has written a story for their creative writing blog. They have asked you to help them with their spelling.

Highlight and list each mistake in their story, then write the mistake and the correct spelling next to it in the table at the bottom of the sheet. The first one has been done for you. There are 24 mistakes altogether!

General Solar and the Plague of Space Salmon

General Solar and his faithful freind Larry the Lepard were hurtling throo space towards Jupiter. Suddenly, a warning light flashed on the dashboard of thier ship.

"I don't beleive it!" cried General Solar. "Those fish are back! That pesky plage of Space Samon has followed us."

Larry growled feircely.

"I thawt we'd fawt them off by Pluto last Wednsday!"

Larry shook his head.

"And I gess we didn't decieve them when we hid behind Saturn an our ago," continued the Genral. "We awt to change course and lead the Space Salmon away from the good peple of Earth. I now what to do. Fasen your seat belt, Larry. This could get ruff."

Larry whimpered and put his big paws over his eyes.

"Don't be frightned, old chap," said Solar. "Prepare for hyper-speed! Let's hope we brawt enuff biscits and deisel with us."

mistake	correction
freind	friend

mistake	correction

mistake	correction

ENGLISH
YEAR 6

38 ANSWERS

STARTER ACTIVITY: WHAT'S MISSING?
Veget̲able; le̲opard; bisc̲uit; diff̲erent; bu̲ild; pe̲ople; gen̲eral; cemet̲ery; fright̲ening; plag̲ue; a̲isle; g̲uess; busi̲ness; Wedne̲sday

MAIN ACTIVITY: SILENT SUBMARINES
I̲sland; k̲night; doub̲t; w̲rist; s̲word; lis̲ten; thumb̲; cup̲board; g̲host; sa̲lmon; mus̲cle; p̲sycho; we̲dge; s̲cissors

MAIN ACTIVITY: TRICKY LETTER STRINGS

1. 'uff': tough; rough; enough
   'oh': though; dough; although
   'oo': through
   'awt': fought; ought; thought; bought; brought; nought
   'uh': borough; thorough
   'off': cough; trough
   'ow': plough; drought; bough

2. a) fie̲rce; b) ce̲iling; c) calorie̲s; d) achie̲vement; e) rece̲ive; f) belie̲f; g) ancie̲nt; h) pie̲ce

HOMEWORK ACTIVITY: SPELLING MISTAKES
General Solar and his faithful friend Larry the Leopard were hurtling through space towards Jupiter. Suddenly, a warning light flashed on the dashboard of their ship.
"I don't believe it!" cried General Solar. "Those fish are back! That pesky plague of Space Salmon has followed us."
Larry growled fiercely.
"I thought we'd fought them off by Pluto last Wednesday!"
Larry shook his head.
"And I guess we didn't deceive them when we hid behind Saturn an hour ago," continued the General. "We ought to change course and lead the Space Salmon away from the good people of Earth. I know what to do. Fasten your seat belt, Larry. This could get rough."
Larry whimpered and put his big paws over his eyes.
"Don't be frightened, old chap," said Solar. "Prepare for hyper-speed! Let's hope we brought enough biscuits and diesel with us."

GLOSSARY
Silent or unstressed letters
A letter or letters in a word whose presence cannot be predicted from the pronunciation of the word.

Published by Pearson Education Limited, 80 Strand, London, WC2R 0RL.

www.pearsonschools.co.uk

Text © Pearson Education Limited 2016
Series consultant: Margaret Reeve
Edited by Jane Cotter
Designed by Andrew Magee
Typeset by Elektra Media Ltd
Produced by Elektra Media Ltd
Original illustrations © Pearson Education Limited 2016
Illustrated by Elektra Media Ltd
Cover design by Andrew Magee

The right of Giles Clare to be identified as author of this work has been asserted by him in accordance with the Copyright, Designs and Patents Act 1988.

First published 2016

19 18 17 16
10 9 8 7 6 5 4 3 2 1

British Library Cataloguing in Publication Data
A catalogue record for this book is available from the British Library.

ISBN 978 1 292 17251 4

Copyright notice
All rights reserved. The material in this publication is copyright. Activity sheets may be freely photocopied for use by the purchasing tutor. However, this material is copyright and under no circumstances may copies be offered for sale. If you wish to use the material in any way other than that specified you must apply in writing to the publishers.

The ActiveBook accompanying this book contains editable Word files. Pearson Education Limited cannot accept responsibility for the quality, accuracy or fitness for purpose of the materials contained in the Word files once edited. To revert to the original Word files, download the files again.

Printed in the United Kingdom by Ashford Colour Press Ltd

Acknowledgements

We would like to thank Tutora for its invaluable help in the development and trialling of this course.

We are grateful to the following for permission to reproduce copyright material:

Text
Poetry 1.1 from *The Complete Poems,* ISBN: 0140423664, Penguin (Rossetti, C. 2001) p. 251, Christina Georgina Rossetti; Poetry 2.1 from *Laughing Time: Collected Nonsense,* ISBN: 0-374-44315-7, Macmillan Children's Publishing Group (Smith, W 1990) used by permission.; Poetry 3.1 from *IT DOESN'T ALWAYS HAVE TO RHYME* (Merriam, E.) Copyright c 1964 Eve Merriam. C Renewed 1992. Used by permission of Marian Reiner.; Poetry 4.1 from *The Best of the West,* Hutchinson (West, C. 1990) (c) Colin West. Reprinted with permission of the poet.

Photographs
SCIENCE PHOTO LIBRARY p23; Getty/Fox Photos/Stringer p24.